Keats's Reading of the Romantic Poets

Keats's Reading of the
Romantic Poets

∽

BETH LAU

Ann Arbor

THE UNIVERSITY OF MICHIGAN PRESS

1994   1993   1992   1991   4   3   2   1

Distributed in the United Kingdom by
Manchester University Press, Oxford Road,
Manchester M13 9PL, UK

Library of Congress Cataloging-in-Publication Data

Lau, Beth, 1951–
    Keats's reading of the romantic poets / Beth Lau.
        p.   cm.
    Includes bibliographical references (p.   ) and index.
    ISBN 0-472-09437-8 (cloth : alk.)
        1. Keats, John, 1795–1821—Books and reading. 2. Keats, John,
1795–1821—Knowledge—Literature. 3. English poetry—19th century—
History and criticism. 4. Romanticism—Great Britain.   I. Keats,
John, 1795–1821.   II. Title.
PR4838.B6L38   1991
821'.7—dc20   91-8936
                                                                                            CIP

British Library Cataloguing in Publication Data
Lau, Beth
    Keats's reading of the romantic poets.
    1. Poetry in English. Keats, John, 1795–1821 — Critical
studies
    I. Title
    821.7

ISBN 0-472-09437-8

Jacket illustration: Woodcut, "John Keats,"
by Vechislav Begidjanov

Acknowledgments

My greatest thanks must go to the many scholars and critics who have written on Keats before me. Individual works are cited below at appropriate points, but I wish here to acknowledge a particular debt to the editions of the writings of Keats and the Keats circle and the biographies of Keats and his friends that I consulted. The present study could not have been written without the aid of these essential texts.

I have also accrued debts of a more personal nature. Jack Stillinger read every chapter as I wrote it and offered extremely helpful commentary, advice, and encouragement. As a teacher and dissertation director, moreover (on a project completely separate from the present one), he introduced me to Keats studies and provided a model of scholarly excellence that continues to guide and inspire (and sometimes intimidate) me. Leon Waldoff also read the entire manuscript and prodded me to engage issues and develop points that would enhance the book's interest and critical significance. Others who read portions of the manuscript and provided valuable feedback are Donald H. Reiman, Charles E. Robinson, Susan Wolfson, Anca Vlasopolos, Christine Gallant, Ronald Sharp, and Mary Quinn. I can only regret that my book does not respond more adequately to all the perceptive suggestions for improvement I received.

Debbie Holdstein performed a valuable service by urging me to get the manuscript off my desk and in the mail to a press. I thank George Bornstein for recommending that I send my book to the University of Michigan Press, as well as for giving me much helpful, practical advice about publishing a book. It has been a pleasure to work with LeAnn Fields, my editor at Michigan Press.

A grant from New Mexico State University allowed for summer travel that resulted in the first chapter of this book. At the other end of the writing process, an NEH Summer Seminar at Johns Hopkins University, directed by Jerome Christensen, provided resources and a congenial environment for writing the introduction and planning final revisions to my manuscript.

An earlier version of "Keats's Reading of Wordsworth" was published in *Studies in Romanticism* 26 (1987): 105–50. Portions of the chapter on "Keats's Reading of Byron" first appeared as "Keats and Byron" in *Critical Essays on John Keats*, edited by Hermione de Almeida (Boston: G. K. Hall, 1990). I am grateful to the editors at *Studies in Romanticism* and G. K. Hall for permission to reprint this material. I also thank Hermione de Almeida for inviting me to submit my essay for her collection. Finally, thanks to Soviet artist Vechislav Begidjanov for permission to use his delightful woodcut of Keats for the dustjacket of my book.

Contents

Introduction

Keats's Reading of the Romantic Poets is designed to serve two major functions. It is, in the first place, a reference source for information about Keats's familiarity with the writings of the other major poets of the early nineteenth century that may assist future influence, intertextual, biographical, or critical studies—any works concerned, either extensively or in part, with interrelationships between Keats and Wordsworth, Coleridge, Byron, and/or Shelley. The subject has been treated in the past by one book, Thora Balslev's *Keats and Wordsworth,* by a number of articles and notes, by Keats's biographers, and by some critical works, especially those like Claude Lee Finney's *The Evolution of Keats's Poetry* that emphasize source and influence study. In addition, annotated editions of Keats's poetry and letters identify quotations and allusions to the other writers and note verbal and conceptual parallels between their works and Keats's own.

My book seeks to improve on the existing state of scholarship in several ways. First, it considers Keats's familiarity with the writings of all four of the other Romantic poets. Previous studies have addressed in isolation Wordsworth's, Coleridge's, Byron's, or Shelley's influence on Keats. Second, it brings together, organizes, and analyzes information scattered throughout many works and thereby makes this material more accessible and meaningful than heretofore. Finally, it attempts to establish a reliable, factual record of what contemporary works Keats read and when he read them. Too often in the past influence studies have based their arguments on tenuous echoes of one writer in another's work, without considering whether the allegedly influenced writer did or could have had access to the other's work. My book, while acknowledging echoes and allusions as one type of evidence, distinguishes these from direct references and quotations and other, less speculative forms of evidence; it also explores such issues as which published versions of poems and prose works Keats could have seen, where he could have acquired copies, when and why he is likely to have read particular works, and how much of certain volumes he knew. The aim has been to establish, as far as is possible, the extent and timing of Keats's reading of the other major Romantic poets and thereby lay a groundwork for more informed future studies of the nature of the other poets' influence on Keats.

The second major goal of this book is to situate Keats in the literary climate of his time. The influences on Keats's poetry to which most attention has been paid are Shakespeare, Milton, Spenser, and other Renaissance and Medieval writers. Certainly, as his letters and friends attest, Keats studied carefully, at times worshipfully, his great literary forebears, and his poetry bears the mark of such reading. Some distortion nonetheless results from viewing Keats—or any writer—solely or disproportionately in relationship to earlier literature. Poets, like people generally, are largely products of their time and culture. Keats's very interest in Renaissance and Medieval literature was common to the age, as is evident from the fact that many of Keats's friends shared and encouraged the poet's fondness for Spenser, Shakespeare, Milton, Chaucer, Dante, Boccaccio, and other early writers.

In a recent study of Wordsworth's literary allusions, Edwin Stein concludes that "Wordsworth's tastes in literary echoes were overwhelmingly eighteenth-century tastes and not decisively different from those of most pre-Romantic poets" (12). Even Wordsworth's frequent allusions to Milton and Shakespeare, Stein argues, are in keeping with late eighteenth-century reverence for those figures. This is not to argue that Keats and Wordsworth lack either individuality or universality. If one wishes to study the influences on a writer's outlook and style, however, one generally will find the richest material among contemporary sources. As Shelley writes in his Preface to *The Revolt of Islam,* "there must be a resemblance, which does not depend upon their own will, between all the writers of any particular age. They cannot escape from subjection to a common influence which arises out of an infinite combination of circumstances belonging to the times in which they live; though each is in a degree the author of the very influence by which his being is thus pervaded" (Hutchinson 35).

Shelley's last point is important: great artists help determine the spirit of the age that informs their work. In his Preface to *Prometheus Unbound,* Shelley further specifies the nature of contemporary influence. "It is true," he writes, "that, not the spirit of [writers'] genius, but the forms in which it has manifested itself, are due less to the peculiarities of their own minds than to the peculiarity of the moral and intellectual condition of the minds among which they have been produced. Thus a number of writers possess the form, whilst they want the spirit of those whom . . . they imitate; because the former is the endowment of the age in which they live, and the latter must be the uncommunicated lightning of their own mind" (Hutchinson 206). Although the style, genres, and themes in which a writer expresses him or herself are largely determined by the climate of the times, great artists are endowed with genius and vision that cannot be borrowed from another. Studying a poet's affinities with his or her contemporaries thus not only clarifies shaping influences on that writer's art; it also points up differences among contemporaries and distinguishes each one's unique literary personality and contribution to the period style.

Keats himself realized that "a mighty providence subdues the mightiest Minds to the service of the time being" and that Milton's concern with theology and Wordsworth's with the human heart are more the result of "the general and gregarious advance of intellect, than individual greatness of Mind" (*Letters* 1:281–82). He also realized that "Great spirits now on earth are sojourning"[1]—that his age was distinguished by an efflorescence of literary talent. Shelley's remarks on contemporary influence make clear that he too was conscious of living in a period of extraordinary artistic achievement. "It is impossible," he writes in the Preface to *Prometheus Unbound,* "that any one who inhabits the same age with such writers as those who stand in the foremost ranks of our own, can conscientiously assure himself that his language and tone of thought may not have been modified by the study of the productions of those extraordinary intellects" (Hutchinson 206).[2] This passage reflects the peculiar advantages and disadvantages of Shelley's and Keats's position within the Romantic movement. The younger poets were able to draw upon the exciting new ideas and styles initiated by Wordsworth, Coleridge, Byron, and other notable living writers, but they also faced the challenge of distinguishing themselves in a literary scene already cluttered with established major figures. As the youngest of all the major Romantic poets, Keats experienced even Shelley as a precursor against whose example he had to contend.[3]

These latter remarks suggest a characteristic of Keats's relationship to his contemporaries that may be responsible for the relative neglect in study of these poets' impact on Keats. Whereas Keats's many references to Shakespeare, Milton, Spenser, and other early writers are almost always appreciative, his comments on Wordsworth, Coleridge, Byron, and Shelley are markedly less frequent and less complimentary. A. C. Bradley at the beginning of this century noted the strain of hostility in Keats's attitude toward his most talented contemporaries, which Bradley attributed to the young poet's "native pugnacity" (210–11). A more far-reaching explanation, however, may be that Keats felt a special anxiety of influence from living writers that he did not feel from those long dead. As W. J. Bate says, poets tend to find "ancestral" past writers less threatening than "parental"—or, I might add, sibling—figures closer to their own generation (*Burden of the Past* 22).[4] Certainly Bate's and Bloom's important studies of literary inheritance have taught us that resistance to other writers or denial of the impression they have created can indicate an oppressive burden rather than a paucity of influence; in fact, love/hate literary relationships may be more dynamic and fruitful than those characterized by static reverence.

Readers may question why I considered only Wordsworth, Coleridge, Byron, and Shelley in this study of Keats and other Romantic writers. Blake certainly is another major figure of the age, but he was little known to the literary establishment of his time, and there is no evidence that Keats read any of his poems. Keats of course did read many works by other living writers such as Scott, Southey, Moore, Campbell, Rogers, and Barry Cornwall, and these contemporaries no doubt played some part in shaping Keats's style and outlook. All scholarly works require selectivity, however, and I focused on the four writers in question for several reasons. First, I was concerned with Keats's reading of contemporary poets rather than prose writers and therefore did not include a chapter on Hazlitt, whose essays were profoundly influential for Keats. Second, I chose the Romantic poets now recognized as most significant and in whose relationship to Keats other scholars and critics are most likely to be interested. Indeed, two questions that provoked my investigation were whether Keats himself shared our present assessment of the greatest poets of his age and whether the major Romantic poets can be said to have functioned as a genuine literary group that helped inspire and shape one another's work. The evidence, I believe, points to an affirmative answer to both questions.

As Jack Stillinger has remarked ("John Keats" 699), minor contemporary and eighteenth-century writers had their greatest impact on Keats's earliest poetry. As his literary tastes matured, Keats recognized the inadequacies of such writers and abandoned them for more challenging models. "Mrs Tighe and Beattie once delighted me," he wrote in December 1818; "now I see through them and can find nothing in them—or weakness" (*Letters* 2:18). References to Wordsworth, Coleridge, Byron, and Shelley, by contrast, persist throughout Keats's career. Keats began reading and praising Wordsworth in the fall of 1816, and his letters and poems through 1820 contain allusions to Wordsworth and parallels in language, genre, and theme to his work. Keats probably read Coleridge's 1797 and *Christabel* volumes before or during 1816, and *Biographia Literaria* and *Sibylline Leaves* in 1817. A significant number of the great poems of 1819, moreover—*The Eve of St. Agnes, La Belle Dame sans Merci, Ode to a Nightingale, Lamia, To Autumn*—are conspicuously indebted to language, imagery, cadences, characters, plots, themes, and structural patterns from Coleridge's poems. Byron's poetry was popular with Keats through 1816 and then dropped out of favor, but Keats thereafter continued to observe and comment on Byron's career and public image. It would appear that Byron remained an important professional model who influenced Keats's sense of what it meant to be a poet in the early nineteenth century. In addition, one of the last poems Keats wrote—*The Jealousies*—imitates Byronic satire, and one of the last poems we know Keats read was *Don Juan,* which he took with him on his voyage to Italy. Even Shelley, for whom there is the least evidence of Keats's reading, remained a figure to reckon with for Keats throughout his short life. In October 1817 Keats declared he "refused to visit Shelley, that I might have my own unfettered scope" (*Letters* 1:170), suggesting that he may have avoided contact with Shelley because he felt particularly vulnerable to Shelley's influence. In the summer of 1820 he read *The Cenci,* annotating it with "many notes" (Rollins, "Fanny Brawne Letter" 375), and a 16 August 1820 letter to Shelley objects to the dominance of theme over style, or moral over aesthetic considerations in the play (*Letters* 2:322–23). Clearly Keats took Shelley's work seriously, and the two men's very areas of disagreement provoked Keats to define his own artistic principles. One cannot point to any other contemporary poets who had as striking and persistent an impact on Keats's poetry and poetic theory as did the four other major Romantics.

Other contemporaries of Keats do enter into my work. One of my chief methods for investigating what Keats read, when, and why, was to consider the libraries and literary tastes of his friends, two of whom—Leigh Hunt and William Hazlitt—are important literary figures in their own right. Others, like Charles Cowden Clarke, George Felton Mathew, Benjamin Robert Haydon, John Hamilton Reynolds, Benjamin Bailey, Charles Wentworth Dilke, Richard Woodhouse, and Charles Armitage Brown, made lesser contributions to English literature, but nonetheless played a significant role in introducing Keats to various works and helping him to develop his opinions about contemporary poetry. Time and again one discovers similarities between a statement of Keats's about Wordsworth, Coleridge, Byron, or Shelley and other statements in the writings of Keats's friends. This is not to say that Keats's friends perpetually furnished him with ideas. Rather, the Keats circle operated as most circles of friends do, providing for each member an interchange of information and ideas and a sounding board for expressing and sorting out his own opinions. In a number of instances, as when Keats, Reynolds, and Haydon all express dissatisfaction with Wordsworth's behavior during his 1817 visit to London, the group probably arrived at its opinions conjointly. So extensively do the attitudes and reading habits of Keats's friends enter into the essays in this book that the work may be considered a study of two levels in Keats's relationship to his contemporaries: his literary relationships with the major poets of his day, and his personal interactions with an immediate circle that helped stimulate and focus his reading and thinking about poetry.

The four chapters that follow contain separate essay and checklist sections. The essays are divided into two parts: one on which of the other poet's works Keats read and the other on when he read them.[5] Each checklist is organized according to the major editions the other poet published in Keats's lifetime. First listed, for each publication, is the most reliable evidence for Keats's reading: direct references or quotations in Keats's poems, letters, essays, and marginalia; entries in Charles Brown's "List of Keats's Books," drawn up after the poet's death (*Keats Circle* 1:253–60); and statements by people who knew Keats. Next comes a list of echoes of and allusions to that work which scholars have discovered in Keats's writing. Entries in this section supply the title and line number(s) of the poem (or, for prose works, the page number[s]) and part or all of the passage proposed as a source; the title, line number(s) (or, for letters, volume and page number[s]), and passage in Keats's work said to reflect influence; and the critics who have advanced or supported the argument for this echo or allusion. Finally, each checklist contains sections on general references to the other poet in Keats's poetry and prose.

The checklists are designed to provide clear and easy access to data on which of the other poet's works Keats read, which passages made the greatest impression upon him, and which of his own poems, throughout his career, were influenced by specific works of the other writers. Readers who wish to determine when Keats read a given work can consult the appropriate essay section on this topic. One can also use the index to trace references throughout the book to particular Keats poems and letters.

The essays that begin each chapter evaluate and draw conclusions from information in the checklists and consider other issues and types of evidence that do not lend themselves to a checklist format. It is here that I explore such questions as who might have introduced Keats to the other poets, where he might have acquired copies of the volumes he read, what editions he is likely to have used, why he read certain works at particular periods of his life, and how personal or temperamental factors may have affected his attitude toward the other writers.

The essays do not always repeat in full quotations or examples of parallel passages listed in the reference section of each chapter. Wherever it seems necessary, I refer the reader to the appropriate checklist section for further reading, but cross referencing every parallel between essays and checklists would have inordinately cluttered the essays and impeded the flow of discussion. Readers should keep in mind that the essays are largely based on material in the checklists, and quotations or other evidence alluded to in the essays can be found by turning to the relevant checklist section.

I have tried to locate all Keats's direct references to or quotations of the other poets. The list of echoes and allusions, however, cannot claim to be exhaustive, though it is as complete as I felt I could reasonably make it. To compile the list I consulted the major annotated editions of Keats's poems (by de Selincourt, Bush, Allott, and Barnard); the major biographies (by Ward, Bate, and Gittings); and books, articles, and notes wholly or largely concerned with the other poets' influence on Keats. I did not, however, comb through every work ever written on Keats, as I should have to have done to garner all the pertinent echoes that have been proposed. For the fact is, as Stillinger explains, "Keats's critics invoke sources on practically every occasion, sometimes without being aware of doing so. . . . and the activity has in fact accelerated rather than slowed down" since the 1950s, despite a widespread suspicion of the value of source study within the academic community ("John Keats" 698–99). If the checklists in this book are not exhaustive, they nonetheless do reflect the central patterns in influence on which scholars agree. A few echoes more or less would not alter the impression that *Endymion* is heavily indebted to both Wordsworth's *Excursion* and Shelley's *Alastor*. A few more echoes, unless they were of major significance, would not convince most Keatsians that canto 3 of *Childe Harold's Pilgrimage* made an important impression on Keats, if he read it at all.

The latter remarks suggest the ways I used the checklists as evidence for Keats's familiarity with various works. In the first place, I did separate the direct references, quotations, statements by people who knew Keats, and items in Brown's "List of Keats's Books" from the more speculative echoes and allusions and considered the former as harder evidence.[6] Within the lists of echoes, it is also possible to distinguish more from less convincing cases. When Keats in *Sleep and Poetry* says, "The blue / Bared its eternal bosom" (lines 189–90), he is undoubtedly echoing "The Sea that bares her bosom to the moon" from Wordsworth's *The world is too much with us,* as a number of scholars have long agreed. The sonnet, moreover, was available to Keats in Wordsworth's 1807 and 1815 editions of poems, for both of which collections there is further evidence of Keats's reading. By contrast, it is much less certain that "In noisome alley, and in pathless wood" from *Addressed to Haydon* echoes "pathless wood" from Shelley's *Queen Mab,* especially since only one scholar has supported this connection (Allott, *Poems* 66), and there is evidence that Keats read only the reworking of parts 1 and 2 of *Queen Mab* published as *The Daemon of the World* in the *Alastor* volume, rather than the complete *Mab* from which "pathless wood" derives.

The practice of searching for echoes and allusions has been criticized for coming up with dubious results that are often of minor literary significance. A supposed echo of one writer in another's work, it has been argued, may be a case of coincidental similarity or of shared poetic language common to the period. In addition, there may be more than one source—nonliterary as well as literary—for a given phrase, image, or plot element, and focusing on an isolated influence produces a distorted impression of the creative process.[7] While I fully agree that any single or even handful of examples of parallel passages is in itself of slight significance, I believe that accumulating a substantial body of such material and judiciously assessing it in the light of other evidence and considerations can permit meaningful conclusions about the extent and nature of one writer's impact on another.

Readers may wonder why I did not simply omit from the checklists the least convincing echoes and allusions. I do, in the essays and notes, remark cases that have been disputed, that fly in the face of known fact, or that seem very slight. I hesitated to reject any material that would contribute to the overall picture of scholarship on the subject, however; if nothing else, the less convincing examples often serve to highlight by contrast the more impressive ones. Also, it is difficult to draw an absolute line between probable and spurious echoes, and opinions may (and obviously do) vary from one scholar to another. I have tried to provide adequate information about each echo (identification of similarity proposed, critics in support, recording of disputes or flaws in reasoning) so that individuals may draw their own informed conclusions.

Finally, I have included what may appear to be dubious parallels in the event that others may find valid uses for them. John Hollander has argued for the legitimacy of echoes "as small as single words, and as elusive as particular cadences," and says that critics up to now simply may not have known how to interpret such material properly (88–89; see also 94–95, 108). Roger Lonsdale points out that even parallels between two poets which stem from an earlier writer both knew or from common poetic practice of the day can still be useful in revealing "new poetic vogues or preoccupations of the period" (xvii). Edwin Stein also argues that, even if an echoed term is part of the common poetic language of the age, it "still may have a fit and noteworthy allusive force" (3). My aim in this book has been to collect, organize, and analyze information in such a way that it may be useful to a broad number of readers for a variety of different purposes. If I have erred on the side of inclusiveness or objectivity, I hope I have thereby produced a reference work that will serve more uses to more people than a more selective or interpretive study would have done.

CHAPTER I

Keats's Reading of Wordsworth

Which of Wordsworth's Works Keats Read

Among the major works or collections that appeared during Keats's life-time, the only Wordsworth publication we know for certain Keats read is *The Excursion*. This he directly quotes or alludes to in several letters, and four of Keats's contemporaries recorded the poet's appreciation of or re-sponse to that work. In addition, scholars have discovered numerous echoes of *The Excursion* in Keats's poems, particularly *Endymion, Hyperion,* and *The Fall of Hyperion* (see checklist, *The Excursion*). As far as we know, Keats did not own a copy of this work, but he could have borrowed one from several friends. Benjamin Robert Haydon's copy of *The Excursion* survives (Healey 13), and Keats read in Benjamin Bailey's copy when he visited at Oxford in September 1817 (see "When Keats Read Words-worth"). Leigh Hunt, who as I explain below is likely to have introduced Keats to *The Excursion,* probably possessed a copy, as did John Hamilton Reynolds, who looked forward to the poem's publication and later wrote a guide to it (Jones 92). Finally, William Hazlitt reviewed *The Excursion* for the *Examiner* in August 1814 and therefore must have owned or had access to the work.

As the checklist shows, abundant evidence exists that Keats also knew poems first published in the first and second editions of *Lyrical Ballads* and in the 1807 *Poems in Two Volumes*. The pieces in all three of these editions, however, were reprinted in Wordsworth's first collected edition of 1815. Keats therefore could have read either two or three separate editions of Wordsworth's shorter poems or only the 1815 volumes.

One potential source of evidence for determining which publication Keats read is the fact that Wordsworth revised many of his poems each time he reprinted them. Formerly published works reprinted in 1815 there-fore are not identical to the same poems as printed in *Lyrical Ballads* or

Poems in Two Volumes; even the *Lyrical Ballads* poems alter somewhat from one edition to the next. Unfortunately, either Keats quotes passages that were not revised within his lifetime, or his references are too general, brief, or transmuted to allow for this kind of close checking of sources. The one conclusion we can draw is that, if Keats read from just one copy of *Lyrical Ballads,* it was either a second (1800), third (1802), or fourth (1805) edition, since his letters and poems allude to several pieces—such as *The Old Cumberland Beggar, The Pet-Lamb, She dwelt among the untrodden ways, To Joanna,* and *The Two April Mornings*—that were not published in the first edition of 1798 (see checklist, *Lyrical Ballads* [1800]: Direct References).

Charles Brown's "List of Keats's Books," drawn up after the poet's death, makes clear that Keats owned an edition of Wordsworth's poems, but does not specify which one. Brown's entry reads merely: "Wordsworth's Poems . . . 8ᵛᵒ—2 vol:" (*Keats Circle* 1:253). Both Rollins and Ward believe Brown refers to the 1807 *Poems in Two Volumes,* from which most of Keats's echoes and allusions derive (*Keats Circle* 1:253n.3; Ward 420n.31). The 1807 volumes, however, are duodecimo rather than octavo. The only two-volume, octavo editions of Wordsworth's poems published during Keats's lifetime are the second, third, and fourth editions of *Lyrical Ballads* and the 1815 *Poems.*[1]

Either edition would have been a logical choice for Keats. The *Lyrical Ballads,* especially the second and later editions that contained the revolutionary Preface, was in Keats's lifetime Wordsworth's most notorious single collection and the one most often mentioned by name. We know Hunt owned or at least read a copy of the fourth edition (1805), for he specifically cites that edition in the notes to his 1814 *The Feast of the Poets* (89). Reynolds almost certainly owned a copy of *Lyrical Ballads,* perhaps, like Hunt, the fourth edition. The fact that, in a 30 July 1814 letter, Reynolds praises the *Lyrical Ballads* Preface as well as the poems indicates he has read a second or later edition (Richardson, *Letters from Lambeth* 120). Jane Reynolds gave a friend a copy of the fourth edition (Healey 11), and in so doing may have followed her brother's recommendation and example. In addition, Leonidas Jones believes Leigh Hunt's 1814 *Feast of the Poets* introduced Reynolds to Wordsworth (Jones 52). If this was the case, Reynolds may well have purchased the edition cited in that work. Perhaps Keats, like his friends, wished to own the last edition of Wordsworth's most famous publication.

On the other hand, throughout Keats's brief career the 1815 edition was the most recent of Wordsworth's collections of poems, and it clearly had an advantage over *Lyrical Ballads* in containing all the short poems from previous collections, in addition to some new ones. As mentioned above, moreover (and as the checklist shows), the majority of Keats's direct or indirect references to Wordsworth poems are to those first published in 1807 and reprinted in 1815, and not to those first published in *Lyrical Ballads*. In addition, Leigh Hunt's 1815 *Feast of the Poets* (89), as well as his 18 February 1816 *Examiner* article "Heaven Made a Party to Earthly Disputes—Mr. Wordsworth's Sonnets on Waterloo," cite Wordsworth's 1815 edition, which Hunt apparently had acquired since he published his 1814 *Feast*. These publications, along with other *Examiner* issues, may have introduced Keats to Wordsworth in late 1815 or 1816 (see "When Keats Read Wordsworth"); if so, they may also have suggested to Keats the edition he ought to purchase. Finally, the entry in Brown's "List of Keats's Books" is closer to the title of the 1815 *Poems, Including Lyrical Ballads* than to *Lyrical Ballads, With Other Poems* (1800) or *Lyrical Ballads, With Pastoral and Other Poems* (1802, 1805). The evidence therefore points to the 1815 edition as the collection Keats is most likely to have possessed.

Nevertheless, I cannot conclude as Gittings confidently does (*John Keats* 52 and note 2) that 1815 definitely was the copy of Wordsworth's poems Keats owned. One problem is that Keats never directly quotes or alludes to any of the pieces that appeared for the first time in 1815. Even the alleged echoes of 1815 poems are rather scanty and tend to be supported by only one scholar (see checklist, *Poems* [1815]: Echoes/Allusions). Direct references and echoes that enjoy consensus support are much more numerous for *Lyrical Ballads* and 1807 poems. If Keats did own the 1815 volumes, he was much more impressed by the reprinted than the new items they contained.

Another problem results from equating the poems Keats read and remembered with those he owned. The truth may be that Keats studied Wordsworth in several different editions, one of which he owned and others that he borrowed from friends. After all, he appears to have read *The Excursion* closely without purchasing that work. And, as this chapter demonstrates, Hunt, Haydon, Reynolds, and Bailey among themselves owned nearly all of Wordsworth's publications up to and including the 1815 edition.

Each of Wordsworth's major collections of poems, moreover, was significant in its own right: *Lyrical Ballads* established Wordsworth's reputation and introduced his new style of poetry; *Poems in Two Volumes* appealed to many people who had not particularly relished the *Lyrical Ballads'* humble, downtrodden characters and also contained the notorious section heading *Moods of My Own Mind,* quoted by Keats, Hunt, Reynolds, and numerous reviewers (see checklist, *Poems in Two Volumes* [1807]: Direct References; Hunt, *Feast of the Poets* 1814, 107; 1815, 106–7; Reynolds 62; Gittings, *John Keats* 56); and the 1815 *Poems* was Wordsworth's first collected edition and included the important "Essay, Supplementary to the Preface," which Reynolds was particularly fond of quoting.[2] It is likely that Keats would have been curious to examine all three of these notable editions and that the libraries of his friends afforded him the opportunity to do so.

Another of Wordsworth's publications to which Keats directly refers is *An Evening Walk* (1793). In the 3 February 1818 letter to Reynolds in which he complains of Wordsworth's egotism, Keats writes, "Old Matthew spoke to [Wordsworth] some years ago on some nothing, & because he happens in an Evening Walk to imagine the figure of the old man—he must stamp it down in black & white, and it is henceforth sacred" (*Letters* 1:224). Because Keats mentions only the title of Wordsworth's poem, his remark does not prove that he actually read the work. If he did read *An Evening Walk,* however, he probably did so in a copy owned by Reynolds. In a 9 December 1815 *Champion* article, Reynolds quotes from the poem and explains in a note that it "was published in [Wordsworth's] youthful days, and is now become very scarce" (Reynolds 26). The note suggests that Reynolds was the proud owner of one of the rare copies of *An Evening Walk;* if this was the case, especially given Reynolds's apparent fondness for the poem, Keats may have been encouraged to borrow the work or at least to look through it while visiting his friend at some point.

Circumstantial evidence exists for Keats's reading of various other Wordsworth works. Benjamin Bailey owned a copy of Wordsworth's pamphlet *Concerning the Convention of Cintra* (1809) (Healey 13), which Keats therefore could have read at Oxford in 1817—although it is unlikely that the dry prose style of the tract would have appealed much to Keats, who was amazed at Bailey's ability to devour Coleridge's *Lay Sermons* (*Letters* 1:175).

A number of Wordsworth's poems and essays appeared in *The Friend,* first issued in 1809–10 and reissued in book form in 1812. Haydon subscribed to *The Friend* upon its first appearance, and Hunt, Shelley, and Hazlitt in their writings refer to the work and may have possessed copies, probably of the 1812 edition, since none appears in surviving lists of subscribers to the original periodical (Coleridge, *The Friend* 2:434–57). The Wordsworth pieces that were published for the first time in *The Friend* are as follows:[3]

The Prelude 1.401–63; 10.79–82, 105–44 (2:258–59, 147–48)

Of mortal parents is the Hero born; Advance–come forth from thy Tyrolean ground (signed "W. W."; 2:153)

The Excursion 1.500–502 (identified as "the Poet's pathetic complaint"), 626 (2:292, 172)

Alas! what boots the long laborious quest (signed "W. W."; 2:183)

"A Reply to 'Mathetes'" (signed "M. M."; 2:229–32, 260–69)

The Land we from our Fathers had in trust; And is it among rude untutor'd vales; O'er the wide earth, on mountain and on plain; On the report of the submission of the TYROLESE ("It was a *moral* end for which they fought") (2:233–35)

Epitaphs Translated from Chiabrera: "There never breath'd a man who when his life," "Destined to war from very infancy"; "Not without heavy grief of heart did He," "Pause, courteous Spirit!—Balbi supplicates"; "Perhaps some needful service of the State," "O Thou who movest onward with a mind" (anon.; 2:248–49, 269–70, 334–35)

"Essay on Epitaphs" (anon.; 2:335–46)

Of these works, only *The Prelude* 10.79–82 and the "Reply to 'Mathetes'" were not reprinted within Keats's lifetime. The "Essay on Epitaphs" was included as a note to *The Excursion,* and all of the sonnets, the two longer extracts from *The Prelude,* and the translations from Chiabrera were reprinted in the 1815 edition.

A number of previously published Wordsworth poems are quoted or printed in full in *The Friend.* They are (the original publication date is included in parenthesis):

My heart leaps up (1807; 2:41n)

September, 1802. Near Dover 9–11 (1807; 2:56)

Tintern Abbey 105–6 (1798; 2:79)

Another year!–another deadly blow! (1807; 2:87)

The Female Vagrant 179–80 (*Guilt and Sorrow* 368–69) (1798; 2:175)

Thought of a Briton on the Subjugation of SWITZERLAND ("Two Voices are there; one is of the Sea") (1807; 2:233)

Ode to Duty 57–64 (1807; 2:269)

Michael 411–12 (1800; 2:327n)

It is possible that Keats read in *The Friend* some of these Wordsworth pieces or passages, though none left a perceptible mark on Keats's own writing.

Scholars have proposed several echoes of *The White Doe of Rylstone*

(1815) in Keats's poems (see checklist, Poems from Other Editions). Rey-
nolds possessed a copy of this work (Healey 15), and Hunt in a footnote to
the 1815 *Feast of the Poets* (109n) reports the poem's publication and gives
his opinion of it, which is mixed. Hunt's note makes clear that he either
owned or had access to *The White Doe*, however, so that Keats could have
acquired a copy from either of his friends.

Three of Wordsworth's sonnets appeared in the *Examiner* during the
first quarter of 1816: *How clear, how keen, how marvellously bright* in the 28
January issue; *While not a leaf seems faded; while the fields* on 11 February; and
To B. R. Haydon ("High is our calling, Friend!—Creative Art") on 31
March (Healey 100). In addition, the 18 February 1816 *Examiner* carried an
article entitled "Heaven Made a Party to Earthly Disputes—Mr. Words-
worth's Sonnets on Waterloo," in which Hunt printed and reviewed three
poems that had appeared two weeks earlier in the *Champion: Occasioned by
the Battle of Waterloo* ("Intrepid sons of Albion! not by you"), *Occasioned by
the Battle of Waterloo* ("The Bard—whose soul is meek as dawning day"),
and *Siege of Vienna Raised by John Sobieski* ("O, for a kindling touch from
that pure flame") (Blunden, *"Examiner" Examined* 57). Keats was a regular
reader of the *Examiner* at this time and probably encountered Wordsworth's
sonnets there. Indeed, Ward believes that Keats "had not heard of [Words-
worth] till Hunt printed a few of his sonnets in the *Examiner*" (69). The
first three sonnets were sent to the *Examiner* by Haydon, who received
them from Wordsworth in a letter dated 21 December 1815 (Wordsworth,
Letters 258). When Haydon received the sonnets on 29 December, he ecsta-
tically recorded the event in his journal and remembered it years afterward
as one of the greatest honors bestowed on him in his life (see *Diary* 1:491–
92; 5:185; *Autobiography* 1:227–29; 2:672). Since Haydon was so proud of
his gift from Wordsworth, he may have shown the manuscript copies to
Keats. *To B. R. Haydon* also appeared in the *Champion* for 31 March 1816
and *Annals of the Fine Arts, for 1817* (1818) (Healey 17); in addition, all six
sonnets were reprinted in *Thanksgiving Ode, With Other Short Pieces* (1816).

In the 20 October 1816 *Champion*, Reynolds favorably reviewed Words-
worth's *Thanksgiving Ode* (Reynolds 76–84). Keats met Reynolds in Octo-
ber 1816, and the aspiring young poet may have been eager to read at this
time both his new friend's recent review and the literary work it extolled.
Benjamin Bailey also possessed a copy of *Thanksgiving Ode* (Healey 18), so
that Keats could have read it for the first or second time while visiting at
Oxford.

Another, rather uncommon Wordsworth publication that Bailey pos-
sessed was *A Letter to a Friend of Robert Burns* (1816) (Healey 17). The work

must have acquired some notoriety for Keats when he heard Hazlitt criticize it at length in his February 1818 lecture "On Burns, and the Old English Ballads" (Hazlitt 5:128–32). The lecture took place after Keats's visit to Bailey, but the poet perhaps could have acquired Wordsworth's pamphlet from Hazlitt or another of his London literary friends. Then again, Keats may have accepted Hazlitt's condemnation of the essay and not have bothered hunting it down.

Although he never reports reading Wordsworth's *Peter Bell* (1819), it would be difficult to imagine Keats did not do so, after the expectation built up by Reynolds's anticipatory parody. Indeed, Jack Stillinger believes that "Reynolds and Keats would be among the earliest readers of the real *Peter Bell* when it came out," and he finds evidence of the poem's influence on *Ode to Psyche* and the other great odes of 1819 ("Wordsworth and Keats" 192–95). Even if Keats did not read the entire *Peter Bell,* he probably saw Hunt's 2 May 1819 *Examiner* review, which contained a number of extracts from the poem (see Hunt, *Literary Criticism* 143–47). In the course of his review Hunt quotes lines 1–7, 143–47, 291–320, 511– 20, and 821–39 of *Peter Bell* and lines 10–14 of the sonnet *Malham Cove,* which was included in the *Peter Bell* volume along with two other sonnets "Suggested by Mr. Westall's Views of the Caves, etc., in Yorkshire" (*Pure element of waters! wheresoe'er; At early dawn, or rather when the air*). These three sonnets had first appeared in *Blackwood's Edinburgh Magazine* in January 1819 (Moorman 372), where Keats might have seen them, although he is unlikely to have read *Blackwood's* with much interest or regularity.

Hyder Rollins (*Letters* 2:78n.4) asserts, without further explanation, that Keats knew Wordsworth's *Vernal Ode,* published in *The River Duddon . . . and Other Poems* (1820). There is no solid evidence that Keats read this poem or any others in *The River Duddon* collection, however, although it appeared in May while Keats was still alive and in England (Moorman 374).

Finally, critics occasionally have proposed that Keats read in manuscript form Wordsworth poems that were not published until after the younger poet's death. Such manuscript reading on Keats's part, however, is extremely unlikely. Keats was not intimate with Wordsworth and never received poems in the mail from Rydal Mount, as Haydon did. Thorpe suggests that, when Wordsworth visited the capital in the winter of 1817–18, he may have read *The Prelude* to his London friends, "gathered at one of the usual meeting places—Haydon's or Hunt's perhaps" ("Wordsworth and Keats" 1022). None of Wordsworth's literary acquaintances mentions any such reading, however, and the accounts that do exist of Wordsworth's 1817–18 London visit describe readings or recitings of published rather than unpublished work (see, for example, Haydon, *Diary* 2:148, 171; Clarke and Clarke 149–50).

The evidence that exists allows us to conclude that Keats read *The Excursion* and either the 1815 edition alone or, more likely, *Lyrical Ballads* (the second, third, or fourth edition), *Poems in Two Volumes* (1807), and the 1815 *Poems*. Of these works, the number and nature of Keats's references indicate that he was most influenced by *The Excursion* and poems first published in 1807, to a lesser extent by those first published in *Lyrical Ballads,* and least of all by those first published in *Poems* (1815).[4] In addition, he may have read other Wordsworth publications that appeared through May 1820. The only principal editions of Wordsworth published during the younger poet's lifetime for which no evidence or arguments for Keats's reading exist are *Descriptive Sketches* (1793) and *The Waggoner* (1819).

When Keats Read Wordsworth

One way to determine when Keats read Wordsworth, especially initially, is to consider the literary tastes of the various friends who influenced the poet's career. Charles Cowden Clarke, by Keats's own admission, "first taught me all the sweets of song" (*To Charles Cowden Clarke,* line 53), and both men have left records of Keats's debt to his schoolmaster and friend for his first acquaintance with Chaucer, Spenser, Shakespeare, Chapman's Homer, and other writers (see *To Charles Cowden Clarke,* and Clarke and Clarke 125–26, 128–31). Wordsworth, however, does not appear to have been one of the poets to whom Clarke introduced Keats. Keats's verse epistle mentions no contemporary writers, except Leigh Hunt, and Clarke's commonplace book, kept from 1810 to October 1818, contains no extracts from Wordsworth (see Coldwell 89). Ward writes that, during the period when Clarke was Keats's mentor, the former's "tastes in poetry were typical of a well-read young schoolmaster of his time, broad but not revolutionary; it is doubtful . . . he yet knew the work of Wordsworth" (29; see also Gittings, *John Keats* 56). It is possible that Clarke learned something about Wordsworth from Hunt, whom he met in 1813 when Hunt's conversion from a detractor to an admirer of Wordsworth had begun.[5] There is no indication, however, that Clarke himself read or recommended Wordsworth at this time. English literature was not part of the school curriculum in Keats's day, and the library at John Clarke's school does not appear to have included contemporary verse (see Clarke and Clarke 123–24). It is therefore unlikely that Keats encountered Wordsworth's poetry as a student at Clarke's school or as an apothecary's apprentice, during which time Clarke remained his chief literary advisor and source of reading material.

George Felton Mathew, with whom Keats enjoyed "a brotherhood in song" in 1815 (*To George Felton Mathew,* line 2), also does not appear to have been an admirer of Wordsworth. Indeed, Gittings believes that Mathew deplored the earliest influence of Wordsworth on Keats's verse and that Wordsworthian elements in *To George Felton Mathew* signaled the end of the two young men's "intellectual friendship" (*John Keats* 57; see also 54– 55). Gittings offers little evidence to support his assertions, and the review Mathew wrote of Keats's 1817 *Poems* suggests that he was familiar with at least *The Excursion* (see checklist, *The Excursion:* Direct References). Still, Wordsworth would not have satisfied Mathew's taste for sentimental, chivalric verse, and one cannot imagine Mathew recommending him to Keats in 1815.

It was not until October of 1816 that Keats met literary men—Haydon, Reynolds, and Hunt at this time—who appreciated Wordsworth's poetry. It is not until November 1816, moreover, that Keats in his poems and letters directly quotes and expresses admiration of the elder poet. Scholars nevertheless have discovered echoes of Wordsworth in poems Keats wrote before October 1816: *On Peace; O come, dearest Emma! the rose is full blown; Woman! when I behold thee flippant, vain; O Solitude; Specimen of an Induction to a Poem; Calidore; To Charles Cowden Clarke;* and *On First Looking into Chapman's Homer.* On the basis of these echoes, one presumes, Gittings (*John Keats* 52) and Allott (*Poems* 23) assert that Keats bought and began reading Wordsworth's *Poems* (1815) in the fall of 1815.

Whether or not one believes Keats read Wordsworth in 1815 depends, of course, on the degree to which one is convinced by the various echoes that have been proposed. Supposing at least some of the echoes are valid, one might wonder what prompted Keats to begin reading Wordsworth at this time. Certainly, as Gittings argues (*John Keats* 56–57), Keats could have discovered the older poet on his own. One possible outside impetus to Keats's initial reading of Wordsworth, however, may have been Leigh Hunt's 1815 edition of *The Feast of the Poets.*

As I mentioned in note 5, the first edition of *The Feast* (1811) ridicules Wordsworth and excludes him from Apollo's banquet. The 1814 edition is more generous, however, and in the 1815 edition, though Hunt in a long note still makes clear his objections to the man's poetry and politics, Wordsworth is celebrated as "the Prince of the Bards of his Time!" (18).[6]

Keats, following Clarke, was in 1815 an ardent admirer of Hunt; one of Keats's earliest poems was *Written on the Day That Mr. Leigh Hunt Left*

Prison on 2 February 1815, and other poems composed before Keats met Hunt extoll the loved "Libertas" (*To My Brother George,* line 24; *To Charles Cowden Clarke,* line 44). In November 1815 Hunt sent Clarke a copy of the latest edition of *The Feast of the Poets* (Clarke and Clarke 192–94; see also Finney 1:72 and Gittings, *John Keats* 55). At this time, Clarke may have been responsible for introducing Keats to Wordsworth via Hunt's *Feast.* Indeed, Gittings believes Keats read *The Feast of the Poets* with Clarke on 9 November 1815, when students at Guy's Hospital were given a holiday (*John Keats* 55). Hunt's praise of Wordsworth in the preface, verse, and notes of the 1815 edition could very well have inspired the young poet to acquire and read his elder contemporary. One should also recall that in January, February, and March of 1816, Hunt further expressed his endorsement of Wordsworth by printing several of the latter's sonnets in the *Examiner.* Moreover, the most convincing echoes of Wordsworth identified in Keats's early poems are those in *O Solitude* and *Specimen of an Induction to a Poem,* both composed in spring 1816 after Keats could have seen *The Feast of the Poets* and the *Examiner* issues containing Wordsworth's sonnets.

If Keats hadn't been encouraged to read Wordsworth by *The Feast of the Poets* or the *Examiner,* however, he almost certainly would have been by Hunt in person after the two men met in October 1816. Hunt's attitude toward Wordsworth during the time he knew Keats is expressed in the 1815 edition of *The Feast of the Poets;* in his review of Keats's 1817 *Poems* (*Examiner* 1 June; 6, 13 July 1817); and in his Preface to *Foliage* (1818). He liked Wordsworth's descriptions of nature and, to a certain extent, his simple language; as he says in his notes to *The Feast of the Poets* (1815), "it is high time for poetry in general to return to nature and to a natural style, and . . . he will perform a great and useful work to society, who shall assist it to do so" (93). In addition, he was profoundly impressed by the account in book 4 of *The Excursion* of the origin of Greek mythology. In his Preface to *Foliage,* Hunt declares that his 1817 poem *The Nymphs* was "founded on that beautiful mythology, which it is not one of the least merits of the new school to be restoring to its proper estimation" (20). As the above remarks suggest, Hunt felt that the Lake Poets, and Wordsworth in particular, were to be credited with reviving "a true taste for nature" in English poetry, which during the eighteenth century had been characterized by "little imagination, of a higher order, no intense feeling of nature, no sentiment, no real music or variety" (review of Keats's 1817 *Poems;* Matthews 56). Nevertheless, Hunt criticized Wordsworth's "morbid" tendency in dwelling on "Idiot Boys, Mad Mothers, Wandering Jews, Visitations of Ague, [and] Indian Women left to die on the road," instead of describing "the beauties of nature and the simplicities of life" (*Feast* 1815, 94). Hunt also thought Wordsworth erred in being too solitary, brooding, and subjective. Wordsworth's penchant for "morbid abstractions," Hunt says, "turns our thoughts away from society and men altogether, and nourishes that eremitical vagueness of sensation,—that making a business of reverie . . . which is the next step to melancholy or indifference"; Wordsworth "thinks us over-active, and would make us over-contemplative. . . . We are, he thinks, too much crowded together, and too subject, in consequence, to high-fevered tastes and worldly infections. Granted:—he, on the other hand, lives too much apart, and is subject, we think, to low-fevered tastes and solitary morbidities" (*Feast* 1815, 97, 107). The chief problem with all of Wordsworth's flaws, in Hunt's opinion, is that they "endanger those great ends of poetry, by which it should assist the uses and refresh the spirits of life" (*Feast* 1815, 90).[7]

Hunt's influence on Keats's reading and understanding of Wordsworth is probably most pronounced in *Sleep and Poetry* and *I stood tip-toe upon a little hill,* both written entirely or in part during the last three months of 1816. Scholars, beginning with Richard Woodhouse, have found in *Sleep and Poetry* numerous echoes of Wordsworth's poems, particularly *Tintern Abbey* (1798), *The world is too much with us* (1807), and *To the Daisy* (1807). Hunt, in his review of Keats's 1817 volume, explains lines 230–47 of *Sleep and Poetry* as an "object[ion] to the morbidity that taints the productions of the Lake Poets" (Matthews 62). Keats's characterization in the same poem of eighteenth-century poets as "Men . . . who could not understand / [Apollo's] glories" (lines 184–85) echoes Hunt's own views, as does Keats's definition of "the great end / Of poesy": "that it should be a friend / To sooth the cares, and lift the thoughts of man" (lines 245–47). It is therefore likely that the young poet at this time also adopted Hunt's opinion of Wordsworth's faults.[8] Keats would have been following Hunt by celebrating Wordsworth's "music" in lines 224–26 of his poem, however, and "Libertas" may very well have encouraged Keats's reading and appreciation of the Wordsworth poems echoed in *Sleep and Poetry*.

From Hunt's review of Keats's first volume we also learn that the last 117 lines of *I stood tip-toe upon a little hill* recount the origin of Greek myth "on the ground suggested by Mr Wordsworth in a beautiful passage of his *Excursion*" (Matthews 59). Aileen Ward believes that Keats in this passage is not echoing *The Excursion* but only what he had heard of that poem from Hunt (421n.8). Ward is alone in arguing this position, however, and it is hard to believe that Keats would accept Hunt's interpretation of Wordsworth's poem without reading the work for himself. Nevertheless, it is

probably fair to say that Hunt introduced Keats to *The Excursion* in the fall
of 1816 and that *I stood tip-toe* largely reflects the older man's understanding
of that work.

Another person Keats met in the fall of 1816 who would have encour-
aged him to read Wordsworth was Benjamin Robert Haydon, who was
personally acquainted with the elder poet. In January 1817 Haydon sent
Wordsworth a copy of Keats's sonnet beginning "Great spirits now on
earth are sojourning," thereby introducing Wordsworth to Keats's poetry,
and in December 1817 he arranged the first meeting between the two poets
at Thomas Monkhouse's residence in London (Bate, *John Keats* 97, 264–65;
Keats Circle 2:143). For Haydon, Wordsworth was a great man—one of the
gods in the artist's pantheon. On 13 June 1815 he wrote in his *Diary,* "I
don't know any man I should be so inclined to worship as a purified being"
(1:451), and, as mentioned above, he counted receiving three sonnets from
Wordsworth in December 1815 as one of the great honors of his life. He
was not above criticizing Wordsworth, especially after 1817, but in 1816
he was generally an ardent supporter.[9]

It is surely significant that the three earliest of Keats's direct references
to or quotations from Wordsworth occur in poems or letters written to
Haydon. In *Addressed to Haydon,* Keats quotes *Character of the Happy Warrior*
(1807), a poem the artist in 1842 listed as one of Wordsworth's "finest
productions" (*Diary* 5:234). *Addressed to the Same,* composed the day after
Keats and Charles Cowden Clarke spent the evening with Haydon, cele-
brates Wordsworth as one of the "Great spirits now on earth."[10] Finally,
the 21 November 1816 letter in which Keats sent Haydon a revised fair
copy of the latter poem concludes, "The Idea of your sending [the sonnet]
to Wordsworth put me out of breath—you know with what Reverence—I
would send my Wellwishes to him" (*Letters* 1:118). Perhaps too it was
partly under the influence of Haydon's outlook and manner of speaking
that Keats inscribed the copy of *Poems* (1817) he sent to Wordsworth, "with
the Author's sincere Reverence" (Bate, *John Keats* 149). Haydon undoubt-
edly contributed to Keats's sense of the elder poet's grandeur and impor-
tance, and he probably encouraged Keats to read some of his (Haydon's)
favorite Wordsworth poems.[11]

John Hamilton Reynolds is best remembered for his 1819 parody of *Peter
Bell,* but in October 1816 when Keats met him he was a confirmed Words-
worthian. Reynolds's 1814 *The Eden of the Imagination* and several poems
in his 1816 collection *The Naiad* reflect Wordsworth's influence, and Rey-
nolds sent copies of both volumes to Rydal Mount (Jones 52, 55, 67, 70,
73–75). Reynolds also published a *Sonnet to Wordsworth* in the 18 February

1816 *Champion* (Reynolds 432). In a number of 1815 and 1816 *Champion* articles, moreover, he comments on and quotes from nearly all of Wordsworth's extant publications: *Lyrical Ballads, Poems in Two Volumes, An Evening Walk,* and *Thanksgiving Ode.* He also quotes extensively Wordsworth's remarks on poetry in the "Essay, Supplementary to the Preface" of 1815.[12] For Reynolds, Wordsworth was the poet *par exellence* of nature and of "gentle tastes, quiet feelings, and innocent affections" ("Mr. Wordsworth's Poetry"; Reynolds 26). More than anything else, however, Reynolds celebrated Wordsworth's "power of calling forth the retired thoughts and fleeting recollections of the mind" ("Mr. Wordsworth's Poetry"; Reynolds 25). Wordsworth, Reynolds writes in another essay, is a "great contemplative genius"; "he gives the intellectual part of those who apply to him, something serious and severe to do. . . . He turns the soul inward, to muse upon and enjoy its own realities" ("Wordsworth's *Thanksgiving Ode*"; Reynolds 81). In his article "On Egotism in Literature," Reynolds approves Wordsworth's introspection, saying "The 'moods' of a great poet's mind are valuable at all times" (Reynolds 62). From Reynolds in 1816 Keats perhaps first came to regard Wordsworth as the chief example of a new type of meditative, subjective, modern poet. It was in letters to Reynolds that Keats later compared Wordsworth's "Egotis[m]" to the Elizabethans' "unobtrusive[ness]" and Wordsworth's concern with human experience to Milton's less sophisticated (in Keats's view) philosophy (letters of 3 February and 3 May 1818, respectively). Reynolds also may have encouraged Keats to read certain Wordsworth poems the younger man hadn't encountered before, such as *An Evening Walk* and *Thanksgiving Ode* (see "Which of Wordsworth's Works Keats Read").

If Keats was open to the suggestions and opinions of his friends in the fall and winter of 1816–17, he appears to have wanted to cut himself off from their—and especially from Hunt's—influence when he began writing *Endymion* in April 1817. He left Hampstead for the Isle of Wight and then Margate, Canterbury, and Hastings to begin book 1, and he finished book 1 and composed book 2 at Hampstead during the summer, apparently keeping fairly much to himself.[13] What reading Keats did at this time was therefore most likely self-directed.

Clearly, as his letters reveal, Keats was reading Shakespeare in April, May, and June of 1817. No such clear evidence exists that he also read Wordsworth, but books 1 and 2 of *Endymion* contain numerous echoes of Wordsworth's poems, particularly *The Excursion.* That fact is not surprising, since book 4 of *The Excursion* apparently gave Keats the idea of retelling one of the Greek myths, and the poem also was an important contemporary example of an ambitious, long narrative work. Keats may simply have recalled lines from *The Excursion* as he worked on *Endymion,* or he may actually have reread passages, especially in book 4, from which most of the alleged echoes derive. One can easily imagine Keats turning to Wordsworth for guidance and inspiration as he embarked on his first major narrative poem.

Keats wrote book 3 of *Endymion* in September 1817 while staying with Benjamin Bailey at Oxford, and for this period we have clear evidence that the young poet was reading Wordsworth. Keats tells Reynolds in a 21 September 1817 letter that he and Bailey "have read Wordsworth" while boating in "Reynolds's Cove" (*Letters* 1:162). In this and earlier letters from Oxford, Keats also directly quotes or refers to *Written in March, While Resting on the Bridge at the Foot of Brother's Water* (1807); *Ode: Intimations of Immortality* (1807); *Personal Talk* (1807); *The Old Cumberland Beggar* (1800); and *Resolution and Independence* (1807). Writing to Milnes in 1849 and apparently referring to this period, Bailey cited passages Keats particularly liked from *Tintern Abbey* (1798); *Ode: Intimations of Immortality* (1807); *She dwelt among the untrodden ways* (1800); and *The Excursion* (see checklist under the appropriate volumes: Direct References). As Thorpe remarks, this list of poems suggests that, at Oxford, Keats and Bailey were reading from a second or later edition of *Lyrical Ballads, Poems in Two Volumes,* and *The Excursion* ("Wordsworth and Keats" 1014).[14] As noted above, Bailey also owned copies of *Concerning the Convention of Cintra* (1809), *A Letter to a Friend of Robert Burns* (1816), and *Thanksgiving Ode* (1816) (Healey 13, 17–18), which Keats may have examined during his Oxford visit.

Bailey clearly was the staunchest Wordsworthian among Keats's friends. As he told Milnes in 1849, "I had always been, (at least from the year 1813) through good & through evil report, one of the few unflinching admirers of Mr Wordsworth's poetry" (*Keats Circle* 2:286). When Keats came to visit him in 1817, Bailey found the young man's appreciation of Wordsworth deficient: "[he] seemed to me to value this great Poet rather in particular passages than in the full length portrait, as it were, of the great imaginative & philosophic Christian Poet, which he really is, & which Keats obviously, not long afterwards, felt him to be" (*Keats Circle* 2:274). Bailey apparently took it upon himself to correct the deficiency he perceived in Keats, both by urging extensive reading in the whole of Wordsworth's corpus and by advancing his own interpretation of those works. Bailey's remarks to Milnes just quoted suggest what this interpretation was. If Hunt enjoyed Wordsworth's descriptions of nature and the origin of Greek myths, Haydon liked his sublimity and ambition, and Reynolds responded to his self-expression, Bailey revered Wordsworth for his morals and ideas: his compassion for suffering humanity; his notion that individuals grow and change, with corresponding losses and gains; his attempt throughout his career to understand human life and thereby lighten "the burthen of the mystery." When Keats quotes the latter phrase from *Tintern Abbey* (1798) and when, in October and November 1817 letters to Bailey, he quotes "years that bring the philosophic mind" and "who has kept watch o'er Man's mortality" from the *Intimations* ode (1807), Keats is reflecting the clergyman's interest in Wordsworth (see checklist, *Lyrical Ballads* [1798] and *Poems in Two Volumes* [1807]: Direct References). This is not to say that Keats was merely echoing Bailey's views. Bailey pointed out to Keats an aspect of Wordsworth that profoundly interested the young man and became a permanent element in his thinking about the nature and function of poetry.[15]

Echoes of Wordsworth in book 4 of *Endymion* and, more important, direct quotations and references in letters, especially to Bailey, suggest that Keats continued his serious reading of Wordsworth throughout the fall of 1817. In particular, a detailed analysis of *Gipsies* (1807) in a 29 October 1817 letter to Bailey reveals close reading of or at least serious thinking about the elder poet at this time. One impetus to Keats's continued study of Wordsworth this fall would have been the latter's impending visit to the capital in December. Clarence Thorpe believes that "the Haydon-Hunt group were reading and discussing Wordsworth at every opportunity" in preparation for the bard's arrival ("Wordsworth and Keats" 1022).

Keats's only meetings with Wordsworth took place this winter, and the younger poet's letters, along with the accounts of several friends, record the series of disappointing events that seems to have tarnished the older man's image in Keats's eyes: the "pretty piece of Paganism" response to Keats's "Hymn to Pan"; Wordsworth's dressing up for a dinner at Deputy Comptroller of Stamps John Kingston's; and his various supercilious statements.[16] It was not long after Wordsworth's visit that, in a 3 February 1818 letter to Reynolds, Keats wrote his strongest criticism of the elder poet's egotism and rejected him along with Hunt in favor of Shakespeare and Milton as literary models. Throughout the spring of 1818, in fact, impatient or critical remarks about Wordsworth occur frequently in Keats's letters.[17]

Wordsworth's visit was not the only reason for the decline in Keats's reverence, however; another strong influence on Keats's thinking about Wordsworth and poets generally at this time was William Hazlitt. Hazlitt had been writing for the *Examiner* since 1814, and Keats probably met him at Hunt's in the winter of 1816–17 (Muir, "Keats and Hazlitt" 139). Nevertheless, Hazlitt's real influence on Keats does not seem to have begun until late September 1817, when the latter reported reading *The Round Table* with Bailey (*Letters* 1:166). One of the essays in this collection was Hazlitt's review of *The Excursion,* first published in the *Examiner* in 1814. Although Hazlitt concludes this essay by refuting Wordsworth's depiction of North England rural folk as pure and wise, he finds a good deal to praise in the poem in the first part of his review. As Allott says ("Keats and Wordsworth" 41–42), this must be the reason why Keats found no contradiction in celebrating together *The Excursion* and "Hazlitt's depth of taste" on 10 and 13 January 1818 (*Letters* 1:203, 204–5). Further evidence that Keats for a time associated Wordsworth with Hazlitt is the fact that he transcribed a quotation from *The Excursion* onto the title page of his copy of Hazlitt's *Characters of Shakespear's Plays* (Forman 5:280).[18] Keats had also read Hazlitt's harsh comments on *Gipsies* (1807) in the *Round Table* essay "On Manner," for he discussed that passage and attempted to mediate between poet and critic in his 29 October 1817 letter to Bailey (*Letters* 1:173–74).

It would seem to have been the criticism of Wordsworth in Hazlitt's lectures on the English poets, delivered at the Surrey Institute from 13 January to 3 March 1818, that particularly impressed Keats and helped alter his own opinion of Wordsworth. As we have seen, on 13 January Keats was still extolling *The Excursion.* Only eight days after attending the lecture "On Milton and Shakespeare," however, he repeats Hazlitt's contrast between the older, selfless poets and the egotistical moderns in his 3 February 1818 letter to Reynolds.[19]

Probably Hazlitt's incisive criticism, the disappointing meeting with Wordsworth, and Keats's independent thinking about poetry combined to make the young man impatient with Wordsworth in the spring of 1818. And yet, even during this period, Keats frequently echoes or quotes approvingly the older poet's works: *The Old Cumberland Beggar* (1800); *Expostulation and Reply* (1798); *The Excursion; To the Men of Kent. October, 1803* (1807); *The Redbreast Chasing the Butterfly* (1807); *Elegiac Stanzas* (1807); *Moods of My Own Mind* (1807); *Tintern Abbey* (1798); and *The Thorn* (1798). Moreover, on 3 May 1818 Keats wrote, again to Reynolds, his most glowing tribute to Wordsworth as a more humane and sophisticated poet than Milton. Clearly Keats was thinking about Wordsworth throughout the spring of 1818; the older man was intimately involved in the younger's reflections on the poet's role and responsibility. Although Keats need not have been reading Wordsworth during this time in order to contemplate the general nature of the latter's poetry, it is likely that the frequent remarks on Wordsworth in the letters were prompted or followed by some reading or rereading of the poems. In particular, one might assume that Keats had been reading Wordsworth shortly before he reassessed the Lake Poet's status in the 3 May letter to Reynolds. Perhaps, as Ward suggests, Keats had been rereading around this time the *Lyrical Ballads,* with their "beggars and gipsies . . . girls abandoned by their lovers and fathers by their sons" (178); his references to *Tintern Abbey* in the 3 May letter, along with his appreciation of Wordsworth's compassion for human suffering, suggest this possibility.[20]

Keats's attitude toward Wordsworth does not appear to have undergone material changes after May 1818: throughout the rest of his brief life, Keats continued to voice periodic annoyance with the older poet's political views, self-centeredness, and prosaic characters, but he acknowledged Wordsworth as a great modern writer and profound influence on his own poetry and poetic theory in recurring quotations, references, and echoes. A few periods during which Keats seems to have particularly felt Wordsworth's influence remain to be considered.

In June and July of 1818, Keats and Charles Brown toured northern England and Scotland. Keats's respect for Wordsworth seems to have returned as he contemplated paying a call at Rydal Mount, but Wordsworth's absence on campaign for Lowther again provoked disappointment (see checklist, General References to Wordsworth in Keats's Writing: Prose). Nevertheless, Keats was impressed by the scenery of the Lake District, and he delighted to recognize a mountain peak described in *To Joanna* (1800). Scholars also have discovered echoes of a number of Wordsworth's poems—*The Excursion, Resolution and Independence* (1807), *Stargazers* (1807), *Ode: Intimations of Immortality* (1807)—in poems Keats composed during the northern tour. Keats had no opportunity to read Wordsworth on this expedition: the only books he and Brown had with them were Cary's translation of Dante and a copy of Milton (Bate, *John Keats* 348). The landscape of the Lake District therefore was most likely responsible for frequently bringing Wordsworth's verses into Keats's mind.

The next Keats poem that significantly reflects Wordsworth's influence is *Hyperion,* composed in the closing months of 1818 and early spring of 1819. Scholars have discovered more echoes of *The Excursion* in this work than in any other of Keats's compositions. As with *Endymion,* one wonders whether Keats was rereading *The Excursion* at this time, or whether the attempt at a long narrative poem called to mind Wordsworth's achievement in the same genre. In addition, *Hyperion's* bare, mountainous setting seems modeled on the scenery of the Lake District and Scotland, and these memories of Wordsworth country may in turn have touched off recollections of the poetry associated with it. Clearly Keats had not needed fresh readings to recall Wordsworth's poetry during the northern tour, and if he had previously studied *The Excursion* closely, he could have written under that poem's influence when he threw himself into a long work even more similar to *The Excursion* in theme and tone than *Endymion* had been. Still, it is possible that Keats did some rereading in *The Excursion* as he sat by his dying brother's bedside throughout that dreary fall. Perhaps he even turned to it in an effort to find solace for his own despondency over Tom's decline.

Another poem remarkable for the number of Wordsworthian echoes attributed to it is *Ode to a Nightingale*. Indeed, scholars have discovered more echoes of Wordsworth in this poem, line for line, than in any other of Keats's works. The variety of Wordsworth poems allegedly echoed is also unusual: *To the Cuckoo* (1807), *Tintern Abbey* (1798), *Resolution and Independence* (1807), *Ode: Intimations of Immortality* (1807), *O Nightingale! thou surely art* (1807), *The Green Linnet* (1807), *The Solitary Reaper* (1807), *The Excursion, Yarrow Visited* (1815), *The Female Vagrant* (1798), *Peter Bell,* and even the Preface to *Poems* (1815). If even a portion of these echoes are valid, one would have to call *Ode to a Nightingale* the most Wordsworthian of Keats's poems; and yet it is quintessentially Keatsian. Perhaps this poem best reflects the way in which Keats could absorb images, phrases, and cadences from another writer and then transform them into poetry uniquely his own. In this case, I should say that *Ode to a Nightingale* reflects not recent reading of Wordsworth, but Keats's entire past reading digested and incorporated into his own thoughts and feelings.

The final poem for which numerous echoes of Wordsworth have been proposed is, not surprisingly, *The Fall of Hyperion*. As with the earlier *Hyperion* poem, *The Excursion* is the work most frequently identified as a source of echoes. The same pattern I have traced before in *Endymion* and *Hyperion* applies to *The Fall:* when he embarked on an epic or long narrative poem, Keats seemed inevitably to turn to other notable works in the same genre for guidance. This he may have done literally—by reading or rereading *The Excursion, Paradise Lost,* and *The Divine Comedy*—or unconsciously, by process of association. There is no doubt that *The Fall of Hyperion,* with its searching debate over the ability of poetry to alleviate human suffering, owes a good deal to Wordsworth's example as a poet "That hath kept watch o'er man's mortality."

In conclusion, one can say that Keats probably began reading Wordsworth late in 1815 or in 1816 and had certainly read some poems by November 1816. He also probably began reading *The Excursion* in the fall of

1816 and may have continued reading or rereading that poem in the spring and summer of the following year. In September 1817 Keats embarked on a course of serious, concentrated reading of Wordsworth's corpus under Bailey's tutelage, and he most likely continued his study of Wordsworth throughout the remaining months of that year. From 1818 to the end of Keats's life it is difficult to pinpoint periods of new reading or rereading; Keats tends to quote or refer to the same poems or at least poems from the same collections throughout this period. Clearly Wordsworth remained an important influence on Keats's thought and art to the end of his career, however, and we can assume that the younger poet periodically renewed his acquaintance with his elder contemporary's compassionate, meditative verse.

An Evening Walk (1793)

DIRECT REFERENCES

"Old Matthew spoke to him some years ago on some nothing, & because he happens in an Evening Walk to imagine the figure of the old man—he must stamp it down in black & white, and it is henceforth sacred" (Keats to Reynolds, 3 February 1818; *Letters* 1:224).

ECHOES/ALLUSIONS

An Evening Walk (1793 Quarto text)	Keats Poem or Letter	Critic
line 23: "youth's wild eye"[21]	*La Belle Dame sans Merci* 16: "her eyes were wild"	Balslev 13n.6

Poems First Published in *Lyrical Ballads* (1798)

DIRECT REFERENCES

The Idiot Boy: characters Susan Gale and Betty Foy
"those three rhyming Graces Alice Fell, Susan Gale and Betty Foy. . . . the more he will hate the coarse Samplers of Betty Foy" (Keats's review of Reynolds's *Peter Bell; Letters* 2:94).

line 289: "Fond lovers! yet not quite hob nob."
"at a distance about 4 feet 'not quite hob nob'—as wordsworth says" (Keats to Woodhouse, 21 September 1819; *Letters* 2:169).

Tintern Abbey
"To this point was Wordsworth come, as far as I can conceive when he wrote 'Tintern Abbey'" (Keats to Reynolds, 3 May 1818; *Letters* 1:281).

lines 37–41
"Again, we often talked of that noble passage in the Lines on Tintern Abbey:—

'That blessed mood,
In which *the burthen of the mystery,*
In which the heavy & the weary weight
Of all this unintelligible world
Is lightened.'"

(Bailey to Milnes, 7 May 1849; *Keats Circle* 2:275)

line 38: "the burthen of the mystery"
"An extensive knowledge . . . helps, by widening speculation, to ease the
Burden of the Mystery. . . . We feel the 'burden of the Mystery'" (Keats to
Reynolds, 3 May 1818; *Letters* 1:277, 281).

ECHOES/ALLUSIONS

Lyrical Ballads (1798)	Keats Poem or Letter	Critic
Expostulation and Reply: philosophy of "wise passiveness"	19 February 1818 letter to Reynolds: "let us open our leaves like a flower and be passive and receptive. . . . I have not read any Books— the Morning said I was right" (*Letters* 1:232–33)	de Selincourt 534; Wigod 390; *Letters* 1:232n.4
Expostulation and Reply, The Tables Turned: "wise passiveness"	*O thou whose face hath felt the winter's wind*	de Selincourt 534; Finney 1: 367–68; Balslev 23–24; Allott, *Poems* 310–11
The Female Vagrant 205–7 (*Guilt and Sorrow* 394–96): " . . . Fretting the fever round the languid heart, / And groans"	*Ode to a Nightingale* 23–24: "The weariness, the fever, and the fret / Here, where men sit and hear each other groan"	Balslev 12
Goody Blake and Harry Gill 6: "Good duffle grey"	February (?) 1820 letter to Fanny Brawne: "Be very careful of . . . going without your duffle grey" (*Letters* 2:262)	*Letters* 2:262n.5

Lyrical Ballads (1798)	Keats Poem or Letter	Critic
Her Eyes Are Wild 1: "Her eyes are wild, her head is bare"	*La Belle Dame sans Merci* 16: "And her eyes were wild"; 31: "her wild wild eyes"	Finney 2:598; Bush, *Selected Poems* 344; Balslev 12; Bloom, *Visionary Company* 386; Allott, *Poems* 504; Wolfson 296
The Idiot Boy 13–14: "let Betty Foy / With girt and stirrup fiddle faddle" (*WPW* 2:68n)	*The Jealousies* 238: "And fiddle-faddle standest while you go"	de Selincourt 561; Balslev 22; Allott, *Poems* 714
The Thorn: various narrative and rhetorical techniques	*La Belle Dame sans Merci*	Wolfson 296–300
lines 65–66, 76–77, 241–42: "'Oh misery! oh misery! / Oh woe is me! oh misery!'"	*Isabella* 235, 503–4: "O misery!"; "'O cruelty . . .'"	Stillinger, *Hoodwinking* 43; Stillinger, "Wordsworth and Keats" 184
lines 69–74: obsession with special object	*Isabella* 417–24	Allott, *Poems* 348; Stillinger, "Wordsworth and Keats" 184
Simon Lee: narrator	*Isabella:* narrator	Wolfson 275–76, 279–80
Tintern Abbey: Nature is Presence that presides over speaker's growth	*Ode to Psyche:* Psyche is Presence that presides over speaker's growth	Waldoff 115–16
"notions about the mind, the feelings, association of ideas, perceiving, creating, remembering" (Stillinger)	22 November 1817 letter to Bailey on the imagination (*Letters* 1:184–85)	Stillinger, "Wordsworth and Keats" 189
lines 5–7: landscape description	*Ode to Psyche* 51, 54–55, 58: landscape	Bloom, *Visionary Company* 404; Waldoff 115; Wolfson 309
line 17: "Green to the very door"	26 June 1818 letter to Tom Keats: "shores and islands green to the marge" (*Letters* 1:298)	Lau (present work)

Lyrical Ballads (1798)	Keats Poem or Letter	Critic
Tintern Abbey 22–30: "These beauteous forms . . ."	*Endymion* 1.1–13: "A thing of beauty is a joy for ever . . ."	Finney 1:297; Wolfson 235
lines 22ff.: memories of landscape have aided speaker in various ways	*Endymion* 1.25–33: nature and poetry "Haunt us till they become a cheering light / Unto our souls"	Bush, *Selected Poems* 317
line 27: "In hours of weariness"	*Ode to a Nightingale* 23: "The weariness, the fever, and the fret"	Rivers
lines 41–42: ". . . In which the affections gently lead us on"	22 November 1817 letter to Bailey: "I am certain of nothing but of the holiness of the Heart's affections" (*Letters* 1: 184)	Stillinger, *Hoodwinking* 152
lines 45–46: "we are laid asleep / In body, and become a living soul"	*Ode on Indolence* 41–50: creative indolence	Vendler 31
line 49: "We see into the life of things"	22 November 1817 letter to Bailey: "the truth of Imagination" (*Letters* 1:184)	Stillinger, *Hoodwinking* 152–53
lines 52–53: "the fretful stir / Unprofitable, and the fever of the world"	*Ode to a Nightingale* 23: "The weariness, the fever, and the fret"	de Selincourt 474; Finney 2:627; Bush, *Selected Poems* 348; Balslev 12; Allott, *Poems* 526; Waldoff 122; Stillinger, "Wordsworth and Keats" 180
lines 65–111: stages of growth	*Sleep and Poetry* 85–162: stages of poetic career; 3 May 1818 letter to Reynolds: "Mansion of Many Apartments" passage (*Letters* 1:280–81)	de Selincourt 406–8; Lowell 1:219–23; Finney 1:163, 397–98; 2:462; Bush, *Selected Poems* 311–12; Balslev 17–19, 74; Allott, "Keats and Wordsworth" 35–37; Allott, *Poems* 73–74; Barnard, *Poems* 551[22]

Lyrical Ballads (1798)	Keats Poem or Letter	Critic
Tintern Abbey 65–111: stages of growth	The Fall of Hyperion book 1: stages of human development	Finney 2:462–65, 716
lines 94–112: sustaining presence in nature	Endymion 1.6–13, 26–28; 3.54–57, 93–96: beauty in nature and art that inspires love and reverence	Balslev 15–17
lines 95–97: "A sense sublime / Of something far more deeply interfused, / Whose dwelling is the light of setting suns"	Dear Reynolds, as last night I lay in bed 67–69: "O that our dreamings . . . Would all their colours from the sunset take: / From something of material sublime"	Bate, John Keats 308; Gittings, John Keats 203; Allott, Poems 323; Barnard, Poems 596; Wolfson 196–97
lines 101–3: ". . . rolls through all things"	Sleep and Poetry 290–91: "yet there ever rolls . . ."	Balslev 134
lines 106–7: "both what they half create, / And what perceive"	22 November 1817 letter to Bailey: "What the imagination seizes as Beauty must be truth . . ." (Letters 1:184)	Stillinger, Hoodwinking 153
lines 112–20: sister's presence	Endymion 1.407–12: sister	Balslev 14
lines 117–19: ". . . the shooting lights / Of thy wild eyes"	La Belle Dame sans Merci 16: "And her eyes were wild"	Balslev 12–13
To My Sister 31–32: "We for the years to come may take / Our temper from to-day"	9 June 1819 letter to Sarah Jeffrey: "You will judge of my 1819 temper when I tell you . . ." (Letters 2:116)	Muir, "Three Notes"; Letters 2:116n.2

Poems First Published in *Lyrical Ballads,* Second Edition (1800)

DIRECT REFERENCES

The Old Cumberland Beggar
"Has Martin met with the Cumberland Beggar" (Keats to Reynolds, 21 September 1817; *Letters* 1:166).

line 77: "a spirit and pulse of good."
"the Benefit done by great Works to the 'Spirit and pulse of good'" (Keats to Reynolds, 19 February 1818; *Letters* 1:231).

line 153: "That we have all of us one human heart."
"But then as Wordsworth says, 'we have all one human heart'" (Keats to George and Georgiana Keats, 19 March 1819; *Letters* 2:80).

The Pet-Lamb: character Barbara Lewthwaite
"to play at bob cherry with Barbara Lewthwaite" (Keats's review of Reynolds's *Peter Bell; Letters* 2:94).

She dwelt among the untrodden ways
"But in those exquisite stanzas:—'She dwelt among the untrodden ways, / Beside the springs of Dove—' ending,—

   'She lived unknown & few could know
      When Lucy ceased to be;
   But she is in her grave, & oh,
      The difference to me'—

the simplicity of the last line [Keats] declared to be the most perfect pathos" (Bailey to Milnes, 7 May 1849; *Keats Circle* 2:275–76).

To Joanna 56: "That ancient Woman seated on Helm-crag."
"[I] discovered without a hint 'that ancient woman seated on Helm Craig'" (Keats to George and Georgiana Keats, 27 June 1818; *Letters* 1:303).

"I discovered 'the ancient woman seated on Helm Crag'" (Keats to Tom Keats, 29 June 1818; *Letters* 1:307).

"[Wordsworth's] line—'That ancient woman seated on Helm Crag' was brought to remembrance as the object itself came in sight" (Charles Brown, "Walks in the North"; *Letters* 1:430).

The Two April Mornings 57–60: "Matthew is in his grave, yet now, / Methinks, I see him stand, / As at that moment, with a bough / Of wilding in his hand."
"Why with Wordsworth's 'Matthew with a bough of wilding in his hand' when we can have Jacques 'under an oak &c'—The secret of the Bough of Wilding will run through your head faster than I can write it—Old Matthew spoke to him some years ago on some nothing, & because he happens in an Evening Walk to imagine the figure of the old man—he must stamp it down in black & white, and it is henceforth sacred" (Keats to Reynolds, 3 February 1818; *Letters* 1:224).

ECHOES/ALLUSIONS

Lyrical Ballads (1800)	Keats Poem or Letter	Critic
Preface	Keats's theory of composition, expressed in various poems and letters	Finney 1:268–72
Hart-Leap Well	*O Solitude! if I must with thee dwell* 7: "the deer's swift leap"	Gittings, *John Keats* 53
lines 12, 109ff.: silent, blighted landscape	*Endymion* 4.963–68: while depressed, Endymion hears no sound	Balslev 124n
It was an April morning: fresh and clear 38–39: "this wild nook, / My EMMA, I will dedicate to thee"	*O come, dearest Emma! the rose is full blown* 1	de Selincourt 563; Gittings, *John Keats* 54; Allott, *Poems* 21–22; Barnard, *Poems* 537
Nutting	*I stood tip-toe upon a little hill* 43–46: "it may haply mourn / That such fair clusters should be rudely torn / From their fresh beds . . ."	Balslev 19–20

Lyrical Ballads (1800)	Keats Poem or Letter	Critic
The Old Cumberland Beggar 6–7, 16: description of old man	The Eve of St. Agnes 91–92, 97: description of Angela	Balslev 20–21
line 153: "we have all of us one human heart"	Why did I laugh tonight? No voice will tell 4: "Then to my human heart I turn"	Balslev 21–22
The Pet-Lamb	Ode on Indolence 54: "A pet-lamb in a sentimental farce!"	Lau (present work)
	9 June 1819 letter to Sarah Jeffrey: "I hope I am a little more of a Philosopher than I was, consequently a little less of a versifying Pet-lamb" (Letters 2:116)	Lau (present work)
A Poet's Epitaph 18–20: "Philosopher!—a fingering slave . . ."	Lamia 2.234–38: "Philosophy will clip an Angel's wings . . ."	Balslev 22
To Joanna 61: "Helvellyn far into the clear blue sky"	Addressed to the Same 3: "Who on Helvellyn's summit"	Allott, Poems 68
line 62: "old Skiddaw"	Endymion 4.394: "Or from old Skiddaw's top"	de Selincourt 573; Bush, Selected Poems 323; Allott, Poems 261

Poems First Published in *Poems in Two Volumes* (1807)

DIRECT REFERENCES

Alice Fell
"those three rhyming Graces Alice Fell, Susan Gale and Betty Foy. . . . the coarse Samplers of . . . Alice Fell" (Review of Reynolds's *Peter Bell; Letters* 2:94).

"Beloved Vale!" I said, "when I shall con" 7–9: "from mine eyes escaped no tears; / Deep thought, or dread remembrance, had I none. / By doubts and thousand petty fancies crost."

"'I shed no tears; / Deep thought, or awful vision, I had none; / By thousand petty fancies I was crossed.' Wordsworth" (Epigraph to *On Some Skulls in Beauley Abbey, near Inverness*).[23]

Character of the Happy Warrior 40: "Keeps faithful with a singleness of aim." "Oft may be found a 'singleness of aim'" (*Addressed to Haydon* 6).

Gipsies
Extended analysis of *Gipsies,* in response to Hazlitt's disparaging remarks on the poem in a note to his *Round Table* essay "On Manner" (Keats to Bailey, 29 October 1817; *Letters* 1:173–74).

Moods of My Own Mind (section title)
"I should judge it [*Gipsies*] to have been written in one of the most comfortable Moods of his Life" (Keats to Bailey, 29 October 1817; *Letters* 1:174).

"I am troubling you with Moods of my own Mind" (Keats to Bailey, 25 May 1818; *Letters* 1:287).

"Moods of one's mind! you know I hate them well" (*Dear Reynolds, as last night I lay in bed* 106).

Ode: Intimations of Immortality 142–50

> "'Not for these I raise
> The song of thanks & praise;
> But for those obstinate questionings
> Of sense & outward things,
> Fallings from us, vanishings;
> Blank misgivings of a creature
> Moving about in worlds not realized,
> *High instincts, before which our mortal nature*
> *Did tremble like a guilty thing surprized.*'

The last lines [Keats] thought were quite awful in their application to a guilty finite creature, like man, in the appalling nature of the feeling which they suggested to a thoughtful mind" (Bailey to Milnes, 7 May 1849; *Keats Circle* 2:275).

line 166: "Though inland far we be"
"'though inland far I be' I now hear the voice most audibly" (Keats to Jane and Mariane Reynolds, 14 September 1817; *Letters* 1:158).

Ode: Intimations of Immortality 181–82: "Though nothing can bring back the hour / Of splendour in the grass, of glory in the flower."
"though the world has taken on a quakerish look with me, which I once thought was impossible—

> 'Nothing can bring back the hour
> Of splendour in the grass and glory in the flower'

I once thought this a Melancholist's dream—" (Keats to Sarah Jeffrey, 31 May 1819; *Letters* 2:113).

line 190: "In years that bring the philosophic mind"
"to whom it is necessary that years should bring the philosophic Mind" (Keats to Bailey, 22 November 1817; *Letters* 1:186).

line 202: "That hath kept watch o'er man's mortality"
"he is the only Man 'who has kept watch on Man's Mortality'" (Keats to Bailey, 29 October 1817; *Letters* 1:173).

Personal Talk 1–2: "I am not One who much or oft delight / To season my fireside with personal talk."
"He [Hunt] agrees with the Northe[r]n Poet in this, 'He is not one of those who much delight to season their fireside with personal talk'" (Keats to Reynolds, 21 September 1817; *Letters* 1:163).

Resolution and Independence
"Has Martin . . . been wondering at the old Leech gatherer?" (Keats to Reynolds, 21 September 1817; *Letters* 1:166).

To the Men of Kent. October, 1803
"When I think of Wordswo[r]th's Sonnet 'Vanguard of Liberty! ye Men of Kent!' the degenerated race about me are Pulvis Ipecac Simplex a strong dose" (Keats to Bailey, 13 March 1818; *Letters* 1:241).

Written in March, While Resting on the Bridge at the Foot of Brother's Water 3–4: "The small birds twitter, / The lake doth glitter."
"Wordsworth sometimes, though in a fine way, gives us sentences in the Style of School exercises—for Instance

The lake doth glitter
Small birds twitter &c."

(Keats to Reynolds, September 1817; *Letters* 1:151)[24]

ECHOES/ALLUSIONS

Poems in Two Volumes (1807)	**Keats Poem or Letter**	**Critic**
The Affliction of Margaret 68–70: "I question things and do not find / One that will answer to my mind"	*Why did I laugh tonight? No voice will tell* 7–8: " . . . To question heaven and hell and heart in vain"	Balslev 59
Alice Fell 57: " 'let it be of duffil grey' "	February (?) 1820 letter to Fanny Brawne: "Be very careful of . . . going without your duffle grey" (*Letters* 2:262)	*Letters* 2:262n.5
Character of the Happy Warrior 3–7: "who, when brought / Among the tasks of real life, hath wrought / Upon the plan that pleased his boyish thought . . ."	*Sleep and Poetry* 96–98: "O for ten years . . . so I may do the deed / That my own soul has to itself decreed"	Balslev 56–57
lines 12–14: "doomed to go in company with Pain, / And Fear . . . glorious gain"	*Sleep and Poetry* 123–25, 128: speaker must take on "the agonies, the strife / Of human hearts"; "glorious fear"	Balslev 57
line 14: "glorious gain"	*On Receiving a Laurel Crown from Leigh Hunt* 6: "glorious gain"	Finney 1:179; Balslev 57
Composed by the Sea-Side, near Calais, August, 1802: "Thou hangest . . . On England's bosom. . . . Bright Star!"	*Bright star, would I were stedfast as thou art* 1, 10: "Pillow'd upon my fair love's ripening breast"	Balslev 54
Elegiac Stanzas: images of painting, castle, and ship	*Dear Reynolds, as last night I lay in bed:* images	Stillinger, "Wordsworth and Keats" 182

Poems in Two Volumes (1807)	Keats Poem or Letter	Critic
theme: cruelty in nature	*Dear Reynolds, as last night I lay in bed* 86–105: theme	Finney 1:391; Bush, *Selected Poems* 327; Balslev 52–53; Stillinger, "Wordsworth and Keats" 182
Fidelity 20, 25–26; note to line 20: references to and definition of "tarn"	*Endymion* 4.693: "mountain tarn"	de Selincourt 451[25]
Great men have been among us; hands that penned 1	*Addressed to the Same* 1: "Great spirits now on earth are sojourning"	Finney 1:148; Bush, *Selected Poems* 309; Balslev 59; Gittings, *John Keats* 99
lines 3–4: "The later Sidney, Marvel, Harrington, / Young Vane"	*Lines Written on 29 May, the Anniversary of Charles's Restoration, on Hearing the Bells Ringing* 5: "'Tis gallant Sydney's, Russell's, Vane's sad knell"	Balslev 59–60
lines 9–10: "France, 'tis strange / Hath brought forth no such souls as we had then"	27 (?) February 1820 letter to Fanny Brawne: ridicules Rousseau and concludes, "Thank God I am born in England with our own great Men before my eyes" (*Letters* 2:266–67)	*Letters* 2:267n.5
The Green Linnet: linnet with its ecstatic song is "Presiding Spirit" or personification of spring	*Ode to a Nightingale:* nightingale is "Dryad" singing happily of summer	Spens 239–40
lines 7–8 (1807 text; *WPW* 2:140n): "a Bird will be the toy / That doth my fancy tether"	*Fancy* 89–94: Fancy personified as bird restrained by a "silken leash"	Balslev 60–61
How sweet it is, when mother Fancy rocks 5: "And wild rose tip-toe upon hawthorne stocks"; theme of nature stimulating imagination	*I stood tip-toe upon a little hill:* opening	Gittings, *John Keats* 71

Poems in Two Volumes (1807)	Keats Poem or Letter	Critic
I wandered lonely as a cloud 23–24: "And then my heart with pleasure fills, / And dances with the daffodils"	Specimen of an Induction to a Poem 51: "And always does my heart with pleasure dance"	de Selincourt 391; Finney 1: 111; Gittings, John Keats 67; Allott, "Keats and Words-worth" 34; Allott, Poems 35; Barnard, Poems 541; Stillin-ger, "Wordsworth and Keats" 178
	Woman! when I behold thee flippant, vain 6–7: "E'en then, elate, my spirit leaps, and prances, / E'en then my soul with exultation dances"	Finney 1:111; Balslev 60
	Specimen of an Induction to a Poem 27–28: "Or when his spirit . . . Leaps"; Calidore 57, 71: "white coursers prancing"; "Anon he leaps along"	Finney 1:111
It is a beauteous evening, calm and free: religious imagery	Bright star, would I were stedfast as thou art: religious imagery	Balslev 53–54
lines 6–8: ". . . a sound like thunder"	Sleep and Poetry 27–28: "Coming sometimes like fearful claps of thunder, / Or the low rumblings earth's re-gions under"	Bate, John Keats 126
Methought I saw the footsteps of a throne: speaker sees and climbs mysterious stairs; be-holds woman's face	The Fall of Hyperion 1.81ff.	Balslev 33–35
My heart leaps up when I be-hold 1	Endymion 4.445: "His heart leapt up"	Allott, Poems 263
Nuns fret not at their convent's narrow room: argues that son-net form not constraining	If by dull rhymes our English must be chain'd: proposes making restrictive sonnet form more congenial	Balslev 51

Poems in Two Volumes (1807)	Keats Poem or Letter	Critic
Nuns fret not at their convent's narrow room 5–7: "bees that soar for bloom, / High as the highest Peak of Furness-fells, / Will murmur by the hour in foxglove bells"	*O Solitude! if I must with thee dwell* 7–8: "where the deer's swift leap / Startles the wild bee from the fox-glove bell"	de Selincourt 397; Finney 1:78; Bush, *Selected Poems* 306; Balslev 50–51; Gittings, *John Keats* 53; Allott, "Keats and Wordsworth" 33; Allott, *Poems* 23
	To My Brother George (epistle) 13–14: reference to "honey bee"	Balslev 51
O Nightingale! thou surely art: speaker prefers "homely tale" of Stock-dove to passionate song of nightingale	*Ode to a Nightingale:* speaker rejects nightingale for "commitment to a world of loss and suffering" (Manning)	Manning 191
lines 5–6: "Thou sing'st as if the God of wine / Had helped thee to a Valentine"	*Ode to a Nightingale* 15, 32: "O for a beaker full of the warm South"; "Not charioted by Bacchus"	Manning 190; Randel 52
line 13: "His voice was buried among trees"	*Ode to a Nightingale* 77–78: "and now 'tis buried deep / In the next valley-glades"	Manning 191; Randel 52[26]
Ode: Intimations of Immortality: conflict between sensation and thought	22 November 1817 letter to Bailey: "O for a Life of Sensations rather than of Thoughts!" (*Letters* 1:185)	Stillinger, "Wordsworth and Keats" 190
"sobered happiness of experience" (de Selincourt)	*Endymion* 4.819: "Perhaps ye are too happy to be glad"	de Selincourt 451
origin and development of soul	21 April 1819 letter to George and Georgiana Keats: world as a "vale of Soul-making" (*Letters* 2:101–2)	Wolfson 198; Stillinger, "Wordsworth and Keats" 191–92
repetitions	*Ode to Psyche* 30–35, 44–50	Vendler 50

Poems in Two Volumes (1807)	Keats Poem or Letter	Critic
Ode: Intimations of Immortality: compensation for loss	To Autumn 23–24: "Where are the songs of spring? . . . Think not of them . . ."	Vendler 236–37
eye/ear imagery	To Autumn	Bloom, Visionary Company 432–33
line 18: "there hath passed away a glory from the earth"	To Leigh Hunt, Esq. 1: "Glory and loveliness have passed away"	Allott, Poems 102
line 25: "The cataracts blow their trumpets from the steep"	Hyperion 2.358–63: ". . . And all the everlasting cataracts"	Bush, Selected Poems 337
lines 25–28: "steep," "mountains," "Winds"	Ode to Psyche 53–55: "wind," "mountains," "steep"	Vendler 59–60
lines 56–57: "Whither is fled the visionary gleam? . . . the glory and the dream?"	Ode to a Nightingale 79: "Was it a vision, or a waking dream?"	Allott, Poems 532; Barnard, Poems 658
line 77: "the light of common day"	Endymion 4.820: "a common day"	Balslev 63
line 168: "hear the mighty waters"	Not Aladdin magian 29: "Here his mighty waters play"	Bush, Selected Poems 331
Personal Talk: speaker sitting before fire	Sleep and Poetry 71–73: "Imaginings will hover / Round my fire-side . . ."	de Selincourt 405; Balslev 61–62
lines 25–26: "sweetest melodies / Are those that are by distance made more sweet"	Ode on a Grecian Urn 11–14: "Heard melodies are sweet, but those unheard / Are sweeter . . ."	de Selincourt 477; Balslev 62
scene described and line 38: "Matter wherein right voluble I am"	To My Brothers: scene described and line 7: "Upon the lore so voluble and deep"	de Selincourt 398; Bush, Selected Poems 309; Balslev 61; Gittings, John Keats 96; Allott, Poems 65

Poems in Two Volumes (1807)	Keats Poem or Letter	Critic
Personal Talk 38: "voluble"	The Eve of St. Agnes 204: "her heart was voluble"	de Selincourt 398
lines 49–50: "my little boat /Rocks in its harbour"	Endymion 1.46–47: "I'll smoothly steer / My little boat"	Gittings, John Keats 130
The Redbreast Chasing the Butterfly	Dear Reynolds, as last night I lay in bed 104–5: "The gentle robin, like a pard or ounce, / Ravening a worm"	Balslev 58–59
lines 3–5, 21–23: "Our little English Robin; / The bird that comes about our doors / When Autumn-winds are sobbing? . . . That, after their bewildering, / Covered with leaves the little children, / So painfully in the wood?"	This pleasant tale is like a little copse 13–14: "Meekly upon the grass, as those whose sobbings / Were heard of none beside the mournful robbins"	de Selincourt 540; Finney 1:182; Balslev 58; Allott, Poems 104
Resolution and Independence: cadence and meter; Burns source of painful reflection; mood of depression	On Visiting the Tomb of Burns	Balslev 41–42
lines 22–28: shift from joy to depression	Sleep and Poetry 155–62: speaker struggles against dejection after vision of charioteer vanishes	Balslev 43–44
lines 55–84: description of old man	Endymion 3.191–217: description of Glaucus	Balslev 40–41; Stillinger, "Wordsworth and Keats" 179
lines 59–60: "Wonder to all who do the same espy, / By what means it could thither come, and whence"	Sleep and Poetry 69–71: ". . . We must ever wonder how, and whence / It came"	Balslev 58[27]
lines 109–10: "seem / dream" rhyme	On Visiting the Tomb of Burns 2–3: "seem / dream"	Balslev 42

Poems in Two Volumes (1807)	Keats Poem or Letter	Critic
Resolution and Independence 115: "Cold, pain, and labour"	*On Visiting the Tomb of Burns* 3, 8: landscape is "cold"; "All is cold beauty; pain is never done"	Balslev 42–43
lines 127–28: "enumeration of qualities belonging to the object of contemplation" (Balslev)	*On Visiting the Tomb of Burns* 1–2	Balslev 42
lines 135–36: "with de-meanour kind, / But stately in the main"	*The Jealousies* 453: "Some-what in sadness, but pleas'd in the main"	de Selincourt 561; Balslev 44
The Solitary Reaper: image of maiden	*Ode to a Nightingale* 66–67: image of Ruth	Bush, *Selected Poems* 348; Balslev 50; Stillinger, "Wordsworth and Keats" 180
line 9: nightingale	*Ode to a Nightingale*	Stillinger, "Wordsworth and Keats" 180
lines 9–12: nightingale con-soles weary travelers	*Ode to a Nightingale* 65–67: nightingale's song heard by homesick Ruth	Allott, *Poems* 530
lines 15–16: "Breaking the si-lence of the seas / Among the farthest Hebrides"	*Ode to a Nightingale* 69–70: "the foam / Of perilous seas . . ."	Balslev 50
line 18: "Perhaps the plain-tive numbers flow"	*Ode to a Nightingale* 75: "thy plaintive anthem fades"	Bush, *Selected Poems* 348; Al-lott, *Poems* 532; Stillinger, "Wordsworth and Keats" 180
lines 18–20: "Perhaps the plaintive numbers flow / For old, unhappy, far-off things . . ."	*Endymion* 1.435: "minstrel memories of times gone by"	Allott, *Poems* 139
lines 30–31: "as I mounted up the hill, / The music in my heart I bore"	*Ode to a Nightingale* 77: "Up the hill-side"	Allott, *Poems* 532

Poems in Two Volumes (1807)	Keats Poem or Letter	Critic
Sonnets Dedicated to Liberty: theme, style, phrases	On Peace	de Selincourt 562; Allott, Poems 5
Star-Gazers 13–28: ". . . Or is it that, when human Souls a journey long have had /And are returned into themselves, they cannot be but sad? . . ." (thought and meter)	There is a joy in footing slow across a silent plain 23ff.: "At such a time the soul's a child, in childhood is the brain . . ."	Murry, "Keats and Wordsworth" 289–90; Balslev 36–39; Allott, "Keats and Wordsworth" 30
	Endymion 2.274–76: ". . . The journey homeward to habitual self"	Balslev 39
To the Cuckoo 3–4, 17–18: "shall I call thee Bird, / Or but a wandering Voice?"; "The same whom in my schoolboy days / I listened to"	Ode to a Nightingale 65: "Perhaps the self-same song"	Allott, Poems 530[28]
lines 29–32: ". . . An unsubstantial, faery place; / That is fit home for Thee"	Ode to a Nightingale 70: "faery lands forlorn"	Muir, "Keats and Hazlitt" 145–46; Balslev 48–49
To the Daisy 70–71: "A happy, genial influence, / Coming one knows not how, or whence"	Sleep and Poetry 69–71: "And many a verse from so strange influence / That we must ever wonder how, and whence / It came"	de Selincourt 405; Bush, Selected Poems 311; Balslev 58; Sperry, "Woodhouse" 153; Allott, Poems 72; Barnard, Poems 551; Stillinger, "Wordsworth and Keats" 178–79
To Sleep ("O gentle Sleep! do they belong to thee")	Endymion 1.453–63: address to sleep	Balslev 29–30
lines 6–8: metaphor of elusive sleep as a fly	Endymion 1.850–53: ". . . atomies / That buzz about our slumbers, like brain-flies . . ."	Balslev 30[29]

Poems in Two Volumes (1807)	Keats Poem or Letter	Critic
With how sad steps, O Moon, thou climb'st the sky 1–2	I stood tip-toe upon a little hill 199–202: sorrowful moon	Allott, "Keats and Words-worth" 38
The world is too much with us; late and soon	16 December 1818 letter to George and Georgiana Keats: "The going[s] on of the world make me dizzy" (Letters 2:5)	Letters 2:5n.9
line 5: "This sea that bares her bosom to the moon"	Sleep and Poetry 189–90: "The blue / Bared its eternal bosom"	de Selincourt 408; Finney 1:166; Bush, Selected Poems 312; Balslev 54–56; Allott, Poems 77; Stillinger, "Words-worth and Keats" 179
line 9: "It moves us not"	Sleep and Poetry 193: "Why were ye not awake? But ye were dead"	Stillinger, "Wordsworth and Keats" 179
line 14: "Or hear old Triton blow his wreathed horn"[30]	Endymion 1.206: "By the dim echoes of old Triton's horn"	de Selincourt 421; Bush, Selected Poems 317; Balslev 56; Allott, Poems 128
Yarrow Unvisited 43–44: swan	To Charles Cowden Clarke 1–2: swan	Allott, Poems 54

The Excursion (1814)

DIRECT REFERENCES

General
"I am convinced that there are three things to rejoice at in this Age—The Excursion Your Pictures, and Hazlitt's depth of Taste" (Keats to Haydon, 10 January 1818; Letters 1:203).

"In a note to Haydon about a week ago . . . I said if there were three things superior in the modern world, they were 'The Excursion.' 'Haydon's pic-tures' & 'Hazlitts depth of Taste'" (Keats to George and Tom Keats, 13 January 1818; Letters 1:204–5).

"The more he may love the sad embroidery of the Excursion" (Keats's review of Reynolds's *Peter Bell; Letters* 2:94).

Prospectus to *The Recluse* 40–41: "the Mind of Man— / My haunt, and the main region of my song."
"And whether Wordsworth has in truth epic passion, and martyrs himself to the human heart, the main region of his song" (Keats to Reynolds, 3 May 1818; *Letters* 1:278–79).

1.169: "The moral properties and scope of things."
Keats wrote this line on the title page of his copy of Hazlitt's *Characters of Shakespear's Plays* (Forman 5:280; Owings 26–27).

4.857–60
"I remember to have been struck . . . by [Keats's] remarks on that well known & often quoted passage of the Excursion upon the Greek Mythology,—where it is said that

'Fancy fetched
Even from the blazing Chariot of the Sun
A beardless youth who touched a golden lute,
And filled the illumined groves with ravishment.'

Keats said the description of Apollo should have ended at the 'golden lute,' & have left it to the imagination to complete the picture,—*how* he 'filled the illumined groves'" (Bailey to Milnes, 7 May 1849; *Keats Circle* 2:276).

4.857–64
"Poor Keats used always to prefer this passage to all others" (Haydon's comment in his copy of *The Excursion;* quoted by Moorman 314–15).

4.718–62, 847–87: account of the origin of Greek myth.
"The first poem [*I stood tip-toe upon a little hill*] consists of a piece of luxury in a rural spot, ending with an allusion to the story of Endymion and to the origin of other lovely tales of mythology, on the ground suggested by Mr Wordsworth in a beautiful passage of his *Excursion*" (Leigh Hunt, review of Keats's *Poems* [1817]; Matthews 59).

"The principal conception of [*I stood tip-toe upon a little hill*] is the same as that of a contemporary author, Mr Wordsworth, and presumes that the most ancient poets, who are the inventors of the Heathen Mythology, imagined those fables chiefly by the personification of many appearances in nature" (George Felton Mathew, review of Keats's *Poems* [1817]; Matthews 52).

ECHOES/ALLUSIONS

The Excursion	Keats Poem or Letter	Critic
Preface: compares *The Recluse* to a gothic church	3 May 1818 letter to Reynolds: compares life to a "Mansion of Many Apartments" (*Letters* 1:280–81)	Gittings, *John Keats* 211–12
Prospectus to *The Recluse* 8–9: "intent to weigh / The good and evil of our mortal state"	*Dear Reynolds, as last night I lay in bed* 73–77: " . . . Oh never will the prize, / High reason, and the lore of good and ill, / Be my award . . ."	Wolfson 197
lines 28, 40–41: "shadowy ground"; "the Mind of Man . . ."	*Ode to Psyche* 51, 65: "region of my mind"; "shadowy thought"	Bloom, *Visionary Company* 402–3; Wolfson 309
lines 42ff.: "Beauty—a living Presence of the earth . . ."	27(?) December 1817 letter to George and Tom Keats: "with a great poet the sense of Beauty overcomes every other consideration" (*Letters* 1:194)	Murry, "Keats and Wordsworth" 282
	Endymion 1.1–33: "A thing of beauty is a joy for ever . . ."	Allott, *Poems* 120; Wolfson 235
	27 June 1818 letter to Tom Keats: " . . . that mass of beauty which is harvested from these grand materials . . ." (*Letters* 1:301)	Murry, "Keats and Wordsworth" 287; Ward 192

The Excursion	**Keats Poem or Letter**	**Critic**
lines 47–48: "Paradise, and groves / Elysian"	*Endymion* 1.177: "groves Elysian"	Bush, *Selected Poems* 317
lines 52–55: ". . . A simple produce of the common day"	*Endymion* 4.820: "O feel as if it were a common day"	de Selincourt 451–52; Balslev 62–63; Allott, *Poems* 278
line 55: "common day"	*Mother of Hermes! and still youthful Maia* 14: "Rich in the simple worship of a day"	Ward 181
lines 62–68: fit between "external World" and "individual Mind"	*Dear Reynolds, as last night I lay in bed* 67–72: ". . . in the world, / We jostle"	Wolfson 196–97
lines 76–77: ". . . Pipe solitary anguish"	*Hyperion* 3.5–6: "A solitary sorrow . . ."	Bush, *Selected Poems* 337
line 86: "metropolitan temple"	*Hyperion* 1.129: "gold clouds metropolitan"	Bush, *Selected Poems* 335
general: myth of fall reinterpreted for contemporary times	*Hyperion*	Sperry, *Keats the Poet* 155–97 (esp. 157–58, 165–79)
general: the Wanderer	*Hyperion:* Oceanus	Wolfson 257
1.15: "With side-long eye"	*To G. A. W.* 1: "Nymph of the downward smile, and sidelong glance"	Wolfson 214
1.77ff.: "Oh! many are the Poets that are sown / By Nature . . ."	*The Fall of Hyperion* 1.8–15: " . . . Since every man whose soul is not a clod / Hath visions, and would speak . . ."	Bush, "Notes" 804; Finney 2:460–61; Murry, "Keats and Wordsworth" 272–73; Bush, *Selected Poems* 356; Balslev 98–99
1.204–5: "And in their silent faces could he read / Unutterable love"	*Hyperion* 3.111–12: "I can read / A wondrous lesson in thy silent face"	Murry, "Keats and Wordsworth" 272–74; Bush, *Selected Poems* 358; Balslev 98

The Excursion	Keats Poem or Letter	Critic
1.480–81: "the strong creative power / Of human passion"	*Endymion* 4.146–81: Indian Maid's song; 22 November 1817 letter to Bailey: "our Passions . . . are . . . creative of essential Beauty" (*Letters* 1:184)	Stillinger, *Hoodwinking* 153–54; "Wordsworth and Keats" 189–90
1.634–36: "wer't not so, / I am a dreamer among men, indeed / An idle dreamer!"	*The Fall of Hyperion* 1.161–62, 168, 198–202: Moneta's condemnation of "dreamers"	Bush, "Notes" 805; Finney 2:461; Murry, "Keats and Wordsworth" 285; Bush, *Selected Poems* 358; Balslev 99–100
1.865–92: Margaret asks passersby about husband	*Isabella* 489–94: Isabella asks pilgrims about basil plant	Balslev 93; Wolfson 279; Stillinger, "Wordsworth and Keats" 184–85
1.949–53: "what we feel of sorrow and despair . . . Appeared an idle dream . . ."	*The Fall of Hyperion* 1.167–69, 198–202: "Thou art a dreaming thing"; " . . . The poet and the dreamer are distinct . . ."	Balslev 99–100
2.40–41: "And in the silence of his face I read / His overflowing spirit"	*Hyperion* 3.111–12: "I can read / A wondrous lesson in thy silent face"	Murry, "Keats and Wordsworth" 274; Bush, *Selected Poems* 338; Balslev 98
2.710: "Music of finer tone"	22 November 1817 letter to Bailey: "we shall enjoy ourselves here after by having what we called happiness on Earth repeated in a finer tone" (*Letters* 1:185)	Lau (present work)
2.710–12: "Music of finer tone . . . though it be the hand / Of silence"	*Ode on a Grecian Urn* 11–14: "Heard melodies are sweet, but those unheard / Are sweeter . . ."	de Selincourt 477; Balslev 62n; Allott, *Poems* 534; Barnard, *Poems* 650
2.830–69: description of mountain scenery when fog clears	*Hyperion* 1.176–82, 217–24, 238: description of Hyperion's palace	Bush, "Notes" 801; Bush, *Selected Poems* 335; Allott, *Poems* 406–7, 409; Barnard, *Poems* 612

The Excursion	Keats Poem or Letter	Critic
2.830–69: description of mountain scenery when fog clears	*Endymion* 2.224–25, 270, 631–38: description of underwater region	Balslev 89–90
2.833: "By waking sense or by the dreaming soul!"	*Ode to a Nightingale* 79: "Was it a vision, or a waking dream?"	Bush, *Selected Poems* 348; Barnard, *Poems* 658
3.50: "a semicirque of turf-clad ground"	*Endymion* 4.769: "its hazel cirque of shedded leaves"	Bush, *Selected Poems* 324; Allott, *Poems* 276
	Hyperion 2.34: "like a dismal cirque"	de Selincourt 507; Bush, *Selected Poems* 336; Allott, *Poems* 419
3.92: "Voiceless the stream descends"	*Hyperion* 1.11: "A stream went voiceless by"	Bush, *Selected Poems* 334
3.232ff.: primitive peoples' cosmologies	*The Fall of Hyperion* 1.2–4: "the savage too . . . Guesses at heaven"	Finney 2:461; Balslev 98–99
3.333–40: ". . . Why should not grave Philosophy be styled, / Herself, a dreamer of a kindred stock, / A dreamer yet more spiritless and dull?"	*The Fall of Hyperion* 1.161–62, 168, 198–202: Moneta's condemnation of "dreamers"	Bush, "Notes" 805; Bush, *Selected Poems* 358; Finney 2:461; Murry, "Keats and Wordsworth" 285; Balslev 100–1; Allott, "Keats and Wordsworth" 31
3.381ff.: "craving peace, / The central feeling of all happiness . . ."	*Hyperion* 2.203–5: ". . . to envisage circumstance, all calm, / That is the top of sovereignty"	Bush, "Notes" 802; Bush, *Selected Poems* 337; Balslev 105n
3.931n: Wordsworth quotes William Gilbert's notes to *The Hurricane* (*WPW* 5:422–23)	*On First Looking into Chapman's Homer* 10–12: ". . . like stout Cortez when with eagle eyes / He star'd at the Pacific"	de Selincourt 565; Allott, *Poems* 62; Barnard, *Poems* 547
4.69–73: "Possessions vanish, and opinions change, / And passions hold a fluctuating seat . . ."	*Hyperion* 2.203–5: ". . . to envisage circumstance, all calm, / That is the top of sovereignty"	Bush, "Notes" 802; Bush, *Selected Poems* 337; Balslev 105n

The Excursion	Keats Poem or Letter	Critic
4.140–45: hopes dissolve like smoke in "thinner air"	*Endymion* 4.650: "too thin breathing"	Bush, *Selected Poems* 324
4.145: "Melts, and dissolves"	*Endymion* 1.501: "Endymion's spirit melt away and thaw"	Bush, *Selected Poems* 318
4.332–35: ". . . explores / All natures,—to the end that he may find / The law that governs each"	*Endymion* 3.699–700: "If he explores all forms and substances / Straight homeward to their symbol-essences"	Finney 1:313; Balslev 87–88
4.418–26: " . . . the vassalage that binds her to the earth . . ."	*Endymion* 1.6–11: ". . . A flowery band to bind us to the earth"	Balslev 84
4.428–30: ". . . the mole contented . . ."	*Endymion* 3.66–68: ". . . The poor patient oyster . . ."	Ward 424n.12
4.440–50: animals flock together from "a strict love of fellowship"	*Endymion* 1.777–80, 807–15: "fellowship with essence" passage	Balslev 85–86
4.609: "the many-chambered school"	3 May 1818 letter to Reynolds: life as a "Mansion of Many Apartments" (*Letters* 1:280–81)	Balslev 153n.43
4.631ff.: origins of ancient religions	*The Fall of Hyperion* 1.2–4: "the savage too . . . Guesses at heaven"	Finney 2:461
	Endymion 2.827–53: origin of myths	Ward 424n.12; Barnard, *Poems* 499
4.687–88: "upon that height / Pure and serene"	*On First Looking into Chapman's Homer* 7: "pure serene"[31]	Ford 456n.6
4.694ff.: "Chaldean Shepherds . . ."	*Endymion* 3.21: "those old Chaldeans"	Bush, *Selected Poems* 321

The Excursion	Keats Poem or Letter	Critic
4.697–700: "Looked on the polar star, as on a guide . . . that never closed / His stedfast eye"	*Endymion* 1.598–99: "lidless-eyed train / Of planets"	Ward 424–25n.12
	26 June 1818 letter to Tom Keats: "a sort of north star which can never cease to be open lidded and stedfast" (*Letters* 1:299); *Bright star, would I were stedfast as thou art* 1–4: ". . . watching, with eternal lids apart . . ."	Ford 457; Ward 425n.12; Gittings, *John Keats* 220; Allott, *Poems* 737–38; Barnard, *Poems* 685
	Hyperion 1.350–53: "on the stars / Lifted his curved lids . . . And still they were the same bright, patient stars"	Ward 425n.12
4.718–62: account of ancient Greek religion of nature	*Endymion* 2.827–53: origin of myth	Ward 424n.12; Barnard, *Poems* 499
4.735–44: sympathy for ancient Greek religion	*Ode to Psyche* 38–45: nostalgia for "happy pieties" of ancient Greeks	Allott, *Poems* 518; Barnard, *Poems* 499
4.760: "While man grows old, and dwindles, and decays"	*Ode to a Nightingale* 26: "Where youth grows pale, and spectre-thin, and dies"	Bush, *Selected Poems* 348; Balslev 91–92; Gittings, *John Keats* 317; Allott, "Keats and Wordsworth" 30–31; Allott, *Poems* 527; Barnard, *Poems* 655; Stillinger, "Wordsworth and Keats" 180
4.760–62: "While man grows old, and dwindles, and decays; / And countless generations of mankind /Depart . . ."	*Ode on a Grecian Urn* 46–47: "When old age shall this generation waste, / Thou shalt remain, in midst of other woe"	Allott, "Keats and Wordsworth" 30–31

The Excursion	Keats Poem or Letter	Critic
4.761–62: "And countless generations of mankind / Depart; and leave no vestige where they trod"	*Ode to a Nightingale* 62: "No hungry generations tread thee down"	de Selincourt 475; Bush, *Selected Poems* 348; Balslev 92; Gittings, *John Keats* 317; Allott, "Keats and Wordsworth" 30–31; Allott, *Poems* 530; Barnard, *Poems* 657; Stillinger, "Wordsworth and Keats" 180
4.769: "Mad Fancy's favourite vassals"	*Fancy* 28: Fancy "has vassals to attend her"	Bush, *Selected Poems* 338
4.847–87: origin of Greek myth	*Endymion* 2.827–53: origin of myth	Ward 424n.12; Barnard, *Poems* 499
4.847–60: origin of Apollo myth	*Hyperion* 2.252–84: Clymene sees Apollo	Balslev 115–18
4.857–60: Apollo's lyre "filled the illumined groves with ravishment"	*Hyperion* 3.62–67, 110: Apollo plays lute in groves and the "universe / Listen'd in pain and pleasure"	Balslev 97
4.861–71: origin of Diana myth	*Endymion* 2.302ff.: prayer to Cynthia	Bush, *Selected Poems* 320; Balslev 88
4.876–85: Oreads "sporting" where "Withered boughs grotesque . . . From depth of shaggy covert [are] peeping forth"	*Endymion* 1.671: "An arch face peep'd,—an Oread as I guess'd"	Balslev 89
4.879–87: ancient Greeks see "the lurking Satyrs . . . or Pan himself"	*Endymion* 1.232–306: hymn to Pan	Ward 424n.12; Barnard, *Poems* 499
4.1070–77: ". . . virtue . . . thus feeds / A calm, a beautiful, and silent fire . . ."	*Hyperion* 2.203–5: ". . . to envisage circumstance, all calm, / That is the top of sovereignty"	Bush, "Notes" 802; Balslev 105n
4.1132–38: child hears "Murmurings" inside "a smooth-lipped shell"	*Hyperion* 2.270–71: Clymene "took a mouthed shell / And murmur'd into it"	Bush, "Notes" 802; Bush, *Selected Poems* 337; Balslev 96

The Excursion	Keats Poem or Letter	Critic
4.1144: "tidings of invisible things"	*I stood tip-toe upon a little hill* 186: "Shapes from the invisible world"	Bush, *Selected Poems* 310; Allott, *Poems* 94
4.1146–47: "And central peace, subsisting at the heart / Of endless agitation"	*Hyperion* 2.203–5: "to bear all naked truths, / And to envisage circumstance, all calm, / That is the top of sovereignty"	Bush, "Notes" 802; Balslev 105n
4.1204–13: loving communion between people and the "Forms / Of nature"	*Endymion* 1.777–80, 807–15: "fellowship with essence" passages	Balslev 85–86
4.1207ff.: person grows wiser and more compassionate by communing with spirit of love in nature[32]	3 May 1818 letter to Reynolds: Chamber of Maiden-Thought (*Letters* 1:281)	Finney 2:464; *Letters* 1:281n.4
4.1266ff.: ". . . Whate'er we see, / Or feel . . . Shall fix, in calmer seats of moral strength, / Earthly desires . . ."	*Hyperion* 2.203–5: "to bear all naked truths, / And to envisage circumstance, all calm, / That is the top of sovereignty"	Bush, "Notes" 802; Balslev 105n
4.1276ff.: ". . . that eloquent harangue . . . Such as, remote, 'mid savage wilderness, / An Indian Chief discharges from his breast"	*The Fall of Hyperion* 1.2–7: ". . . the savage too . . . Guesses at heaven . . ."	Bush, "Notes" 804; Bush, *Selected Poems* 356
4.1281–83: "hushed / As the unbreathing air, when not a leaf / Stirs in the mighty woods"	*Hyperion* 1.7–10: "No stir of air was there . . ."	Balslev 95–96; Allott, *Poems* 397
5.6–11: quiet, shady "Primeval forests"	*Hyperion* 1.1–10: quiet, shady vale	Balslev 95
5.145: "large and massy; for duration built"	*The Fall of Hyperion* 1.83: "The embossed roof, the silent massy range"	Bush, *Selected Poems* 357

The Excursion	Keats Poem or Letter	Critic
5.333–36: ". . . Choose for your emblems whatsoe'er ye find / Of safest guidance . . . The torch, the star, the anchor"	*Hyperion* 2.61: "as Hope upon her anchor leans"	Bush, *Selected Poems* 336
5.391ff.: "in the life of man . . . we see as in a glass / A true reflection of the circling year, / With all its seasons . . ."	*Four seasons fill the measure of the year*	Finney 1:383–84; Bonnerot; Bush, *Selected Poems* 327; Balslev 92–93; Gittings, *John Keats* 199
5.400: "And mellow Autumn, charged with bounteous fruit"	*To Autumn* 1: "Season of mists and mellow fruitfulness"	Bonnerot; Muir, "Three Notes"; Allott, *Poems* 651; Barnard, *Poems* 675
5.465–67: ". . . Do generations press / On generations, without progress made?"	*Hyperion* 2.173ff.: Oceanus' speech	Bush, "Notes" 801; Balslev 105n
	Ode to a Nightingale 62: "No hungry generations tread thee down"	de Selincourt 577; Bush, *Selected Poems* 348
5.469–78: speculation on good and evil, reason and will	*Dear Reynolds, as last night I lay in bed* 73–77: ". . . High reason, and the lore of good and ill . . . Things cannot to the will / Be settled"	Balslev 102–3
5.500–4: reason is "an attribute of sovereign power"	*Hyperion* 2.203–5: ". . . That is the top of sovereignty"	Bush, "Notes" 802; Balslev 105n
6.545–46: "Fictions in form, but in their substance truths, / Tremendous truths!"	*Endymion* 4.770–73: ". . . Truth the best music in a first-born song"	Allott, "Keats and Wordsworth" 39
6.763–66: " 'That glorious star . . . will shine / As now it shines, when we are laid in earth . . .' "	*Bright star, would I were stedfast as thou art*	Balslev 54n.26

The Excursion	Keats Poem or Letter	Critic
6.814, 987: unwed mother called "a weeping Magdalene" and "a rueful Magdalene"	Eve of St. Agnes, rejected stanza 7 (Poems 301): "no weeping Magdalen"	Stillinger, Hoodwinking 163
6.886–87: "how far / His darkness doth transcend our fickle light!"	O thou whose face hath felt the winter's wind 5–7: "the light / Of supreme darkness . . ."	Allott, "Keats and Words-worth" 30
7.5–7: "When, in the hollow of some shadowy vale . . ."	Hyperion 1.1–10: "Deep in the shady sadness of a vale . . ."	Balslev 95
7.976–78: "So fails, so lan-guishes, grows dim, and dies . . ."	Ode to a Nightingale 24–26: ". . . Where youth grows pale, and spectre-thin, and dies"	Allott, "Keats and Words-worth" 30–31
7.999ff.: "The vast Frame / Of social nature changes ev-ermore . . ."	Hyperion 2.173ff.: theme of evolution in Oceanus' speech	Bush, "Notes" 801; Balslev 105n
8.143–47: ". . . the blessed Isle, / Truth's consecrated residence, the seat / Impreg-nable of Liberty and Peace"	On Peace	Balslev 93–94
9.1–9: "To every Form of being is assigned . . . An ac-tive Principle . . ."	Hyperion 1.316–18: "sym-bols divine, / Manifestations of that beauteous life / Dif-fus'd unseen throughout eternal space"	Allott, Poems 413
9.9: "The moving waters, and the invisible air"	Bright star, would I were stedfast as thou art 5: "The moving waters at their priestlike task"	Ward 425n.12; Allott, Poems 738
9.55ff., 69ff.: "a place of power, / A throne . . ."; "For on that superior height . . ."	Hyperion 2.203–5: "for to bear all naked truths . . . That is the top of sover-eignty"	Bush, "Notes" 802; Balslev 105n

Poems First Published in *Poems* (1815)

ECHOES/ALLUSIONS

Poems (1815)	Keats Poem or Letter	Critic
Preface[33]: discussion of fancy and imagination	*Endymion* 1.850–57: beliefs about love "are true, / And never can be born of atomies . . . Leaving us fancy-sick"; 8 October 1817 letter to Bailey: "Fancy is the Sails, and Imagination the Rudder" (*Letters* 1:170)	Balslev 30–33
Essay, Supplementary to the Preface (*WPW* 2:429): contempt for public opinion	*Lamia* 1.392; 2.150–56: "curious" public; "The herd" gawks at interior of Lamia's and Lycius' house	Wolfson 335
Composed While the Author Was Engaged in Writing a Tract Occasioned by the Convention of Cintra ("Not 'mid the World's vain objects that enslave") 5–8: "in dark wood and rocky cave, / And hollow vale which foaming torrents fill . . ."	*Hyperion* 2.360–65: "gulf . . . chasm . . . headlong torrents . . . huge shade"	Allott, *Poems* 433
The fairest, brightest, hues of ether fade: "The sweetest notes must terminate and die . . ."; sound of flute	*Ode on a Grecian Urn* 11–14: "Heard melodies are sweet, but those unheard / Are sweeter; therefore, ye soft pipes, play on . . ."	Balslev 65–66
Inscriptions: In the Grounds of Coleorton . . .; In a Garden of the Same; Written at the Request of Sir George Beaumont . . . for an Urn . . .; For a Seat in the Groves of Coleorton: short epistles addressed to fellow artist	*To George Felton Mathew*	Gittings, *John Keats* 56

Poems (1815)	Keats Poem or Letter	Critic
The Shepherd, looking east-ward, softly said: shepherd addresses moon and sees it cast away its cloud veil	*I stood tip-toe upon a little hill* 181ff.: origin of Endymion and Cynthia myth	Gittings, *John Keats* 76
lines 2–6: ". . . that little cloud, in ether spread" over bright moon	*Calidore* 157: "Lovely the moon in ether, all alone"	Allott, "Keats and Wordsworth" 34; Allott, *Poems* 42
lines 13–14: "meekly yields . . . modest pride"	*I stood tip-toe upon a little hill* 204: "And gave meek Cynthia her Endymion"	Allott, *Poems* 95
Stanzas Written in My Pocket-Copy of Thomson's "Castle of Indolence": whimsical description of friend; Spenserian stanzas	*Character of C. B.*	Allott, *Poems* 496
Upon the Sight of a Beautiful Picture: theme (permanence of art contrasted to flux and mortality of natural life)[34]	*Ode on a Grecian Urn:* theme	de Selincourt 476–77; Finney 2:637; Murry, "Keats and Wordsworth" 289; Balslev 64–65
Yarrow Visited 3: "waking dream"	*Ode to a Nightingale* 79–80: "Was it a vision, or a waking dream . . ."	Bush, *Selected Poems* 348; Barnard, *Poems* 658
Yew-Trees 23–28: ". . . ghostly Shapes . . ."	*Sleep and Poetry* 138–40: "Shapes of delight, of mystery, and fear . . ."	Allott, "Keats and Wordsworth" 36; Allott, *Poems* 75

Poems from Other Editions

ECHOES/ALLUSIONS

Wordsworth Poem	Keats Poem or Letter	Critic
The White Doe of Rylstone (1815) 1.43: "the fervent din"	*Endymion* 3.54: "a holier din"	de Selincourt 437; Balslev 66

Wordsworth Poem	Keats Poem or Letter	Critic
The White Doe of Rylstone 1.43: "the fervent din"	*Endymion* 4.198: "merry din"	Allott, *Poems* 254[35]
lines 2.346–57: Emily embroiders religious "imagery" on father's banner	*The Eve of St. Mark* 24ff.: Bertha reads legend of St. Mark in book decorated with "golden broideries" and "saintly imageries"	Balslev 67
line 4.987: "And cirque and crescent framed by wall"	*Hyperion* 2.34: "like a dismal cirque"	Balslev 96n.19
lines 4.973–74: "feeding /On the green herb, and nothing heeding"	*When they were come unto the Faery's court* 74: "But the Mule grasing on the herbage green"	de Selincourt 558; *Letters* 2: 87n.2; Balslev 66n.44; Allott, *Poems* 494
To B.R. Haydon (*Examiner*, 31 March 1816; *Champion* 31 March 1816; *Thanksgiving Ode, With Other Short Pieces* [1816]; *Annals of the Fine Arts, for 1817* [1818]): praises Haydon's heroic dedication to his art[36]	*Addressed to Haydon:* honors Haydon's "stedfast genius, toiling gallantly"	Allott, *Poems* 66
Two Addresses to the Freeholders of Westmorland (1818): reference to Robert Saunders Dundas, second Viscount Melville	*All gentle folks who owe a grudge* 30: "Better than Mr. D——"	Forman 4:145n; Allott, *Poems* 367; Barnard, *Poems* 604[37]
Peter Bell, Prologue: excursion-return structure	*Ode to a Nightingale, Ode on a Grecian Urn*	Stillinger, "Wordsworth and Keats" 195
lines 116–52: "modernist stance" (Stillinger); idea and some language	*Ode to Psyche* 36–41	Stillinger, "Wordsworth and Keats" 193–94
lines 116–52: importance of human mind	*Ode to Psyche* 50–67	Stillinger, "Wordsworth and Keats" 194–95

Wordsworth Poem	Keats Poem or Letter	Critic
Peter Bell 412 (*WPW* 2:347n): "A new-peeled sapling white as cream"	*When they were come unto the Faery's court* 42: "Peel'd the brown hazel twig to lilly white"	de Selincourt 558; Balslev 66n.44[38]
Vernal Ode 86 (*The River Duddon . . . and Other Poems* [1820]): "wrapped in a fit of pleasing indolence"	7, 19 March 1819 letter to George and Georgiana Keats: "An indolent day . . . is bearable and even pleasant alone. . . . This morning I am in a sort of temper indolent and supremely careless . . ." (*Letters* 2:77–78)	*Letters* 2:78n.4
A POET!—He hath put his heart to school (*Poems of Early and Late Years* [1842]): poets chastised for abandoning nature and writing according to rules established by critics	*Sleep and Poetry* 193–96: eighteenth-century poets "were closely wed / To musty laws lined out with wretched rule"	Balslev 67–68
Thoughts Suggested the Day Following, on the Banks of Nith, near the Poet's Residence 43–54 (*Poems of Early and Late Years* [1842]): Burns survives "in the general heart of men" and therefore has no need of afterlife in heaven	*Bards of passion and of mirth* 1–4, 37–40: poets have double immortality, on earth and in heaven	Forman 3:172–73n; Balslev 67
The Prelude (1850) 3.168–69: "by an unrelenting agency / Did bind my feelings even as in a chain"	*Endymion* 1.6–7: "Therefore, on every morrow, are we wreathing / A flowery band to bind us to the earth"	Balslev 84n

General References to Wordsworth in Keats's Writing

POETRY

Addressed to the Same ("Great spirits now on earth are sojourning") 2–4: "He of the cloud, the cataract, the lake, / Who on Helvellyn's summit, wide awake, / Catches the freshness from archangel's wing."

Woodhouse notes in his copy of Keats's 1817 *Poems*, "Wordsworth, who resides near Mount Helvellyn in Cumberland" (Sperry, "Woodhouse" 151).

Sleep and Poetry 224–26: "[music] has been upstirr'd / From out its crystal dwelling in a lake, / By a swan's ebon bill; from a thick brake."
    Woodhouse identifies the reference to "Wordsworth, who resides near one of the lakes in Cumberland" (Sperry, "Woodhouse" 155).[39]

Sleep and Poetry 230–47: "yet in truth we've had / Strange thunders from the potency of song . . ."
    Leigh Hunt, in his review of Keats's 1817 *Poems,* says these lines "object to the morbidity that taints the productions of the Lake Poets" (Matthews 62).[40]

All gentle folks who owe a grudge 31: "Better than Wordsworth too, I ween."

PROSE

"The Idea of your sending [*Addressed to the Same*] to Wordsworth put me out of breath—you know with what Reverence—I would send my Wellwishes to him" (21 November 1816 letter to Haydon; *Letters* 1:118).

"I long to see Wordsworth's [head] as well as to have mine in [Haydon's painting]. . . . I begin to think that detracting from [the Duke of Wellington] as well as from Wordsworth is the same thing. . . . Give my respects the next time you write to the North" (11 May 1817 letter to Haydon; *Letters* 1:143–45).

"I met a friend the other day who had seen Wordsworth's House" (August 1817 letter to Haydon; *Letters* 1:149).

"I am quite disgusted with literary Men and will never know another except Wordsworth" (8 October 1817 letter to Bailey; *Letters* 1:169).

"[Kean] feels his being as deeply as Wordsworth, or any other of our intellectual monopolists" (Keats's review of Edmund Kean, *Champion,* 21 December 1817; Forman 5:231).

"I met Wordsworth on Hampstead Heath this Morning" (31 December 1817 letter to Haydon; *Letters* 1:195).

"This day I promised to dine with Wordsworth and the Weather is so bad that I am undecided for he lives at Mortimer street I had an invitation to meet him at Kingstons—but not liking that place I sent my excuse—What I think of doing to day is to dine in Mortimer Street (words^{th}). . . . On Saturday I called on Wordsworth before he went to Kingston's and was surp[r]ised to find him with a stiff Collar." Keats also mentions Wordsworth as one of the company at Haydon's "immortal dinner" of 28 December 1817 (5 January 1818 letter to George and Tom Keats; *Letters* 1:197–98).

"I have seen Wordsworth frequently—Dined with him last Monday" (10 January 1818 letter to Taylor; *Letters* 1:202).

"I have seen a good deal of Wordsworth" (23 January 1818 letter to Bailey; *Letters* 1:212).

"I know not whether Wordsworth has left town" (23 January 1818 letter to George and Tom Keats; *Letters* 1:214).

"It may be said that we ought to read our Contemporaries. that Wordsworth &c should have their due from us. but for the sake of a few fine imaginative or domestic passages, are we to be bullied into a certain Philosophy engendered in the whims of an Egotist." Passage continues to criticize further Wordsworth's egotism. (3 February 1818 letter to Reynolds; *Letters* 1:223–24)

"I am sorry that Wordsworth has left a bad impression where-ever he visited in Town—by his egotism, Vanity and bigotry—yet he is a great Poet if not a Philosopher" (21 February 1818 letter to George and Tom Keats; *Letters* 1:237).

"I have never had your Sermon from Wordsworth" (13 March 1818 letter to Bailey; *Letters* 1:242).

"It has as yet been a Mystery to me how and when Wordsworth went—I cant help thinking he has retu[r]ned to his Shell—with his beautiful Wife and his enchanting Sister. . . . Wordsworth ha[s] damned the lakes" (21 March 1818 letter to Haydon; *Letters* 1:251–52).

"I am affraid Wordsworth went rather huff'd out of Town—I am sorry for it. he cannot expect his fireside Divan to be infallible he cannot expect but that every Man of worth is as proud as himself. O that he had not fit with a Warrener that is din'd at Kingston's" (8 April 1818 letter to Haydon; *Letters* 1:265–66).

"My Branchings out therefrom have been numerous: one of them is the consideration of Wordsworth's genius and as a help . . . how he differs from Milton." Passage continues with extended comparison of Wordsworth and Milton (3 May 1818 letter to Reynolds; *Letters* 1:278–82).

"I was very much gratified in hearing from Haydon that you so great a Lover of Wordsworth should be pleased with any part of my Poem. In hopes of seeing you soon after my return [from the northern tour], and Speaking of my visit to Rydal" (21 June 1818 letter to Thomas Monkhouse; *Letters* 1:297).

"I enquired of the waiter for Wordsworth—he said he knew him, and that he had been here a few days ago, canvassing for the Lowthers. What think you of that—Wordsworth versus Brougham!! Sad—sad—sad—and yet the family has been his friend always. . . . But Lord Wordsworth, instead of being in retirement, has himself and his house full in the thick of fashionable visitors. . . . We arose this morning at six, because we call it a day of rest, having to call on Wordsworth who lives only two miles hence" (26–27 June 1818 letter to Tom Keats; *Letters* 1:299–300).

"We slept at Ambleside not above two Miles from Rydal the Residence of Wordsworth. . . . after [breakfast we] proceeded to Wordsworths He was not at home nor was any Member of his family—I was much disappointed" (27 June 1818 letter to George and Georgiana Keats; *Letters* 1:302).

"we proceeded from Ambleside to Rydal, saw the Waterfalls there, & called on Wordsworth, who was not at home. nor was any one of his family. I wrote a note & left it on the Mantlepiece" (29 June 1818 letter to Tom Keats; *Letters* 1:305–6).

"Wordsworth's house is situated just on the rise of the foot of mount Rydall, his parlor window looks directly down Winandermere" (29 June 1818 letter to Tom Keats; *Letters* 1:307).

"As to the poetical Character itself, (I mean that sort of which, if I am any thing, I am a Member; that sort distinguished from the wordsworthian or egotistical sublime; which is a thing per se and stands alone)" (27 October 1818 letter to Woodhouse; *Letters* 1:386–87).

"Conversation is not a search after knowledge, but an endeavour at effect. In this respect two most opposite men, Wordsworth and Hunt, are the same" (8 March 1819 letter to Haydon; *Letters* 2:43).

"the undersigned . . . liketh half of Wordsworth" (3 [?] March 1819 letter to George and Georgiana Keats; *Letters* 2:69).

"Wordsworth is going to publish a Poem called Peter Bell—what a perverse fellow it is! Why wilt he talk about Peter Bells" (15 April 1819 letter to George and Georgiana Keats; *Letters* 2:83).

"I met xxx in town a few days ago, who invited me to supper to meet Wordsworth, Southey, Lamb, Haydon, and some more; I was too careful of my health to risk being out at night" (about 21 June 1820 letter to Brown; *Letters* 2:298–99).

CHAPTER 2

Keats's Reading of Coleridge

Which of Coleridge's Works Keats Read

Nearly all of the Coleridge poems for which there is evidence of Keats's reading were included in one of the principal editions Coleridge published before 1821: the first (1796), second (1797), and third (1803) editions of his early *Poems; Lyrical Ballads* (1798, 1800, 1802, 1805); *Christabel; Kubla Khan, A Vision; The Pains of Sleep* (1816); and *Sibylline Leaves* (1817). Within Keats's lifetime Coleridge also published a great deal of verse and prose in newspapers, magazines, anthologies, pamphlets, and other people's works. It is unlikely, however, that Keats ever read Coleridge in these sources. Most of the poems Coleridge published in newspapers and periodicals appeared before 1803 when Keats was still a child, and his later journalism advanced conservative political views that were anathema to the liberal circle in which Keats moved. The present work therefore concentrates on Keats's reading of Coleridge's published volumes of poetry and prose.[1]

We know from Charles Brown's "List of Keats's Books" that Keats possessed a copy of the second, 1797 edition of *Poems, by S. T. Coleridge . . . To Which Are Now Added Poems by Charles Lamb, and Charles Lloyd.* Brown's entry reads "Coleridge Lamb & Lloyd 8vo–1 [vol] (bound)" (*Keats Circle* 1:256), and 1797 is the only edition of Coleridge's poems that includes Lamb and Lloyd in its title. Further evidence that Keats owned this edition is the fact that, in the original preface to *Endymion*, he directly quotes "a bowed mind" from the 1797 text of *Ode to the Departing Year* (*Poems* 738). This poem was not included in the 1796 *Poems on Various Subjects,* and in 1803 the phrase was altered to "submitted mind" (*CPW* 1:160).

A few poems proposed as influences on Keats—*Sonnets on Eminent Characters* and *To the Nightingale*—were published in 1796 and 1803 but not in 1797. If Keats read these poems, he therefore would have done so in a collection other than the 1797 volume he owned. All but one of the poems said to echo *Sonnets on Eminent Characters* and *To the Nightingale* were written before Keats met most of his literary friends, but Charles Cowden Clarke or, more likely, George Felton Mathew might have owned a copy of 1796 or 1803 that Keats could have borrowed (see "When Keats Read Coleridge").

We know from his references to Wordsworth that Keats almost certainly read one or more editions of *Lyrical Ballads,* which included several Coleridge poems. *The Rime of the Ancient Mariner, The Foster-Mother's Tale,* and *The Nightingale: A Conversation Poem* appeared in all editions of *Lyrical Ballads; The Dungeon* in 1798 and 1800; and *Love* in 1800, 1802, and 1805. Keats makes no direct references to any of these poems, but numerous echoes of *The Ancient Mariner, The Nightingale,* and *Love* have been discovered in Keats's verse. These three poems, however, were reprinted in *Sibylline Leaves,* where Keats might have read them for the first time. Coleridge's name never appeared on the title page of *Lyrical Ballads,* and in the Preface to the second edition, reprinted in 1802 and 1805, Wordsworth attributed Coleridge's poems merely to "a Friend" (Brett and Jones 42). Keats may as a result have paid less attention to these scattered, anonymous works than to the acknowledged Wordsworth poems in the collection. Nearly all of the proposed echoes of *The Ancient Mariner, The Nightingale,* and *Love,* moreover, occur in poems Keats wrote after *Sibylline Leaves* was published.

The only echo of a *Lyrical Ballads* poem that could not have derived from a reading of *Sibylline Leaves* is the word "leafits" in line 432 of *Isabella.* Coleridge used "leafits" in the 1798 text of *The Nightingale* but in later editions replaced it with the more common "leaflets" (Brett and Jones 42). As the OED makes clear, however, "leafits" occurs in botanical writing of the eighteenth and early nineteenth centuries, so that Keats need not have discovered the word in Coleridge's poem. Moreover, Reynolds, Woodhouse, and Taylor all read Keats's draft of *Isabella* and made numerous suggestions for revision, "amounting to coauthorship" according to Stillinger (*Poems* 604), and yet none queried "leafits," as they are likely to have done if the word was virtually unknown outside Coleridge's 1798 text. Since no other evidence points to Keats's familiarity with the first edition of *Lyrical Ballads,* it seems likely that the young poet learned "leafits" from another source; the word may even have been in fairly common circulation among educated people.

Benjamin Robert Haydon subscribed to *The Friend* upon its first appearance in 1809–10, and Hunt, Shelley, and Hazlitt may also have owned copies, probably of the first collected edition of 1812 since none appears in surviving lists of subscribers to the periodical (*The Friend* 2:434–57). Keats could have read *Hymn before Sun-Rise, in the Vale of Chamouni* in one of his friends' copies of this work (see discussion in "When Keats Read Coleridge" and in checklist, Poems from Other Publications/Problematic Cases). Besides a proposed echo of the *Hymn*, however, no evidence exists for Keats's reading of *The Friend*.[2]

We are on much surer ground in assuming that Keats read Coleridge's *Christabel* volume, which went through three editions in 1816. *Christabel* enjoyed a great deal of prepublication publicity, having been circulated widely in manuscript form, imitated by Sir Walter Scott in *The Lay of the Last Minstrel*, imitated and praised by Byron in *The Siege of Corinth*, and even supplied with a sequel before it appeared in print. Since Keats at the beginning of his career admired Byron's work he may have read *The Siege of Corinth*, and he may also have seen the anticipatory sequel *Christobell*, which was published in the April 1815 issue of the *European Magazine*—a journal to which Keats's friend Mathew contributed poems and, in November 1816, a review of *Christabel; Kubla Khan . . . The Pains of Sleep* (Reiman, "Christobell" 288).

Besides Mathew, two other friends of Keats reviewed the *Christabel* volume: Hazlitt in the 2 June 1816 *Examiner* (Jackson 205–9), and Reynolds in the 26 May 1816 *Champion* (Reynolds 451n.162). Mathew was the only one of these reviewers to praise *Christabel*, but as he pointed out, even if the poem were attacked and ridiculed, "it has been read, it has been talked of, and it is at least not blighted by the cold overhanging atmosphere of neglect" (Jackson 236). Keats was probably one of the many who read Coleridge's popular 1816 collection; certainly several of his friends could have made the work available to him.

The strongest proof of Keats's reading of the 1816 volume, however, is his own writing. Keats directly quotes *Christabel* twice, and this poem is cited more often than any of Coleridge's other works as an influence on Keats's poetry, particularly *The Eve of St. Agnes*. In addition, several echoes of *Kubla Khan* have been discovered in Keats's verse. No one, however, has yet proposed any evidence of Keats's familiarity with *The Pains of Sleep*.

In a 30 October 1817 letter to Benjamin Bailey, Keats comments on Bailey's reading of "Coleridge's Lays" (*Letters* 1:175), or *The Statesman's Manual*, published in 1816, and its companion volume *A Lay Sermon*, which appeared in 1817. No doubt Keats had seen these volumes at Bailey's in September 1817, but there is little evidence that he read in them extensively. Hazlitt wrote some of his most scathing criticism of Coleridge in *Examiner* reviews of *The Statesman's Manual* in the fall and early winter of 1816–17.[3] If these and similar criticisms voiced by others in the Hunt–Hazlitt circle did not discourage Keats from reading *The Statesman's Manual*, they probably contributed to a poor impression of the work. Robert Ryan (99) believes Hazlitt's and Hunt's antagonism toward *The Statesman's Manual* may have been one of the factors prompting Keats to write his 22 December 1816 sonnet *Written in Disgust of Vulgar Superstition*. Ryan also argues (144–45) that a passage in *The Statesman's Manual* helped shape the notion Keats expresses in his December 1817 "Negative Capability" letter that Coleridge is "incapable of remaining content with half knowledge" (*Letters* 1:194). The only passage in *A Lay Sermon* that has been advanced as an influence on Keats is the "Allegoric Vision," which appears in the introduction. Keats may have read this brief narrative section at the beginning of the 1817 volume and have quickly lost interest in the "sermon" that follows.

Biographia Literaria also appeared in 1817, and scholars have detected its influence on several passages in Keats's letters. Since its subject was more interesting to him, Keats probably read further in this work than he did in either of the *Lay Sermons*. In addition, Bailey and Dilke, with whom Keats almost certainly discussed the *Biographia* and from whom he may have borrowed the work, were more appreciative of Coleridge's prose works than Hunt or Hazlitt were (see "When Keats Read Coleridge"). Bailey's and Dilke's influence therefore may have contributed to a more extensive and open-minded reading of *Biographia Literaria* than Keats gave to Coleridge's theological volumes—although, as I explain below, Keats's response to the *Biographia* was by no means uniformly positive.

The final collection of Coleridge's poetry that Keats almost certainly read is *Sibylline Leaves*, which appeared in July 1817. Keats sent a note to the Dilkes in November 1817 asking to borrow this work (*Letters* 1:183), and there is no reason to suppose that his request was denied. The checklist shows the many allusions scholars have discovered in Keats's work to *Sibylline Leaves* poems not published in one of Coleridge's earlier collections. *Dejection* and *Frost at Midnight*, for example, appear to have significantly influenced the structure, mood, imagery, and language of a number of Keats's poems, especially *Ode to a Nightingale* and *To Autumn*, respectively. Verbal echoes of *Fears in Solitude*, *France: An Ode*, *This Lime-Tree Bower My Prison*, and *Melancholy* also have been detected, as well as echoes of lines from *The Eolian Harp* first included in *Sibylline Leaves*. In addition, as I remarked above, Keats may have read or reread in the 1817 volume poems previously published in *Lyrical Ballads*.

Since Keats had ambitions to become a playwright and began composing plays near the end of his life, one wonders if he ever read Coleridge's dramatic works. Allott (*Poems* 545) says that Keats and Brown intended *Otho the Great* to capitalize on "the popular taste for strongly flavoured tragedies based on German history" such as Schiller's *Die Piccolomini* and *Wallensteins Tod,* which Coleridge translated and published in 1800. Allott finds some influence of Schiller's plays on the relationship between the emperor and his son Ludolph in *Otho*.

Coleridge's most successful drama was *Remorse,* published and first produced in 1813. Although no direct or indirect references to this play have been discovered in Keats's work, we do know that several of Keats's friends were familiar with it. Mathew mentions it in his 1816 review of *Christabel* (Jackson 241), and in a 24 December 1815 *Champion* article Reynolds says, alluding to *Remorse,* that "Coleridge, some time back, gave one fine proof that he had the ability" to "write for the Stage" (Reynolds 132, 453n.9). Finally, in the *Examiner* for 5 February 1815, Hunt praises *Remorse* as "the only tragedy touched with real poetry for the last fifty years" (Hunt, *Literary Criticism* 644). Because *Remorse* had such a solid reputation in 1815–20, even with people like Hunt and Reynolds who more often ridiculed than praised Coleridge's works during this period, Keats may have been motivated to read this play.

Coleridge's last drama, *Zapolya,* was published in November 1817 and reviewed, for the most part unfavorably, by Reynolds in the 16 November 1817 *Champion* (Reynolds 120–26). Bernice Slote (95) finds echoes of this review in the articles Keats wrote for the *Champion* in December 1817 and January 1818. If Keats read Reynolds's review he may also have read the play under consideration; but then again he may have accepted Reynolds's judgment of *Zapolya* as a poor work and declined to read it. Only one echo of *Zapolya* in Keats's poetry has been proposed.

In summary, Keats possessed a copy of Coleridge's 1797 *Poems,* and he almost certainly read both the 1816 *Christabel* volume and *Sibylline Leaves.* He may also have read some of Coleridge's works in the first (1796) or third (1803) edition of *Poems* and in one or more editions of *Lyrical Ballads.* Coleridge's prose works do not appear to have had much appeal for Keats, but there is evidence that he read at least parts of *Biographia Literaria, The Friend,* and the *Lay Sermons.* Finally, although one might think that Keats would have been interested in Coleridge's plays, only scant, circumstantial evidence exists for his reading of those works.

When Keats Read Coleridge

The edition of *Poems* Keats owned contained few of the works now re-garded as Coleridge's best. The 1797 volume collects Coleridge's earliest poetry and features sentimental sonnets, declamatory odes, and allegorical figures throughout. Such works would have been most appealing to Keats at the beginning of his poetic career and, although the first direct quotation of a 1797 text does not occur until March 1818 in the original preface to *Endymion,* echoes of *Monody on the Death of Chatterton* and *On Observing a Blossom on the First of February 1796* have been detected in poems Keats wrote in 1815 and 1816.

It is possible that Charles Cowden Clarke introduced Keats to Coleridge's early poetry, for Clarke was fond of eighteenth-century writers like Charlotte Smith, William Cowper, and Mary Tighe, who wrote in the same style as the youthful Coleridge (see Finney 1:25–26). Richard Altick also compares some of Clarke's own early compositions to Coleridge's conversation poems (20). Nevertheless, no concrete evidence exists for Clarke's familiarity with Coleridge's poetry during the period when Keats was a student or frequent visitor to Enfield. Coleridge is not included in Clarke's 1810–18 commonplace book (Coldwell 89), and most of the Coleridge works quoted or alluded to in *Recollections of Writers* were not published until 1817 or later (Clarke and Clarke 30–34, 63).

If Clarke did not introduce Keats to Coleridge, George Felton Mathew almost certainly did. In November 1816 Mathew published an enthusiastic review of *Christabel* that reflects familiarity with and approval of Coleridge's work generally (Jackson 236–44).[4] It is possible that Mathew inspired Keats to buy and read the second edition of Coleridge's *Poems* in 1815, and he may himself have owned a copy of the first (1796) or third (1803) edition, in which Keats could have read *To the Nightingale* and other poems not published in 1797 that have been cited as influences on his work. In addition, Keats may have been exposed to *Remorse* through Mathew, for the latter mentions this play in his *Christabel* review (Jackson 241). Finally, Keats perhaps read *Christabel; Kubla Khan, A Vision; The Pains of Sleep* for the first time in Mathew's copy.

By the time the *Christabel* volume appeared in May 1816 and certainly by the time the November review was published, however, Keats was no longer intimate with Mathew. Keats's first documented reference to *Chris-tabel,* moreover, reflects not Mathew's opinion of the poem but that of the new set of friends Keats met in October 1816. The passage in question occurs in *Sleep and Poetry* and criticizes literature that delights in "trees uptorn, / Darkness, and worms, and shrouds, and sepulchres" (lines 242–43). Hunt said these lines "object to the morbidity that taints the productions of the Lake Poets" (Matthews 62), and Woodhouse glossed the lines as an "Allusion to Lord Byron, & his terrific stile of poetry—to Christabel by Coleridge &c." (Sperry, "Woodhouse" 155).

Mathew in his 1816 review praises *Christabel* for its "mild . . . tenderhearted . . . virtuous . . . [and] amiable" heroine and its delightful "domestic" incidents (Jackson 236–37, 240). By contrast Hunt, as indicated by his comment on *Sleep and Poetry,* and others in his circle regarded Coleridge's poem as morbid and grotesque. Hazlitt, for example, in a 2 June 1816 *Examiner* review of *Christabel* says, "There is something disgusting at the bottom of his subject, which is but ill glossed over by a veil of Della Cruscan sentiment and fine writing—like moon-beams playing on a charnel-house, or flowers strewed on a dead body" (Jackson 207). Reynolds, obviously alluding to *Christabel,* similarly writes in his November 1817 review of *Zapolya:* "a sort of Della Cruscan spell has ever tied the tips of [Coleridge's] wings together. . . . He seems as enamoured of a serpent's coil, as of [a] nightingale; and would think it no small delight to be eyebound, for a short season, by a rattle-snake" (Reynolds 121). In *Sleep and Poetry* Keats clearly concurs with Hunt's, Hazlitt's, and Reynolds's rather than Mathew's view of *Christabel,* and he may not have read the work until after he met Hunt and his circle in October 1816.

Unfortunately, most of Keats's new acquaintances were unlikely to have encouraged the young poet to read or appreciate other Coleridge works in the fall and winter of 1816–17. Hazlitt, who despised his former mentor and friend for his turncoat politics, was then publishing some of his most caustic attacks on Coleridge in the *Examiner* (see note 2). As editor of the *Examiner,* Leigh Hunt countenanced Hazlitt's abuse, and Hunt's own published writings for 1813–18 make clear that he too thought poorly of Coleridge at this time. Coleridge, like Wordsworth, appears in *The Feast of the Poets,* and like Wordsworth too he receives somewhat better treatment in each new edition. Hunt's praise of Coleridge in *The Feast* nonetheless remains more limited and reserved than his praise of Wordsworth. In the 1815 edition, which Keats probably read (see "When Keats Read Wordsworth"), Coleridge is represented as having "vex'd" Apollo "By his idling, and gabbling, and muddling in prose" (14). In a note to these lines, while acknowledging that "Mr. Coleridge is a man of great natural talents," Hunt goes on to qualify the compliment by concluding, "as those who most lament his waste of them, are the readiest to acknowledge" (83–84). Hunt's verses and notes also attack Coleridge's political views as expressed in *The Friend* and "in pamphlets and newspapers" (14, 78, 86– 87). Finally, although Apollo invites Coleridge to his banquet he does so begrudgingly, saying, "There, you lazy dog, sit you down too" (18). Three years later in the Preface to *Foliage* (1818), Hunt delivers another backhanded compliment by calling Coleridge "a man who has been the real oracle of the time in more than one respect, and who ought to have been the greatest visible person in it, instead of a hopeless and dreary sophist" (10–11).

It is not until an 1821 "Sketches of the Living Poets" essay that Hunt expresses genuine appreciation of Coleridge's poetry.[5] Before that time, and especially during the period when he exerted the most influence on Keats, Hunt appears actually to have read very little of Coleridge's verse. Most of his criticisms in *The Feast of the Poets* are aimed at Coleridge's prose. He did not care for the early poems (see *Imagination and Fancy* 282) and did not discover until 1814 and 1815 that Coleridge had written some of the *Lyrical Ballads* (*Feast* 1814, 94–95 and note; 1815, 89n). Houtchens and Houtchens remark that if Hunt knew *Christabel* and *Kubla Khan* in 1817, "he betrays none of his later enthusiasm for them" (Hunt, *Literary Criticism* 644). In 1816 and 1817 Hunt could have introduced Keats to a few of Coleridge's *Lyrical Ballads* poems and the *Christabel* volume. The record indicates that Hunt at this time had little interest in or familiarity with Coleridge's poetry, however, and that he regarded Coleridge chiefly as a metaphysical and political writer.

Although Reynolds too was generally irreverent in his treatment of Coleridge, he at least appears to have been familiar with the poetry. As various *Champion* articles from 1815 to 1817 make clear, Reynolds read Coleridge's early sonnets and odes (Reynolds 48–49, 62, 93, 121); *Remorse* (132); *The Nightingale* and *The Ancient Mariner* from *Lyrical Ballads* (26, 53); *Christabel; Kubla Khan . . . The Pains of Sleep* (93–94, 97–98, 121–22, 126); *Sibylline Leaves* (121); and *Zapolya* (120–26). Reynolds seems to have read all of Coleridge's major publications soon after they appeared and to have found some worth in each.[6]

Because of his greater knowledge and appreciation of the poetry, Reynolds is more likely than Hunt to have introduced Keats in 1816 or 1817 to Coleridge's *Lyrical Ballads* poems and *Christabel* volume. Reynolds's influence on Keats's reading of *Christabel* may have been particularly strong, for all of Keats's direct references to that poem have a parallel in some published comment by Reynolds. The similarity between Keats's and Reynolds's criticism of *Christabel*'s Gothic elements has already been noted. When Keats filled in for Reynolds as dramatic reviewer for the *Champion,* he included a slight misquotation of line 253 of *Christabel* in his 21 December 1817 essay on Kean (Forman 5:229). In an 1822 *London Magazine* article, Reynolds misquotes the line in exactly the same way, writing "a thing to dream of" rather than "a sight to dream of" (Reynolds 365). Of course, since Reynolds is writing later he might have been influenced by Keats, but it is also possible that Reynolds had for years misquoted the line in this way and that Keats echoed him in the December *Champion* piece, when Reynolds's habitual style and attitudes were likely to have been vividly present to the young poet writing his first journalistic essay as substitute for his friend.[7]

In other cases of similarity between the two men's references to *Christabel*, Reynolds's remarks come first. In "The Arithmetic of Poetry," published in the 16 February 1817 *Champion*, Reynolds quotes lines 9–12 as an example of "feeble," prosaic poetry (Reynolds 97–98). In a 13 July 1818 letter to Reynolds, Keats slightly misquotes line 10—"Four for the quarters and twelve for the hour"—in describing the insufferable drunken attendant at Burns's cottage (*Letters* 1:324). Finally, Reynolds's 16 November 1817 review of *Zapolya* (Reynolds 126) quotes a description of a silver lamp in *Christabel* (lines 180–82) that is frequently cited as a source for line 357 of *The Eve of St. Agnes*. The evidence suggests that Reynolds influenced Keats's response to *Christabel* or at least brought certain passages to his attention.

Benjamin Robert Haydon, who played a significant role in shaping Keats's attitude toward Wordsworth, was unlikely to have exerted much influence on the young poet's reading of Coleridge. Haydon knew Coleridge but apparently not very well. There is no mention of Coleridge in Haydon's *Autobiography* and only scattered references in his *Diary* (3:550; 4:142–43); one of these, in a 26 March 1825 entry, describes meeting Coleridge for the first time in seventeen years (3:12).[8]

We do know, however, that Haydon subscribed to *The Friend* in 1809–10 and that he wrote Coleridge on 10 November 1809 to convey his enthusiasm for *Hymn before Sun-Rise, in the Vale of Chamouni*, published in issue Number 11 (*The Friend* 1:lxiv, n.3; 2:434; see also checklist, Poems from Other Publications/Problematic Cases). If "pure serene" in line 7 of *On First Looking into Chapman's Homer* was influenced by *Hymn before Sun-Rise* as some scholars suppose, Haydon is one of the most likely of Keats's friends to have introduced the young man to Coleridge's poem in 1816.

Another person who could have introduced Keats to *Hymn before Sun-Rise* is Shelley. As Charles Robinson has demonstrated ("Shelley Circle"), Shelley and the women in his household refer to *The Friend* in private and published writing dating from 1814 through 1816. In a 17 July 1816 letter

to Peacock, Shelley asks for news about England's literary scene, adding
"of which when I speak Coleridge is in my thoughts" (Shelley, *Letters* 1:
490), and Shelley's *Mont Blanc,* composed shortly after the letter to Pea-
cock, has often been thought to reflect the influence of *Hymn before Sun-
Rise, in the Vale of Chamouni.* Robinson believes Shelley and Byron read *The
Friend* and discussed Coleridge while the two men were neighbors in Ge-
neva in the summer of 1816 ("Shelley Circle" 273). Keats met Shelley in
December 1816 and saw him fairly often over the next several months. It
is quite possible that Shelley conveyed his enthusiasm for Coleridge to
Keats and others in Hunt's circle and that Keats read *Hymn before Sun-Rise*
in Shelley's copy of *The Friend.*

The record from Keats's own writing for the fall and winter of 1816–
17 reveals virtually no conscious or unconscious Coleridgean influence.
Aside from the reference to *Christabel* in *Sleep and Poetry,* documented by
Hunt and Woodhouse, and the possible echo of *Hymn before Sun-Rise* in the
Chapman's Homer sonnet, we have only two scraps of questionable evidence
for Keats's reading of Coleridge during this period. That evidence consists
of proposed echoes of *The Eolian Harp* and *Frost at Midnight* in *Sleep and
Poetry* and *On the Grasshopper and Cricket,* respectively (see checklist, Po-
ems from Other Publications/Problematic Cases).

Another questionable source of evidence for Coleridge's influence on
Keats at this time is a letter Reynolds wrote to Richard Monckton Milnes
in 1848, claiming that the meeting between Keats and Coleridge described
in the latter's *Table Talk* (14 August 1832) took place in Leigh Hunt's
company "when [Keats] was first known to Leigh Hunt & myself" (Lange
769)—presumably in late 1816 or early 1817. Most scholars, however, have
assumed that Coleridge's *Table Talk* account refers to the same meeting
Keats describes in a 15 April 1819 letter to his brother and sister-in-law
(*Letters* 2:88–89). This encounter took place on 11 April 1819 in a lane near
Caen Wood, where Coleridge was walking with Joseph Henry Green.
Donald Lange, who prints Reynolds's letter, concludes that "there is no
strong reason for giving [Reynolds's] late comment . . . any particular
authority or for accepting it as accurate" (772).

It is not until books 1 and 2 of *Endymion,* written between April and
August 1817 (*Poems* 571), that echoes of Coleridge poems begin to appear
with some regularity in Keats's work. Since *Kubla Khan* is the Coleridge
poem most often cited as an influence on the first half of *Endymion,* espe-
cially book 2, and since there is no evidence of his earlier reading of that
work, Keats perhaps read *Kubla Khan* for the first time—or read it seriously
for the first time—in the spring or summer of 1817.

In November 1817 Keats asked the Dilkes to send him *Sibylline Leaves,* and de Selincourt (447–48), Finney (1:280), and Gittings (*John Keats* 158) believe echoes of *The Ancient Mariner* and *Dejection* in book 4 of *Endymion* can be traced to Keats's November reading of Coleridge's 1817 collection. Keats was writing book 4 in October as well as November, however, and echoes of *The Ancient Mariner* have been discovered throughout that book, not just in later passages. In addition, Frank Pearce argues convincingly for similarities between *The Ancient Mariner* and the Glaucus episode in book 3 of *Endymion,* composed in September 1817 (see checklist, *Lyrical Ballads,* Echoes/Allusions).

If Keats did read *The Ancient Mariner* before November 1817, the most likely place for such reading to have occurred is Oxford, where Keats visited Benjamin Bailey in September of that year. Bailey seems to have been one of the most appreciative readers of Coleridge, especially of his prose, among Keats's friends. In a letter to Bailey written shortly after he returned from his visit to Oxford, Keats refers humorously to his friend's avid reading of the *Lay Sermons* (*Letters* 1:175). Coleridge is mentioned in Bailey's 1817 sermon, *A Discourse Inscribed to the Memory of the Princess Charlotte Augusta,* a copy of which Bailey sent to Coleridge. In February 1818 Bailey received an "odd" but cordial letter in reply, which he described to John Taylor (*Keats Circle* 1:10) and may also have described to Keats. Bailey made arrangements for acquiring the manuscript of Coleridge's 1818 lectures on general literature, and in 1824 he eagerly looked forward to receiving *Aids to Reflection* from Taylor and Hessey (*Keats Circle* 1:11, 281; 2:453–54, 456). In later life he quoted from *Table Talk* and *Biographia Literaria,* composed a poem on Coleridge's death, and corresponded with Coleridge's daughter (*Keats Circle* 2:268, 272, 310).

Bailey almost certainly owned a copy of *Lyrical Ballads* (see chap. 1, "When Keats Read Wordsworth" and note 14), and since *The Ancient Mariner* appeared in all editions of that collection, Keats very well may have read the poem at Bailey's, perhaps for the first time. Keats probably at least flipped through Bailey's copies of *The Statesman's Manual* and *A Lay Sermon.* Since Bailey seems to have been eager to acquire Coleridge's prose works as they appeared, he also may have possessed the recently published *Biographia Literaria* when Keats visited him. Aileen Ward (128) believes that Bailey and Keats discussed "Coleridge's ideas on the imagination" while boating on the Isis, and the first purported allusion to *Biographia Literaria* occurs in a 22 November 1817 letter to Bailey (see checklist, *Biographia Literaria*).

Reading and discussion of Coleridge's work at Bailey's, reading of *Sibyl-*

line Leaves, and conscious and unconscious references to Coleridge in po-
ems and letters all point to fall 1817 as a period in which Keats was studying
his elder contemporary. This period culminates in the Negative Capability
letter of December 1817, where Keats claims that Coleridge cannot exist
"in uncertainties, Mysteries, doubts, without any irritable reaching after
fact & reason" and "would let go by a fine isolated verisimilitude caught
from the Penetralium of mystery, from being incapable of remaining con-
tent with half knowledge" (*Letters* 1:93–94).

As W. J. Bate says (*John Keats* 249n.16), this statement "seems ludi-
crously inept" to anyone familiar with Coleridge's writing and character.
Coleridge himself described his thought process as "reverie-ish & streamy"
(*Notebooks* 1: #1833) rather than relentlessly logical, and during Keats's
lifetime Coleridge was frequently charged with writing mystical, ob-
scure—even nonsensical—and inconclusive prose. Hazlitt, for example, in
one of his reviews of *The Statesman's Manual,* constructs a portrait of
Coleridge that is the antithesis of the one Keats sketches in his December
1817 letter:

> we suspect . . . that our author has not made up his own mind on any of
> the subjects of which he professes to treat. . . . Plain sense and plain
> speaking would put an end to those "thick-coming fancies," that lull him
> to repose. It is in this sort of waking dream, this giddy maze of opinions,
> started, and left, and resumed—this momentary pursuit of truths, as if
> they were butterflies—that Mr. Coleridge's pleasure, and . . . chief fac-
> ulty, lies. He has a thousand shadowy thoughts that rise before
> him. . . . a thousand self-created fancies that glitter and burst like bub-
> bles. In the world of shadows, in the succession of bubbles, there is no
> preference but of the most shadowy, no attachment but to the shortest-
> lived. (*Edinburgh Review,* December 1816; Jackson 264–65)

What then was Keats thinking of when he accused Coleridge of lacking
Negative Capability; which of Coleridge's writings provoked this curious
charge? A number of sources, both verse and prose, have been suggested.
Thayer (271–72) believes that Keats was offended by the poem *Love,* whose
haunting and mysterious central tale is (in Thayer's opinion) marred by an
unnecessary, insipid frame story. Hardy (299) argues that Coleridge's own
diagnosis of his malaise in lines 89–92 of *Dejection* inspired Keats's remarks.
And Barnard ("Echo of Keats" 313) feels that "Coleridge's constant need
to explore the metaphysical dimensions of his imaginative experiences," as
exemplified by the new lines (26–33) added to the *Sibylline Leaves* text of

The Eolian Harp, provoked Keats's criticism. A passage in Leigh Hunt's 1821 "Sketches of the Living Poets" essay complains of a tendency in Coleridge's poetry similar to the one Thayer and especially Barnard describe. Coleridge, says Hunt,

> precedes [*The Ancient Mariner*] with a critico-philosophical extract from Burnet's *Archaeologia*.... In the same spirit he interrupts his "Christabel" with an explanation of the wish sometimes felt to give pain to the innocent; and instead of being content to have written finely under the influence of laudanum, recommends "Kubla Khan" to his readers, not as a poem, but as "a psychological curiosity." (*Literary Criticism* 171)

Keats's charge that Coleridge could not rest in "mystery" or "half knowledge" perhaps was provoked by a variety of poems whose magic is encumbered by intrusive frame devices and metaphysical or psychological explanations. Moreover, Keats may have discussed this characteristic of Coleridge's poetry with Leigh Hunt or other friends before he wrote the December letter.

A number of prose works also have been cited as influences on Keats's opinion of Coleridge as expressed in the Negative Capability letter. Ryan (144–45) proposes a passage in *The Statesman's Manual* that recommends analysis and interpretation of the Scriptures, instead of passive acquiescence in their truth. Both Finney (1:243) and Muir ("Keats and Hazlitt" 143) believe Hazlitt's August 1817 review of *Biographia Literaria* influenced Keats's concept of Coleridge. Beer (*Coleridge the Visionary* 320–21n.20) and Stillinger ("Keats and Coleridge" 24 and note 25) cite a review of *Biographia Literaria* in the October 1817 issue of *Blackwood's Edinburgh Magazine,* which describes Coleridge as a man who "presumptuously came forward to officiate as High Priest at mysteries beyond his ken, and who carried himself as if he had been familiarly admitted into the Penetralia of Nature, when in truth he kept perpetually stumbling at the very Threshold" (Jackson 330–31).[9] Other critics (Watson 256n.3; Stillinger, *Hoodwinking* 152n.3; Stillinger, "Keats and Coleridge" 22–29; Gittings, *John Keats* 175) argue for the *Biographia* itself as a source for Keats's remarks. Here, in chapters 17–22, Coleridge exhaustively develops some rather carping, unsympathetic criticisms of Wordsworth's poems and Preface to *Lyrical Ballads.* In the closing months of 1817 Keats's reverence for Wordsworth had never been higher, and if he read *Biographia Literaria* at this time he might well have been offended by the way in which Coleridge "murder[s] to dissect" Wordsworth's poetry, as in the following passage on lines 110–19 of the *Intimations* ode:

> Now here, not to stop at the daring spirit of metaphor which connects the epithets "deaf and silent," with the apostrophized *eye:* or (if we are to refer it to the preceding word, philosopher) the faulty and equivocal syntax of the passage; and without examining the propriety of making a "master *brood* o'er a slave," or the *day* brood *at all;* we will merely ask, what does all this mean? In what sense is a child of that age a *philosopher*? In what sense does he *read* "the eternal deep?" ... By reflection? by knowledge? by conscious intuition? or by *any* form or modification of consciousness? (*Biographia Literaria* 2:138)

In this passage, Coleridge does display "an irritable reaching after fact & reason" that causes him to overlook the beauty and poetic truth of Wordsworth's lines.

Two final potential influences on Keats's remarks in the Negative Capability letter are his friends Benjamin Bailey and Charles Wentworth Dilke. As mentioned above, Bailey probably introduced Keats to a number of Coleridge's works, and he may have discussed them in a way that led the younger man to characterize Coleridge as an obsessive reasoner. In his well-known November 1817 letter to Bailey on the imagination, Keats describes his friend in terms similar to those he uses to describe Coleridge in the December letter. Bailey, according to Keats, "hunger[s] ... after Truth" and relies upon fallible "consequitive reasoning" instead of imaginative perception and "sensation" (*Letters* 1:185).

Another man Keats characterized in this way was Dilke. "Dilke," writes Keats in September 1819, "[is] a Man who cannot feel he has a personal identity unless he has made up his Mind about every thing. ... [He] will never come at a truth as long as he lives; because he is always trying at it" (*Letters* 2:213). It was from Dilke that Keats wished to acquire a copy of *Sibylline Leaves* and with whom he had the "disquisition" that prompted the remarks on Negative Capability. Dilke could have enlisted Coleridge on his side of the disquisition during that December walk home from the theater or in earlier conversations have represented Coleridge as a thinker like himself. Bailey and Dilke were probably the most sympathetic of Keats's friends to Coleridge the philosopher, and the evidence suggests that all three men were associated in Keats's mind—perhaps to Coleridge's disadvantage.

From 27 January to 13 March 1818, Coleridge delivered a series of lectures on general literature at the Philosophical Society in London. Keats, however, attended not these but Hazlitt's Lectures on the English Poets, delivered at the Surrey Institute every Tuesday from 13 January to 3 March 1818. Hazlitt was in high favor with Keats at this time, as the latter makes clear when he twice in January celebrates "Hazlitt's depth of Taste" as one of "three things to rejoice at in this Age" (*Letters* 1:203, 205). Whatever influence Hazlitt might have had on Keats's attitude toward Coleridge during this period was likely to have been negative. Some of Hazlitt's published criticism of Coleridge in 1816–17 has already been mentioned (see note 2). In 1818 the attacks continued, less frequently than when Hazlitt was provoked by a recent Coleridge publication, but in the same spirit as earlier essays. In two *Yellow Dwarf* articles for 3 and 14 February 1818, Hazlitt makes his usual disparaging remarks about Coleridge's political views and character generally (Hazlitt 19:202–10). Keats almost certainly read at least the second of these pieces, for he praises an article Reynolds published in the same issue (*Letters* 1:228). In addition, Hazlitt ended his lecture series with a brief discussion of Coleridge's poetry, little of which he deemed worthy of praise (Hazlitt 5:165–67). A note of nostalgia and more than a hint of Hazlitt's former admiration of Coleridge does emerge in the last paragraph of the lecture, when Hazlitt says, "[Coleridge] is the only person I ever knew who answered to the idea of a man of genius. . . . He was the first poet I ever knew. His genius at that time had angelic wings, and fed on manna. He talked on for ever; and you wished him to talk on for ever" (5:167). These remarks and perhaps others like them uttered in conversation could have enhanced Keats's image of Coleridge or at least have sown some seeds of appreciation. It should be mentioned too that Keats did not always enter into Hazlitt's vituperative attacks on the Lake Poets. He disagreed, for example, with Hazlitt's unsympathetic analysis of Wordsworth's *Gipsies* and regretted the cutting reference in another article to Southey's "few contemptible grey hairs" (*Letters* 1:173–74, 137 and note 2, 144). Still, Hazlitt in 1818 was unlikely to have inspired Keats to read and enjoy Coleridge's poetry or prose.

In February 1818 Keats reported to his brothers that "Mr Robinson a great friend of Coleridges called on me" (*Letters* 1:227). It is interesting that Keats refers to Henry Crabb Robinson as the friend of Coleridge rather than of Wordsworth, as he is more commonly known. Robinson must have spoken well of Coleridge to convey this impression. Unfortunately, Robinson left no record of his visit to Keats, so we do not know what the two men discussed. If they did discuss Coleridge, however, the conversation seems to have had little effect on Keats's reading and writing, for the only references to Coleridge throughout the spring of 1818 are a quotation of *Ode to the Departing Year* in the original preface to *Endymion* and a possible echo in *Isabella* of the word "leafits" from the 1798 text of *The Nightingale*.

In the first half of 1818 Coleridge, acting for H. F. Cary, negotiated with Taylor and Hessey for the publication of Cary's translation of *The Divine Comedy*. Coleridge was favorably impressed with Taylor and Hessey; Taylor and Hessey were impressed with Cary's translation; and on 11 May 1818 all four men met in Coleridge's rooms at Highgate and signed an agreement whereby Taylor and Hessey were to buy and reissue the remainder of the 1814 edition and later publish a new edition, which eventually appeared in 1819 (see Chilcott 80–83). Keats was aware of Taylor's and Hessey's negotiations with Cary (*Letters* 1:296) and took a copy of either the original or the reissued 1814 edition of Cary's Dante with him on his tour of northern England and Scotland in the summer of 1818. He therefore probably knew about Coleridge's role in getting the volumes republished, and since everyone concerned seems to have been pleased with the arrangements, whatever Keats heard was likely to have been positive. As was the case with Robinson, however, if Keats's publishers spoke favorably of Coleridge they do not seem to have thereby prompted Keats to renewed reading or thinking about the man's verse. A quotation of *Christabel* in a 13 July letter and possible echoes of *Dejection* in the poem *On Visiting the Tomb of Burns* constitute all of Keats's references to Coleridge's poetry throughout the summer of 1818. Passing through the countryside described in *Christabel,* part 2, and *Dejection* no doubt would have helped bring these poems into Keats's mind.

If 1818 was an arid or fallow year in Keats's reading of and response to Coleridge, however, 1819 was an extremely fruitful one. A greater number of convincing echoes of Coleridge poems have been discovered in Keats's 1819 works than in those from any previous year. These echoes, moreover, begin in January with *The Eve of St. Agnes* and persist fairly steadily in poems written throughout the spring, summer, and fall.

Charles Lamb in 1820 was the first in a long line of critics to compare *The Eve of St. Agnes* to *Christabel* (Matthews 157). In fact, scholars are nearly unanimous in agreeing that *Christabel* influenced *The Eve of St. Agnes* and *The Eve of St. Mark,* composed shortly after *St. Agnes* in February 1819. Keats probably read *Christabel* in the summer or fall of 1816, and the 1819 echoes do not necessarily imply recent rereading. Nonetheless, the striking number of purported allusions to Coleridge's Gothic poem does suggest a subsequent reading more serious and sympathetic than Keats's first. Allott

(*Poems* 445) finds an echo of *Christabel* in Keats's *Fancy,* composed near the end of 1818. If Keats did reread the poem before he wrote *St. Agnes,* he might have done so in the closing months of 1818.

Between December 1818 and March 1819, Coleridge was once again lecturing on philosophy and literature in London. As far as we know Keats did not attend, though he might have read John Thelwall's reports in the *Champion* on a few of the early lectures (Coleridge, *Shakespearean Criticism* 2:318–23).

On 11 April 1819 Keats met Coleridge, probably for the first and only time, walking in a lane near Highgate with Joseph Henry Green, who had been a demonstrator at Guy's Hospital when Keats was a student there. Keats described the meeting in a letter to his brother and sister-in-law and included a list of some of the topics Coleridge covered while Keats walked alongside him:

> Nightingales, Poetry—on Poetical sensation—Metaphysics—Different genera and species of Dreams—Nightmare—a Dream accompanied by a sense of touch—single and double touch—A dream related—First and second consciousness—the difference explained between will and Volition—so m[any] metaphysicians from a want of smoking the second consciousness—Monsters—the Kraken—Mermaids—southey believes in them—southeys belief too much diluted—A Ghost story. (*Letters* 2:88–89)

Coleridge's power as a talker has been amply attested by contemporaries, and the very fact that Keats retained an accurate memory of the many subjects raised suggests that he was impressed by the performance. This encounter may have helped to dispel Keats's previous impression of Coleridge and to replace it with one more sympathetic. The man who drifted in his conversation from nightingales to poetry to dreams to mermaids surely did not strike Keats as a "consequitive reason[er]" (*Letters* 1: 185). In addition, Leigh Hunt, obviously referring to this meeting, records that Coleridge "delighted the late Mr. Keats, in the course of conversation, with adding, after he had alluded to it, 'if there is any thing I have written which may be *called poetry*'" (*Literary Criticism* 170).

Coleridge's modesty and meandering discourse on a variety of suggestive, out-of-the-way topics were almost certain to have impressed Keats favorably. It is logical too to suppose, as many critics have, that the encounter prompted Keats to remember, read, or reread a number of Coleridge poems.[10] This assumption is supported by the fact that *La Belle Dame sans*

Merci, Ode to Psyche, and *Ode to a Nightingale,* all written shortly after the meeting with Coleridge, contain many echoes of such poems as *The Rime of the Ancient Mariner (Lyrical Ballads), Love (Lyrical Ballads), Kubla Khan* (1816), *France: An Ode (Sibylline Leaves), The Nightingale (Lyrical Ballads), To the Nightingale* (1796), *Fears in Solitude (Sibylline Leaves), Reflections on Having Left a Place of Retirement* (1797), *Christabel* (1816), and *Dejection (Sibylline Leaves).* Since the *Lyrical Ballads* and 1797 poems were reprinted in *Sibylline Leaves,* Keats is likely to have used that collection if he did read Coleridge's poetry in the spring of 1819.

Similarities in plot and characterization frequently have been noted between *Christabel* and *Lamia,* which Keats composed in July and August 1819. It would not have been necessary for Keats to reread Coleridge's poem to recall its basic elements, however, especially if he had read it closely less than a year before.

In *To Autumn,* written in September 1819, critics have discovered a number of close verbal parallels to Coleridge's *Frost at Midnight,* whose influence has not been detected in any of Keats's earlier works.[11] Keats therefore may have read *Frost at Midnight* shortly before he composed his last ode, though there is always the possibility that the seasonal motif of Keats's poem simply evoked images and phrases from Coleridge's treatment of a similar theme.

Keats came of age at a time when Coleridge's reputation was at a low ebb, even in enlightened literary circles. Few of Keats's friends appreciated Coleridge's work, and those who did—Mathew, Bailey, and Dilke—may have represented it to Keats in an unfortunate way, so that Coleridge became associated with the other men's biases. Many of the best poems remained unpublished or buried in old newspaper and periodical issues until 1816 and 1817, a fact which helps explain Coleridge's inferior status as a poet until around 1819, when a large number of people had had time to read and appreciate his masterpieces. Finally, his reputation as a weak-willed, lazy man who had not lived up to his early promise would no doubt have alienated the ardent, ambitious Keats; certainly Coleridge was never one of Keats's inspirational "Presider[s]" or role models (*Letters* 1:142). Given all these handicaps it is not surprising that we find so few references to Coleridge in Keats's writing; the wonder, perhaps, is that we find as many as we do. For, although Keats in his letters never openly declares that he is reading Coleridge or discusses his reaction to such reading, as he does with Wordsworth, various forms of evidence suggest that he did read several volumes of poetry and prose, starting at an early stage of his poetic career. It attests to the power of Coleridge's verse that it wrought an effect on Keats's own writing without conscious emulation on the younger poet's part.

The checklist of evidence for Keats's reading of Coleridge differs slightly from the Wordsworth checklist. Because Coleridge's poems were reprinted so often and because the earliest publication is not always the most likely source for Keats's reading, I have cross-referenced poems that appeared in two or more editions published during Keats's lifetime. In addition, Coleridge's few *Lyrical Ballads* poems are organized together, but a note after the first entry for each poem states which edition it first appeared in and when it was reprinted.

Poems Published in *Poems on Various Subjects* (1796)

ECHOES/ALLUSIONS

Poems on Various Subjects (1796)	Keats Poem	Critic
The Eolian Harp (rpt. 1797, 1803, 1817) 11: "The stilly murmur of the distant Sea" (line differs in 1803)	*Endymion* 1.121: "The surgy murmurs of the lonely sea"	de Selincourt 565; Bush, *Selected Poems* 317
line 24: "Footless and wild, like birds of Paradise" (line omitted in 1803)	*The Eve of St. Mark* 80: "And legless birds of paradise"	de Selincourt 565; Bush, *Selected Poems* 342

See also entries for *The Eolian Harp* in *Sibylline Leaves* (1817) and Poems from Other Publications/Problematic Cases.

Monody on the Death of Chatterton (rpt. 1797, 1803)	*Oh Chatterton! how very sad thy fate:* "All of the ideas and almost all of the words" echo Coleridge's poem	Finney 1:55
lines 21–24: "Amid the shining Host of the Forgiven / Thou at the throne of mercy and thy God . . . dost hymn . . ."	*Oh Chatterton! how very sad thy fate* 9–11: "Thou art among the stars / Of highest heaven; to the rolling spheres / Thou sweetly singest"	Allott, *Poems* 10–11
lines 64–65: "And now, indignant 'grasps the patriot steel' . . ." (lines omitted 1797, 1803)	*To My Brother George* 73–74: "The patriot shall feel / My stern alarum and unsheath his steel"	Bush, *Selected Poems* 307
Sonnets on Eminent Characters (rpt. 1803): patriotic subject; irregular rhyme scheme and elevated diction	*On Peace*	Finney 1:42; Allott, *Poems* 5
To the Nightingale (rpt. 1803) 1: "Sister of love-lorn Poets, Philomel!"	*To one who has been long in city pent* 10: "Catching the notes of Philomel"	Bush, "Some Notes" 313

Poems on Various Subjects (1796)	Keats Poem	Critic
To the Nightingale 2: "How many Bards in city garret pent"[12]	To one who has been long in city pent 1	de Selincourt 565; Bush, Selected Poems 307; Allott, Poems 45; Barnard, Poems 542
	How many bards gild the lapses of time 1	de Selincourt 565; Bush, Selected Poems 307; Allott, Poems 59
lines 7–8: ". . . the full-orb'd Queen that shines above"	Ode to a Nightingale 36: "haply the Queen-Moon is on her throne"	Allott, Poems 527; Barnard, Poems 656
line 16: "Oft will I tell thee, Minstrel of the Moon!"	Ode to a Nightingale 36: "haply the Queen-Moon is on her throne"	Barnard, Poems 656

Poems Published in *Poems*, Second Edition (1797)

DIRECT REFERENCES

Poems, by S. T. Coleridge, Second Edition. To Which Are Now Added Poems by Charles Lamb, and Charles Lloyd.
Item in Charles Brown's "List of Keats's Books": "Coleridge Lamb & Lloyd 8ᵛᵒ1 [vol.] (bound)" (*Keats Circle* 1:256).

Ode to the Departing Year 6: "With inward stillness, and a bowed mind" "Inscribed, / with every feeling of pride and regret, / and with 'a bowed mind' / To the memory of . . . Thomas Chatterton" (original preface to *Endymion; Poems* 738).

ECHOES/ALLUSIONS

Poems (1797)	Keats Poem	Critic
The Eolian Harp (see Poems on Various Subjects [1796])		
Monody on the Death of Chatterton (see Poems on Various Subjects [1796])		

Poems (1797)	Keats Poem	Critic
On Observing a Blossom on the First of February 1796 (rpt. 1803, 1817) 13–15: "An amaranth, which earth scarce seem'd to own, / Till disappointment came, and pelting wrong / Beat it to earth"	*Oh Chatterton! how very sad thy fate* 7–8: "Thou didst die / A half-blown flower, which cold blasts amate"	Allott, *Poems* 10
Reflections on Having Left a Place of Retirement (rpt. 1803, 1817) 19–21: "the viewless sky-lark's note / (Viewless, or haply for a moment seen / Gleaming on sunny wings)"	*Ode to a Nightingale* 33: "But on the viewless wings of Poesy"	McFarland 139

Poems Published in *Lyrical Ballads* (1798, 1800, 1802, 1805)

ECHOES/ALLUSIONS

Lyrical Ballads	Keats Poem or Letter	Critic
general: ballad form and meter	*La Belle Dame sans Merci*	de Selincourt 527; Barnard, *Poems* 637
The Ancient Mariner (1798; rpt. 1800, 1802, 1805, 1817): nightmare atmosphere	*La Belle Dame sans Merci*	Gittings, *John Keats* 302
excursion-return structure	odes, especially *To a Nightingale* and *Grecian Urn*	Stillinger, "Keats and Coleridge" 19
passage unspecified	*Endymion* 4.182–272: march of Bacchus	Finney 1:227; Bush, *Selected Poems* 323
passage unspecified	*Endymion* 4.405–6: "Slowly they sail, slowly as icy isle /Upon a calm sea drifting"	Gittings, *John Keats* 158n.3
line 8: "May'st hear the merry din"	*Endymion* 4.198: "From kissing cymbals made a merry din"	de Selincourt 573; Allott, *Poems* 254

Lyrical Ballads	Keats Poem or Letter	Critic
The Ancient Mariner 8: "May'st hear the merry din"	Endymion 1.40; 3.54: "the city's din"; "old boughs lisp forth a holier din"	Allott, Poems 122, 208
lines 112–14: "The bloody Sun, at noon, / Right up above the mast did stand, / No bigger than the Moon"	Endymion 4.497–98: "The moon put forth a little diamond peak, / No bigger than an unobserved star"	de Selincourt 447
line 143: "There passed a weary time"	Endymion 3.639: "Now let me pass a cruel, cruel time"	Pearce 13–14
lines 154–56: "And still it neared and neared . . . It plunged and tacked and veered"	Endymion 3.647–50: "I saw grow up from the horizon's brink / A gallant vessel: soon she seem'd to sink / Away from me again . . ."	Pearce 13–14
lines 162–66: ". . . all at once their breath drew in, / As they were drinking all"	Endymion 3.843–44: "Copious wonder-draughts / Each gazer drank"	Pearce 14
line 169: "Withouten wind, withouten tide" (1798 text)	Endymion 4.250: "Nor care for wind and tide"	de Selincourt 447; Finney 1: 289; Gittings, John Keats 158n.3
line 171: "The western wave was all a-flame"	Endymion 4.201: "faces all on flame"	de Selincourt 447
lines 190–91: "Her lips were red, her looks were free . . ."	La Belle Dame sans Merci 15–16: "Her hair was long, her foot was light . . ."	Bloom, Visionary Company 386; Barnard, Poems 638
lines 192–94: "Her skin was white as leprosy, / The Nightmare LIFE-IN-DEATH was she . . ."	The Fall of Hyperion 1.257: "bright blanch'd / By an immortal sickness which kills not"	Allott, Poems 674
lines 195–98: Life-in-Death wins Mariner's soul in dice game	Endymion 3.562–64: "disgust, and hate, / And terrors manifold divided me / A spoil amongst them"	Pearce 13

Lyrical Ballads	Keats Poem or Letter	Critic
The Ancient Mariner 209–12: ". . . The horned Moon, with one bright star / Within the nether tip . . ."	*Endymion* 4.497–98: "The moon put forth a little diamond peak, / No bigger than an unobserved star"	de Selincourt 448
lines 216–19: "Four times fifty living men . . . dropped down one by one"	*Endymion* 3.665–66: "The crew had gone / By one and one, to pale oblivion"	Pearce 14
line 254: "Nor rot nor reek did they"	*Endymion* 3.740: "All ruddy,—for here death no blossom nips"	Pearce 14
lines 273–87: Mariner sees and blesses colorful water-snakes	*Endymion* 3.343–52: friendly sea animals let Glaucus feel "their scales of gold and green" and save him from waterspouts	Pearce 13
lines 277–81: description of water snakes	*Lamia* 1.47ff.: description of Lamia as colorful snake	Finney 2:671; Routh 35
lines 309ff.: ship brought home by supernatural forces	*Endymion* 3.604–6: Glaucus returned home by supernatural forces	Pearce 13
lines 354–66: sweet sounds issue from sailors' animated corpses	*Endymion* 3.790–92, 798–800: beautiful music arises after Endymion brings drowned people to life	Pearce 14
lines 490–96: "A man all light, a seraph-man . . ."	*To George Felton Mathew* 24: "a rapt seraph"	Bush, "Notes" 791; Bush, *Selected Poems* 306
lines 533–36: "Brown skeletons of leaves . . . And the owlet whoops to the wolf below"	*Endymion* 1.182: "And think of yellow leaves, of owlet's cry"	Bush, *Selected Poems* 317
line 570: "all in my own countree"	*Endymion* 4 (draft), btwn. lines 221–22: "We follow Bacchus from a far country" (*Poems* 199)	de Selincourt 447; Gittings, *John Keats* 158n.3

Lyrical Ballads	Keats Poem or Letter	Critic
Love (1800; rpt. 1802, 1805, 1817): frame story	27(?) December 1817 letter to George and Tom Keats: remarks on Coleridge in Negative Capability passage (Letters 1:193–94)	Thayer 271–72
atmosphere, stanza form, rhyme scheme, and meter	La Belle Dame sans Merci	Thayer 270–71
line 33: Knight "pined"	La Belle Dame sans Merci 6: Knight "So haggard and so woebegone"	Thayer 270
line 57: "And how she wept, and clasped his knees"	La Belle Dame sans Merci 30: "And there she wept, and sigh'd full sore"	Thayer 270
line 61: "And that she nursed him in a cave"	La Belle Dame sans Merci 29: "She took me to her elfin grot"	Thayer 270
lines 63–64: "on the yellow forest-leaves / A dying man he lay"	La Belle Dame sans Merci 1–12: signs of late autumn and knight's imminent death	Thayer 270
The Nightingale: A Conversation Poem (1798; rpt. 1800, 1802, 1817) 4: "Come, we will rest on this old mossy bridge!"	Ode to a Nightingale 40: "winding mossy ways"	Finney 2:628; Bush, Selected Poems 348; Barnard, Poems 656
lines 5–11: ". . . But hear no murmuring: it flows silently, / O'er its soft bed of verdure. All is still, / A balmy night! . . ."	Ode to a Nightingale 38–50: "But here there is no light . . . The murmurous haunt of flies on summer eves"	de Selincourt 474; Finney 2:628; Bush, Selected Poems 348; Allott, Poems 528; Barnard, Poems 656; Randel 52
lines 8, 11: "though the stars be dim"; "A pleasure in the dimness of the stars"	Ode to a Nightingale 20: "the forest dim"	Finney 2:628; Randel 52

Lyrical Ballads	Keats Poem or Letter	Critic
The Nightingale 13ff.: nightingale not melancholy	*Ode to a Nightingale* 5ff.: nightingale happy	Finney 2:622–23; Murry, "Keats and Coleridge" 5; Gittings, *John Keats* 317; Randel 51; Vendler 81; Sato, "'Nightingales'" 15–22[13]
lines 25–30: language of stretching limbs, surrendering, forgetting	*Ode to a Nightingale* 1ff.: language of drowsiness, sinking, fading, forgetting	Randel 52
line 26: "Beside a brook in mossy forest-dell"	*Ode to a Nightingale* 40: "winding mossy ways"	Finney 2:628; Bush, *Selected Poems* 348; Barnard, *Poems* 656
lines 52–57: description of tangled grove	*Ode to a Nightingale* 38–50: catalogue of vegetation	Finney 2:628; Bush, *Selected Poems* 348; Barnard, *Poems* 656
line 65: "Whose dewy leafits are but half disclosed" (1798 text; see Brett and Jones 42)	*Isabella* 432: "in perfumed leafits spread"	de Selincourt 461; Finney 2: 623; Bush, *Selected Poems* 329[14]
lines 68–69 (lines omitted 1800): "while many a glow-worm in the shade / Lights up her love-torch"	*Ode to Psyche* 27, 66–67: "amorous glow-worm of the sky"; "A bright torch, and a casement ope at night, / To let the warm Love in!"	Bush, *Selected Poems* 346–47
lines 96–105: moonlight stops Hartley's crying	*Endymion* 3.142–74: address to the moon	de Selincourt 438; Finney 2: 623; Bush, *Selected Poems* 321

The Piccolomini, or the First Part of Wallenstein (1800); *The Death of Wallenstein* (1800)
Translated from the German of Frederick Schiller by S. T. Coleridge

ECHOES/ALLUSIONS

Coleridge Play	Keats Play	Critic
The Piccolomini and *The Death of Wallenstein* (passages unspecified)	*Otho the Great:* Otho's relationship with his son Ludolph	Allott, *Poems* 545

Christabel; Kubla Khan, A Vision; The Pains of Sleep, Three Editions (1816)

DIRECT REFERENCES

Christabel

Woodhouse notes that line 231 of *Sleep and Poetry* ("Strange thunders from the potency of song") is an "Allusion to Lord Byron, & his terrific stile of poetry—to Christabel by Coleridge &c." (Sperry, "Woodhouse" 155).[15]

line 10: "Four for the quarters, and twelve for the hour."
"He drinks glasses five for the Quarter and twelve for the hour" (Keats to Reynolds, 13 July 1818; *Letters* 1:324).

line 253: "A sight to dream of, not to tell!"
"'A thing to dream of, not to tell!'" (Keats's review of Edmund Kean, *Champion*, 21 December 1817; Forman 5:229)

ECHOES/ALLUSIONS

Christabel	Keats Poem	Critic
Medieval atmosphere	*The Eve of St. Agnes*	Bush, *Selected Poems* 339; Allott, *Poems* 451; Maier 66–67; Barnard, *Poems* 621
two-part structure	*Lamia:* structure	Stillinger, "Keats and Coleridge" 17
Geraldine, Leoline	*The Eve of St. Agnes:* Madeline (similar sounding name)	Routh 35
frequent repetition	*The Eve of St. Mark* 57, 67	Allott, *Poems* 484
meter	*The Eve of St. Mark*	de Selincourt 526; Finney 2:570; Bush, *Selected Poems* 341; Allott, *Poems* 481; Barnard, *Poems* 629
Geraldine as serpent woman	*Lamia:* Lamia as serpent woman	Routh 34; Bush, *Selected Poems* 352; Stillinger, "Keats and Coleridge" 17

Christabel	Keats Poem	Critic
Geraldine as vampire	*The Eve of St. Agnes:* Porphyro as vampire	Twitchell
Geraldine sympathetic figure	*Lamia:* Lamia sympathetic figure	Allott, *Poems* 614; Barnard, *Poems* 665
Geraldine both to be feared and pitied	*Lamia:* Lamia both to be feared and pitied	Bloom, *Visionary Company* 388; Stillinger, "Keats and Coleridge" 17
Christabel dreams of her betrothed lover	*The Eve of St. Agnes:* Madeline dreams of her betrothed lover	Stillinger, "Keats and Coleridge" 15
Geraldine introduced in a forest, in state of distress	*Lamia:* Lamia introduced in a forest, in state of distress	Routh 34, 35; Stillinger, "Keats and Coleridge" 17
maiden's father hostile to family of intruder; events take place in part at night while father ignorant of what is passing	*The Eve of St. Agnes:* maiden's kinsmen hostile to family of intruder; events take place at night; kinsmen ignorant	Routh 35
frequent references to moonlight	*The Eve of St. Agnes:* moonlight	Stillinger, "Keats and Coleridge" 14
"ineffectively protective females" (Stillinger): Christabel's mother	*The Eve of St. Agnes:* Angela	Stillinger, "Keats and Coleridge" 15
Christabel entranced	*The Eve of St. Agnes:* Madeline entranced	Stillinger, "Keats and Coleridge" 15
	Lamia: Lycius entranced	Routh 34; Stillinger, "Keats and Coleridge" 17
Christabel a willing or participating victim	*The Eve of St. Agnes:* Madeline in part responsible for own fall from innocence	Maier 67ff.; Stillinger, "Keats and Coleridge" 15
	Lamia: Lycius willing victim	Stillinger, "Keats and Coleridge" 17

Christabel	Keats Poem	Critic
Bard Bracy sees through Geraldine's disguise	Lamia: Apollonius sees through Lamia's disguise	Routh 34; Stillinger, "Keats and Coleridge" 17
line 1: " 'Tis the middle of night"	The Eve of St. Agnes 49: "Upon the honey'd middle of the night"	McFarland 143–44
line 2: reference to owls	The Eve of St. Agnes 2: reference to owl	Routh 35; McFarland 143
line 7: "a toothless mastiff bitch"	The Eve of St. Agnes 365: "The wakeful bloodhound"	Routh 35; de Selincourt 469n; Maier 64; McFarland 143
line 15: "The night is chilly, but not dark"	The Eve of St. Agnes 1: "St. Agnes' Eve—Ah, bitter chill it was!"	McFarland 144
line 46: "ringlet curl"	The Eve of St. Agnes 148: "soft ringlets"	Maier 65; Stillinger, "Keats and Coleridge" 15
lines 54, 69: religious oaths	The Eve of St. Agnes (draft): religious oaths (Poems 303, 305)	Stillinger, "Keats and Coleridge" 15
line 63: "Her blue-veined feet"	Endymion 1.624–25: "her hovering feet, / More bluely veined"	Bush, Selected Poems 318
lines 65–67: gems in hair, "rich" clothing	The Eve of St. Agnes 227, 230	Maier 64–65; Stillinger, "Keats and Coleridge" 15
lines 81–87: description of warriors and steeds	La Belle Dame sans Merci	Stillinger, "Keats and Coleridge" 17n.17
line 120: "move as if in stealth" (1816: "creep in stealth")	The Eve of St. Agnes 249–50: Porphyro "from the closet crept, / Noiseless as fear . . ."	Stillinger, "Keats and Coleridge" 15
lines 124–25: door opened with key	The Eve of St. Agnes 369: key turns, door opens	Stillinger, "Keats and Coleridge" 15

Christabel	**Keats Poem**	**Critic**
lines 145–53: "Outside her kennel, the mastiff old . . ."	*The Eve of St. Agnes* 365: "The wakeful bloodhound rose, and shook his hide"	Routh 35; de Selincourt 469n; Bush, *Selected Poems* 341; Sperry, *Keats the Poet* 217
line 148: mastiff "an angry moan did make"	*The Eve of St. Agnes* 366: mastiff recognizes Madeline and does not bark	Maier 64
lines 149, 153, 207, 470, 538: variations on phrase "what can ail"	*La Belle Dame sans Merci* 1, 5: "O what can ail thee"	Sato, "Extemporization" 11–12
line 150: "Never till now she uttered yell"	*The Eve of St. Agnes* 170: "Never on such a night have lovers met"	Stillinger, "Keats and Coleridge" 15
line 161: "And nothing else saw she thereby"	*La Belle Dame sans Merci* 22: "And nothing else saw all day long"	Sato, "Extemporization" 11; Stillinger, "Keats and Coleridge" 17n.17
lines 162, 435: references to shields and heraldry	*The Eve of St. Agnes* 214, 216	Maier 65; Stillinger, "Keats and Coleridge" 15
lines 178–80: "The chamber carved so curiously, /Carved with figures strange and sweet, / All made out of the carver's brain"	*The Eve of St. Agnes* 34: "The carved angels, ever eager-eyed"	de Selincourt 469n; Bush, *Selected Poems* 339; Maier 64
line 179: "Carved with figures strange and sweet"	*The Eve of St. Agnes* 209: "All garlanded with carven imag'ries"	McFarland 144
line 182: "The lamp with twofold silver chain"	*The Eve of St. Agnes* 357: "A chain-droop'd lamp was flickering by each door"	de Selincourt 469n; Bush, *Selected Poems* 341; Allott, *Poems* 478; Maier 64; McFarland 144
line 184: "The silver lamp burns dead and dim"	*The Eve of St. Agnes* 357: "A chain-droop'd lamp was flickering by each door"	Allott, *Poems* 478; Maier 64

Christabel	Keats Poem	Critic
lines 184–86: repetitions	The Eve of St. Agnes 361–62: chiasmus	Allott, Poems 478
lines 195–96: "maiden most forlorn. . . . Woe is me!"	The Eve of St. Agnes 328, 333: "woe is mine," "dove forlorn"	Stillinger, "Keats and Coleridge" 16
lines 200–201: spirit of Christabel's mother will "hear the castle-bell / Strike twelve upon [Christabel's] wedding-day"	The Eve of St. Agnes 156: Angela's "passing bell may ere the midnight toll"	Maier 65; Stillinger, "Keats and Coleridge" 15
line 205: "Off, wandering mother! Peak and pine!"	The Fall of Hyperion 1.257: "Not pin'd by human sorrows"	Allott, Poems 674
lines 215, 290: Christabel's blue eyes	The Eve of St. Agnes 296: Madeline's blue eyes	Stillinger, "Keats and Coleridge" 15
line 218: "The lady wiped her moist cold brow"	La Belle Dame sans Merci 9–10: "I see a lily on thy brow / With anguish moist and fever dew"	Sato, "Extemporization" 11[16]
lines 248–52: "she unbound / The cincture from beneath her breast: / Her silken robe, and inner vest, / Dropt to her feet, and full in view, / Behold! her bosom and half her side—"	Fancy 84–87: "With a waist and with a side / White as Hebe's, when her zone / Slipt its golden clasp, and down / Fell her kirtle to her feet"	Allott, Poems 445
lines 248–59: description of Geraldine undressing (lines 255–61 first published 1828)	The Eve of St. Agnes 226–34: description of Madeline undressing	Routh 35; Stillinger, "Keats and Coleridge" 15
line 275: "low moaning"	La Belle Dame sans Merci 20: "made sweet moan"	Stillinger, "Keats and Coleridge" 17n.17
lines 279–91: description of Christabel praying	The Eve of St. Agnes 220–24: description of Madeline praying	Stillinger, "Keats and Coleridge" 15, 16

Christabel	Keats Poem	Critic
line 286: "Her slender palms together prest"	The Eve of St. Agnes 220, 241: "hands, together prest"; "Clasp'd like a missal"	Stillinger, "Keats and Coleridge" 15–16
lines 292–93: Christabel dreams with eyes open	The Eve of St. Agnes 296, 298–99: Madeline opens eyes and sees "the vision of her dream"	Stillinger, "Keats and Coleridge" 16–17
line 302: "A star hath set"	The Eve of St. Agnes 324: "St. Agnes' moon hath set"	Stillinger, "Keats and Coleridge" 15
line 320: Christabel compared to a "hermitess"	The Eve of St. Agnes 339: Porphyro compared to a "pilgrim"	Stillinger, "Keats and Coleridge" 15
line 321: "Beauteous in a wilderness"	The Eve of St. Agnes 250: "Noiseless as fear in a wide wilderness"	Stillinger, "Keats and Coleridge" 16
lines 332–33: "Each matin bell, the Baron saith, /Knells us back to a world of death"	Ode to a Nightingale 71–72: "Forlorn! the very word is like a bell / To toll me back from thee to my sole self!"	Davenport 100n
lines 339–42: reference to sacristan	The Eve of St. Agnes 5–28, 377–78: references to beadsman	Routh 35; Maier 64
line 416: "Each spake words of high disdain"	The Eve of St. Agnes 61: "not cool'd by high disdain"	de Selincourt 467; Bush, Selected Poems 339; Maier 63[17]
lines 475–76: "Yet he, who saw this Geraldine, / Had deemed her sure a thing divine"	Lamia 2.86–87: "ever thinking thee, / Not mortal, but of heavenly progeny"	Stillinger, "Keats and Coleridge" 17
lines 530–31: Bard Bracy "Warned by a vision in my rest . . ."	La Belle Dame sans Merci 37–44: knight dreams of kings and princes warning him	Sato, "Extemporization" 11–12
lines 531ff.: heroine associated with dove	The Eve of St. Agnes 198, 333	Stillinger, "Keats and Coleridge" 15

Christabel	Keats Poem	Critic
lines 549–54: description of snake in Bard Bracy's dream	*Lamia* 1.46–58: description of snake	Routh 35; Stillinger, "Keats and Coleridge" 17
lines 583–85: Geraldine has evil eye	*Lamia* 2.245–48, 277–90, 295–96: Apollonius has evil eye	Routh 35
line 598: "She nothing sees— no sight but one"	*La Belle Dame sans Merci* 22: "And nothing else saw all day long"	Sato, "Extemporization" 11
line 621: "Why is thy cheek so wan and wild"	*La Belle Dame sans Merci* 11–12, 31: "And on thy cheeks a fading rose / Fast withereth too"; "And there I shut her wild wild eyes"	Sato, "Extemporization" 11

Kubla Khan	Keats Poem	Critic
passage unspecified	*Endymion* 4.182–272: march of Bacchus	Finney 1:229, 277; Bush, *Selected Poems* 323
Preface: "the Author has frequently purposed to finish for himself what had been originally, as it were, given to him" (296–97)	Woodhouse's account of Keats's description of how *Hyperion* 3.81 was composed: "It seemed to come by chance or magic—to be as it were something given to him" (*Keats Circle* 1:129)	Levinson, *Romantic Fragment Poem* 169; Stillinger, "Keats and Coleridge" 12
passim: name "Kubla," earth goddess images	*Endymion* 2.639–49: description of Cybele	Gerber 386–89
lines 1–5, 31–36: imagery of caverns, subterranean streams, domes, fountains	*Endymion* 2.593–635: underwater region	Gerber 380–84
lines 3–5, 24–28: Alph the sacred river	*Endymion* 2.912ff.: Alpheus / Arethusa sequence	Gerber 389

Kubla Khan	**Keats Poem**	**Critic**
lines 14–16: "A savage place! as holy and enchanted / As e'er beneath a waning moon was haunted / By woman wailing for her demon-lover!"	*Endymion* 4.188–92: ". . . I sat a weeping: what ena-mour'd bride, / Cheated by shadowy wooer from the clouds, / But hides and shrouds . . ."; *The Eve of St. Agnes* 171: "Since Merlin paid his Demon all the mon-strous debt"	Finney 1:279–80; 2:552
line 16: "woman wailing for her demonlover"	*Lamia* 1.55–56: ". . . Some demon's mistress, or the de-mon's self"	Finney 2:672
lines 17–19: "from this chasm, with ceaseless tur-moil seething, / As if this earth in fast thick pants were breathing, / A mighty foun-tain momently was forced"	*Endymion* 2.601–4: "Enor-mous chasms, where, all foam and roar, / Streams subterranean tease their gran-ite beds, / Then heighten'd just above the silvery heads / Of a thousand fountains"	Allott, *Poems* 187–88; Bar-nard, *Poems* 574
line 39: "It was an Abyssi-nian maid"	*Endymion* 4.259: "I saw parch'd Abyssinia rouse and sing"	Finney 1:290
line 53: "he on honey-dew hath fed"	*Endymion* 1.766: "He seem'd to taste a drop of manna-dew"; *Endymion* 2.7: "One kiss brings honey-dew from buried days"	Allott, *Poems* 153, 164
	La Belle Dame sans Merci 26: "And honey wild, and manna dew"	Finney 2:598; Bush, *Selected Poems* 344; Bloom, *Vision-ary Company* 386; Allott, *Po-ems* 504; Barnard, *Poems* 639

The Statesman's Manual (1816); A Lay Sermon (1817)

DIRECT REFERENCES

"I would not for 40 shillings be Coleridge's Lays in your way" (Keats to Bailey, 30 October 1817; *Letters* 1:175).

ECHOES/ALLUSIONS

Coleridge Work	Keats Poem or Letter	Critic
The Statesman's Manual: advocates questioning and interpreting scriptures (45–48)	27 (?) December 1817 letter to George and Tom Keats: "Coleridge, for instance, would let go by a fine isolated verisimilitude caught from the Penetralium of mystery, from being incapable of remaining content with half knowledge" (*Letters* 1:193–94)	Ryan 144–45
A Lay Sermon, "Allegoric Vision": traveler relates vision in which he enters a temple and sees goddess of superstition, then goes outside and encounters majestic goddess of religion (131–37)	*The Fall of Hyperion* 1.1–290: frame story relating narrator's dream-vision entry into temple and encounter with goddess Moneta	O'Loughlin; Bush, *Selected Poems* 358

Biographia Literaria (1817)

ECHOES/ALLUSIONS

Biographia Literaria	Keats Letter	Critic
passage unspecified	27 (?) December 1817 letter to George and Tom Keats: Coleridge and Negative Capability (*Letters* 1:193–94)	Stillinger, *Hoodwinking* 152n.3
chap. 2: poets' "assurance of permanent fame" and indifference "to immediate reputation" (1:33)	14 October 1818 letter to George and Georgiana Keats: "I shall be among the English Poets after my death" (*Letters* 1:394)	Kohli 24–25

Biographia Literaria	Keats Letter	Critic
chap. 2: "indifference to public opinion" (1:44)	27 February 1818 letter to Taylor: friends "will attribute any change in my Life and Temper . . . to a cowering under the Wings of great Poets rather than to a Bitterness that I am not appreciated" (*Letters* 1:239); 8 October 1818 letter to Hessey: "Praise or blame has but a momentary effect on the man whose love of beauty in the abstract makes him a severe critic on his own Works" (*Letters* 1:373)	Kohli 25
chaps. 13–14: secondary imagination incapable of creating new ideas	22 November 1817 letter to Bailey: remarks on imagination (*Letters* 1:184–85)	Stillinger, *Hoodwinking* 152; Stillinger, "Keats and Coleridge" 22–23
chap. 14: "willing suspension of disbelief" (2:6)	27 (?) December 1817 letter to George and Tom Keats: Negative Capability (*Letters* 1:193–94)	Stillinger, "Keats and Coleridge" 27
chap. 15: Shakespeare as compared to Milton lacks individuality; has Protean nature	22 November 1817 letter to Bailey: "Men of Genius . . . have not any individuality" (*Letters* 1:184); 27 (?) December 1817 letter to George and Tom Keats: Negative Capability (*Letters* 1:193–94); 27 October 1818 letter to Woodhouse: "camelion Poet" (*Letters* 1:386–87)	Kohli 22–23; Stillinger, "Keats and Coleridge" 24–26[18]
chaps. 17–20, 22: analysis of Wordsworth's poetry	27 (?) December letter to George and Tom Keats: Coleridge and Negative Capability (*Letters* 1:193–94)	Gittings, *John Keats* 175

Biographia Literaria	Keats Letter	Critic
chaps. 22 and 23: "negative faith" (2:134, 214)	27 (?) December 1817 letter to George and Tom Keats: Negative Capability (*Letters* 1:193–94)	Watson 256n.3; Stillinger, "Keats and Coleridge" 26–27

See also entry for *The Ballad of the Dark Ladie* in Poems from Other Publications/Problematic Cases.

Poems Published in *Sibylline Leaves* (1817)

DIRECT REFERENCES

"Mrs Dilke or Mr Wm Dilke whoever of you shall receive this present have the kindness to send p^r Bearer—'*Sybilline Leaves*'" (Keats to the Dilkes, 5 or 12 [?] November 1817; *Letters* 1:183).

ECHOES/ALLUSIONS

Sibylline Leaves (1817)	Keats Poem or Letter	Critic
The Ancient Mariner (see *Lyrical Ballads*)		
conversation poems (*The Eolian Harp, This Lime-Tree Bower My Prison, Frost at Midnight, Dejection*): form, style, structure, subject matter, themes	Keats's odes	Stillinger, "Keats and Coleridge" 18–21
Dejection: An Ode (lines unspecified)	*In drear nighted December* 21: "The feel of not to feel it"	Gittings, *John Keats* 164
mood of torpor	*On Visiting the Tomb of Burns:* mood	Finney 2:412; Bush, *Selected Poems* 330
psychological structure	*Ode to a Nightingale:* structure	Daniel 137–38
line 18: "And sent my soul abroad"	*Ode to a Nightingale* 57: "While thou art pouring forth thy soul abroad"	Murry, "Keats and Coleridge" 6; Daniel 134

Sibylline Leaves (1817)	Keats Poem or Letter	Critic
Dejection 20: "dull pain"	Ode to a Nightingale 34: "dull brain"	Daniel 136
lines 20–22: ". . . A stifled, drowsy, unimpassioned grief"	Ode to a Nightingale 1–3: "My heart aches, and a drowsy numbness pains / My sense . . ."	Daniel 134–35
lines 26–29: throstle and green sky	Ode to a Nightingale 7–10: nightingale and "beechen green"	Daniel 136
line 31: "those thin clouds above, in flakes and bars"	To Autumn 25: "While barred clouds bloom the soft-dying day"	Allott, Poems 653
lines 35–36: moon	Ode to a Nightingale 36–37: Queen Moon	Daniel 136
line 38: "I see, not feel, how beautiful they are!"	On Visiting the Tomb of Burns: "inability to establish . . . rapport with the scene [speaker] contemplates" (Sperry)	Sperry, Keats the Poet 140
lines 42–43: "It were a vain endeavour, / Though I should gaze for ever"	On Seeing a Lock of Milton's Hair 5–6: "For ever, and for ever: / O, what a mad endeavour"	de Selincourt 565; Bush, Selected Poems 325
lines 51–52: "Than that inanimate cold world allowed / To the poor loveless everanxious crowd"	Ode to a Nightingale 23–24: "The weariness, the fever, and the fret / Here, where men sit and hear each other groan"	Daniel 135–36
lines 78–79: "all misfortunes were but as the stuff / Whence Fancy made me dreams of happiness"	Ode to a Nightingale 73–74: ". . . the fancy cannot cheat so well / As she is fam'd to do . . ."	Daniel 136–37

Sibylline Leaves (1817)	Keats Poem or Letter	Critic
Dejection 87, 94–95: desire to escape thoughts and world of actuality	Ode to a Nightingale 19ff.: desire to escape	Daniel 136
lines 89–93: "And haply by abstruse research to steal / From my own nature all the natural man. . . ."	27 (?) December 1817 letter to George and Tom Keats: Coleridge and Negative Capability (Letters 1:193–94)	Hardy 299
line 100: "mountain-tairn" (see also entry for Wordsworth's Fidelity [Poems in Two Volumes, chap. 1)	Endymion 4.693: "mountain tarn"	Gittings, John Keats 158
lines 112–13: "With groans, of trampled men . . . At once they groan with pain . . ."	Ode to a Nightingale 23–24: ". . . Here, where men sit and hear each other groan"	Daniel 135–36
line 128: "Visit her, gentle Sleep! with wings of healing"	Ode to a Nightingale 33: "wings of Poesy"	Daniel 136

See also entry for Dejection in Poems from Other Publications/Problematic Cases.

The Eolian Harp 26–33: "O! the one Life within us and abroad . . ." (lines first appeared in Errata of 1817; CPW 1:101)	27 (?) December 1817 letter to George and Tom Keats: Coleridge and Negative Capability (Letters 1:193–94)	Barnard, "Echo of Keats" 313

See also entries for The Eolian Harp in Poems on Various Subjects (1796) and Poems from Other Publications/Problematic Cases.

Fears in Solitude 87: "perilous seas" (for this poem's earlier publication history, see Poems from Other Publications/Problematic Cases)	Ode to a Nightingale 70: "perilous seas"	Ford 456; Bush, Selected Poems 348

Sibylline Leaves (1817)	Keats Poem or Letter	Critic
France: An Ode 9–14: speaker, "like a man beloved of God," wanders "Through glooms, which never woodman trod" (for this poem's earlier publication history see Poems from Other Publications/Problematic Cases)	*Ode to Psyche* 50–55: "Yes, I will be thy priest, and build a fane / In some untrodden region of my mind . . . Far, far around shall those dark-cluster'd trees / Fledge the wild-ridged mountains steep by steep"	Blunden, "Keats's Odes" 42
Frost at Midnight 65–74: "Therefore all seasons shall be sweet to thee . . ."	*To Autumn* 23–24: "Where are the songs of spring? Ay, where are they? / Think not of them, thou hast thy music too"	Vendler 235–36
	To Autumn (lines unspecified)	Davenport 100; Barnard, *Poems* 674
line 67: "or the redbreast sit and sing"	*To Autumn* 32: "The redbreast whistles from a garden-croft"	Allott, *Poems* 654; Vendler 236; McFarland 138
line 69: "mossy apple-tree"	*To Autumn* 5: "the moss'd cottage-trees"	Allott, *Poems* 651; Vendler 236
lines 69–70: "Of mossy apple-tree, while the nigh thatch / Smokes in the sun-thaw; whether the eave-drops fall"	*To Autumn* 4: "With fruit the vines that round the thatch-eves run"	Allott, *Poems* 651; Vendler 236

See also entries for *Frost at Midnight* in Poems from Other Publications/ Problematic Cases.

Hymn before Sun-Rise, in the Vale of Chamouni (see Poems from Other Publications/ Problematic Cases)

Sibylline Leaves (1817)	Keats Poem or Letter	Critic
Melancholy 5–8: ". . . The dark green Adder's Tongue was there . . . The long lank leaf bow'd fluttering o'er her cheek"	*Lamia* 2.224: "The leaves of willow and of adder's tongue"	Allott, *Poems* 645
Love (see *Lyrical Ballads*)		
The Nightingale (see *Lyrical Ballads*)		
On Observing a Blossom on the First of February 1796 (see *Poems* [1797])		
Reflections on Having Left a Place of Retirement (see *Poems* [1797])		
This Lime-Tree Bower My Prison 56–57: " . . not a swallow twitters"	*To Autumn* 33: "gathering swallows twitter in the skies"	McFarland 138

See also entries for *This Lime-Tree Bower* in Poems from Other Publications/Problematic Cases.

Zapolya (1817)

ECHOES/ALLUSIONS

Zapolya	Keats Poem	Critic
part 2, 2.1.74–81: bird sings, "Adieu! adieu! / Love's dreams prove seldom true. / The blossoms, they make no delay: / The sparkling dew-drops will not stay. . . . We must away; / Far, far away! / Today! to-day!"	*Shed no tear—O shed no tear* 17–19: "Adieu—adieu—I fly, adieu! / I vanish in the heaven's blue— / Adieu, adieu!"	Allott, *Poems* 490 (citing D. G. Rossetti)

Poems from Other Publications/Problematic Cases

Echoes/Allusions

Coleridge Poem	Keats Poem	Critic
The Ballad of the Dark Ladie	*Endymion* 4.145 (draft): "The ladye" (*Poems* 196); 4.886: "kind lady" (accent on last syllable)	de Selincourt 447

The Ballad of the Dark Ladie was first published in the collected edition of 1834. Coleridge's poem *Love,* however, appeared in the 21 December 1799 *Morning Post* with the title *Introduction to the Tale of the Dark Ladie.* In addition, Coleridge mentions "the 'Dark Ladie' " in chapter 14 of *Biographia Literaria* (see *CPW* 1:293, 330; *Biographia Literaria* 2:7 and note, 238n.3). The latter is the more likely place for Keats to have seen the poem's title.

Dejection: An Ode 86: "My shaping spirit of Imagination"	*Endymion* 1:568: "And shaping visions all about my sight"	Allott, *Poems* 145

Book 1 of *Endymion* was written before *Dejection* appeared in *Sibylline Leaves.* Coleridge's poem was published earlier in the 4 October 1802 *Morning Post* (*CPW* 1:362). It is doubtful, however, that Keats read the newspaper text of *Dejection,* which appeared when he was only six years old.

The Eolian Harp 32–33: "the mute still air / Is Music slumbering on her instrument"	*Sleep and Poetry* 237: " 'Tis might half slumb'ring on its own right arm"	de Selincourt 565; Bush, *Selected Poems* 312; Allott, *Poems* 79

Lines 32–33 of *The Eolian Harp* first appeared in the *Sibylline Leaves* (1817) errata sheet. Barnard ("Echo of Keats" 311; *Poems* 553) accurately points out that *Sleep and Poetry* was published before *Sibylline Leaves,* so that Keats could not have been echoing Coleridge. Barnard claims that the reverse is the case: that lines 32–33 of *The Eolian Harp* echo line 237 of *Sleep and Poetry.* In 1830, however, Coleridge told John Frere that of Keats's works he had read only two sonnets and "a poem with a classical name" (quoted by Bate, *John Keats* 468n). Either Coleridge's memory in 1830 was faulty or neither *The Eolian Harp* nor *Sleep and Poetry* reflects the other poem's influence.

Coleridge Poem	Keats Poem	Critic
Frost at Midnight 1–2: "The Frost performs its secret ministry, / Unhelped by any wind"; 8–12: ". . . extreme silentness . . ."	*On the Grasshopper and Cricket* 10–11: "On a lone winter evening, when the frost / Has wrought a silence"	Davenport 100n; Allott, *Poems* 98
line 2: "The owlet's cry"	*Endymion* 1.182: "owlet's cry"	Bush, *Selected Poems* 317

Frost at Midnight was included in *Sibylline Leaves,* but that collection was not published until July 1817. *On the Grasshopper and Cricket* was written on 30 December 1816 and book 1 of *Endymion* in the spring and summer of 1817 (*Poems* 560, 571). Because line 182 occurs in the first fifth of *Endymion*'s book 1 and was not revised (*Poems* 108), it was almost certainly written in the spring of 1817 before *Sibylline Leaves* was available to Keats.

Frost at Midnight did appear in several pre-1817 publications. It was first published in 1798 in a quarto pamphlet that also included *Fears in Solitude* and *France: An Ode.* The same three poems were printed in 1812 both in *The Poetical Register, and Repository of Fugitive Poetry, for 1808–09* and in a privately printed pamphlet (see Wise, *Coleridge* 52–56; *CPW* 1:240; 2:1148–49).

None of these publications, however, would have been easy for Keats to obtain; the two pamphlets would have been especially rare. Coleridge complained to Southey in December 1799 that "not above two hundred" copies of the original pamphlet had been sold (Coleridge, *Letters* 1:550), and E. H. Coleridge says of the second, privately printed one, "There is no . . . evidence that [it] was placed on the market" (*CPW* 2:1149).

Hymn before Sun-Rise, in the Vale of Chamouni 72: "glittering through the pure serene"	*On First Looking into Chapman's Homer* 7: "Yet did I never breathe its pure serene"	Bush, "Some Notes" 313; Dudley 463; Ford 456; Murry, "Keats and Coleridge" 6–7; Bush, *Selected Poems* 309; Bate, *John Keats* 88n; Allott, *Poems* 61; Barnard, *Poems* 546

Hymn before Sun-Rise was published in *Sibylline Leaves,* but as Murry points out ("Keats and Coleridge" 7), that volume appeared months after the *Chapman's Homer* sonnet was written in October 1816. Coleridge's poem was first published in the 11 September 1802 *Morning Post* and reprinted in

1803 in the *Poetical Register* for 1802 (*CPW* 1:376). A more likely source for Keats's 1816 reading of *Hymn before Sun-Rise,* however, is *The Friend.* The poem appeared both in issue Number 11 (26 October 1809) of the original periodical *Friend* and in the first collected edition of 1812. Line 72 did not appear in the issue Number 11 text, but it was included in Number 13 (16 November 1809) in a list of corrections and additions to the poem (*The Friend* 2:158, 183).

Murry believes that Keats read *Hymn before Sun-Rise* in a copy of *The Friend* owned by Leigh Hunt ("Keats and Coleridge" 7). More likely sources for Keats's acquisition of *The Friend,* however, are Haydon and Shelley, both of whom were more appreciative of the work than Hunt was (see "When Keats Read Coleridge").

When Keats composed the *Chapman's Homer* sonnet he had not met Hunt, Haydon, or Shelley. The line containing the phrase "pure serene," however, was added later—some time after 1 December 1816 when the sonnet with the original line was printed in the *Examiner* (*Poems* 64, 553). By 1 December Keats was friendly with Hunt and Haydon, and he met Shelley shortly thereafter, probably on 11 December (Reiman, "Keats and Shelley" 403). It is therefore possible that Keats read *Hymn before Sun-Rise* in Hunt's, Haydon's, or Shelley's copy of *The Friend* and that this reading influenced the revised line 7 of *On First Looking into Chapman's Homer.* One should nonetheless keep in mind that other sources for the phrase "pure serene" have been proposed (see Allott, *Poems* 61; Ford 456n.6). Bate, moreover, regards "pure serene" as "a fairly conventional eighteenth-century phrase" (*John Keats* 88n). Keats need not have read Coleridge to have written the words in question.

Coleridge Poem	Keats Poem	Critic
This Lime-Tree Bower My Prison	*Calidore* 155: "Grateful the incense from the lime-tree flower"	Allott, *Poems* 42
lines 28–30: "thou hast pined / And hunger'd after Nature, many a year, / In the great City pent"	*To one who has been long in city pent*	Bush, "Some Notes" 313; Allott, *Poems* 45

Both *Calidore* and *To one who has been long in city pent* were written in 1816 (*Poems* 549) before *This Lime-Tree Bower My Prison* appeared in *Sibylline Leaves.* Coleridge's poem was first published in the *Annual Anthology* in

1800 and reprinted in Mylius' *Poetical Classbook* in 1810 (*CPW* 1:178). It should be noted, however, that Allott makes only a tentative claim for *This Lime-Tree Bower*'s influence on *Calidore*, and several other sources have been proposed for the title and first line of *To one who has been long in city pent*, including Coleridge's *To the Nightingale*, published in the 1796 *Poems on Various Subjects*—a collection that would have been much more accessible to Keats than either the *Annual Anthology* or *Poetical Classbook*.

General References to Coleridge in Keats's Writing

POETRY

Sleep and Poetry 230–47: "yet in truth we've had / Strange thunders from the potency of song . . . in clear truth the themes / Are ugly clubs, the poets Polyphemes / Disturbing the grand sea. . . ."

Leigh Hunt, in his review of Keats's 1817 *Poems,* says these lines "object to the morbidity that taints the productions of the Lake Poets" (Matthews 62).[19]

PROSE

"Coleridge, for instance, would let go by a fine isolated verisimilitude caught from the Penetralium of mystery, from being incapable of remaining content with half knowledge" (27 [?] December 1817 letter to George and Tom Keats; *Letters* 1:193–94).

"Mr Robinson a great friend of Coleridges called on me (14 [?] February 1818 letter to George and Tom Keats; *Letters* 1:227).

"Last Sunday I took a Walk towards highgate and in the lane that winds by the side of Lord Mansfield's park I met Mr Green our Demonstrator at Guy's in conversation with Coleridge—I joined them, after enquiring by a look whether it would be agreeable—I walked with him a[t] his alderman-after dinner pace for near two miles I suppose In those two Miles he broached a thousand things—let me see if I can give you a list—Nightingales, Poetry—on Poetical sensation—Metaphysics—Different genera and species of Dreams—Nightmare—a Dream accompanied by a sense of touch—single and double touch—A dream related—First and second consciousness—the difference explained between will and Volition—so m[any] metaphysicians from a want of smoking the second consciousness—Mon-

sters—the Kraken—Mermaids—southey believes in them—southeys belief
too much diluted—A Ghost story—Good morning—I heard his voice as
he came towards me—I heard it as he moved away—I had heard it all the
interval—if it may be called so. He was civil enough to ask me to call on
him at Highgate" (15 April 1819 letter to George and Georgiana Keats;
Letters 2:88–89).

CHAPTER 3

Keats's Reading of Byron

Which of Byron's Works Keats Read

Although Keats's letters and poems contain a fair number of remarks on Byron the literary figure, direct references to or quotations of Byron's poetry are rather scarce in Keats's writing. The only Byron works Keats specifically mentions or quotes are *Fare Thee Well* (1816), *Manfred* (1817), *Childe Harold*, canto 4 (1818), and *Don Juan*, cantos 1 and 2 (1819). Evidence nonetheless suggests that for a time Byron was one of Keats's favorite authors.

Keats's sonnet *To Lord Byron*, dated December 1814 in both surviving manuscripts (*Poems* 543), celebrates the "sweetly sad" strains of Byron's poetry and urges the noble poet to "still tell the tale, / The enchanting tale—the tale of pleasing woe." The fact that he would compose a sonnet to Byron surely implies, as Lowell says, that Keats "fairly soaked in Byron at this period" (1:59). Other poems composed in 1814 and 1815 salute Spenser (*Imitation of Spenser*) and Chatterton (*Oh Chatterton! how very sad thy fate*), and these poets are recognized as major influences on the youthful Keats. Moreover, Henry Stephens, who roomed with the poet in 1815 and 1816, names Byron and Spenser as the two writers most "in favor" with Keats at this time. He also reports that Keats "used to go with his neck nearly bare á lá [*sic*] Byron" (*Keats Circle* 2:209, 211).

Unfortunately, neither *To Lord Byron* nor Henry Stephens specifies which poems the young Keats read and responded to so enthusiastically. Two of Byron's pre-1814 publications have been proposed as the impetus for Keats's sonnet. Finney argues that *Hours of Idleness* (1807) is the work alluded to in the poem and finds other of Keats's early compositions influenced by Byron's first volume (1:53; 33, 45–46, 69, 105). De Selincourt also states that, in his 1813 and 1814 poems, Keats "showed himself to be momentarily affected by the *Juvenilia* of Byron" (xxiii). Gittings ("Byron and Keats's Eremite" 8–9; *John Keats* 43) and Ward (40), however, believe that Keats's sonnet alludes to *Childe Harold,* cantos 1 and 2. Indeed, Gittings confidently asserts that *To Lord Byron* "is clearly based not on Byron's work as a whole, but on *Childe Harold* in particular. In fact it is a sonnet not so much about Byron as about cantos I and II of *Childe Harold"* ("Byron and Keats's Eremite" 8–9).

The main evidence for determining which work or works Keats had in mind when he wrote his sonnet is the poem's characterization of Byron's verse. First, the sonnet specifically urges Byron to continue "tell[ing] *the tale* . . . of pleasing woe" (my italics). *Childe Harold,* with its narrative frame, is much more likely to be referred to as a "tale" than are the *Hours of Idleness* lyrics. Secondly, the chief aspect of Byron's poetry celebrated in the sonnet is its melancholy: its "sweetly sad . . . melody" and touching expressions of the poet's "o'ershading sorrow," "griefs," and "woe." A number of Byron's *Hours of Idleness* poems do express sorrow, especially the pain of unrequited love and nostalgia for boyhood days. Most of these lamentations are fairly conventional, however, and no one seems to have specially commented on the collection's melancholy tone. Henry Brougham, for example, in his notoriously hostile *Edinburgh Review* notice of the volume, criticized Byron's schoolboyish translations, imitations of other writers, and frequent references to his rank and lineage, his youth, and his school and college experiences, but said nothing about excessive melancholy in the verses (see Rutherford 27–32).

It was *Childe Harold's Pilgrimage* that first popularized the solitary, world-weary Byronic hero who is haunted by secret pain and remorse. In addition, the first two cantos of *Childe Harold* were published with a number of decidedly melancholy lyrics, particularly those in the "Thyrza" group lamenting a beloved's death.[1] In the second decade of the nineteenth century, these emotional short poems were among Byron's most popular works, and they may have played a significant role in shaping Byron's reputation as a grief-stricken, tormented soul. Among Keats's friends, for example, Leigh Hunt declared that "Of all his lordship's productions, I confess I am still most taken with the little effusions at the end of the Childe Harold. It is here . . . that the soul of him is to be found, and that he has most given himself up to those natural words and native impressions, which are the truest test of poetry. His lordship has evidently suffered as well as thought" (*Feast* 1814, 133; 1815, 130–31). J. H. Reynolds, in a 2 June 1816 *Champion* essay "On Egotism in Literature," similarly remarks that "The little pieces to Thyrza are the favourites of all his Lordship's poems, because they appear to be records of his private feelings" (Reynolds

62). Finally, Benjamin Robert Haydon in his diary quotes *Stanzas* ("And thou art dead, as young and fair") and, twice, *Euthanasia,* a poem often associated with the "Thyrza" group (*Diary* 4:184; 3:108; 5:335).[2]

If one had to choose between the two publications, it would therefore seem more likely that *To Lord Byron* alludes to *Childe Harold* and the lyrics published with it than to *Hours of Idleness* poems. When Keats wrote his sonnet, *Childe Harold* was certainly the more popular work and, having attained an eighth edition, the more accessible. Of course, Keats might have read both of Byron's volumes by December 1814. Critics have discovered echoes of *Childish Recollections* and *To a Beautiful Quaker,* both published in Byron's first volume, in Keats's August 1814 *Fill for me a brimming bowl. Childish Recollections* and *To a Beautiful Quaker* were not reprinted in the 1808 *Poems on Various Occasions,* which was the source for all subsequent, unauthorized editions of Byron's early poems published in Keats's lifetime. If Keats did read the two poems cited as influences on *Fill for me a brimming bowl,* he therefore did so in a copy of *Hours of Idleness* and not in a later edition of Byron's juvenilia.

Other works Keats may have read and had in mind when he wrote *To Lord Byron* are the romances published in 1813–14: *The Giaour, The Bride of Abydos, The Corsair,* and *Lara.* These works, even more than *Childe Harold's Pilgrimage,* would fit the designation of "tale," the term used in Keats's sonnet to refer to Byron's poetry. In addition, all of the romances feature a gloomy, secretly suffering protagonist similar to Childe Harold; in fact, contemporary critics never tired of pointing out the similarities among Byron's heroes and, as they thought, Byron himself (see Hazlitt 5:153; Chew 78; Brooks 56, 61n.44). Keats therefore could have been thinking of any of the Eastern tales when he characterized Byron's poetry as "sweetly sad." If Stephens was correct in asserting that in 1815 and 1816 Byron was one of Keats's favorite poets, moreover, the young man is almost certain to have read some of these enormously popular works. Charles Cowden Clarke in his commonplace book quotes and praises a passage from *The Giaour* (Coldwell 89). In 1813 when this poem was published Keats was living in Edmonton and regularly visiting Clarke to borrow and discuss books. *The Giaour* and other of Byron's romances may have been among the works Keats encountered at Clarke's.

George Felton Mathew's poem about Keats, *To a Poetical Friend,* speculates that the young poet

> Perhaps . . . hast traversed the glorious East;
>   And like the warm breath of its sun, and its gales,

That wander 'mid gardens of flowers to feast,
   Are tinctured with every rich sweet that prevails.

                              (lines 17–20; Murry, *Studies in Keats* 1)

Although the sources behind this general reference to exotic Eastern lands could be the *Arabian Nights* tales or any number of other popular works of the time with Eastern settings, like James Weber's *Tales of the East* or William Beckford's *Vathek,* Byron's oriental romances might also have contributed to the passage. Mathew does seem to have appreciated Byron, for he objected to the statement in Reynolds's review of Keats's 1817 *Poems* that Keats would eclipse Byron and other popular writers (for Mathew's remark see Matthews 51; for Reynolds's, Matthews 45). Finney (1:33, 45, 46, 51, 53) believes Mathew and Keats read Byron together in 1815. Perhaps the sensational romances were among the works enjoyed by these Eastern enthusiasts.

Despite the strong probability that Keats read several of Byron's best-selling romances, the only evidence for such reading in Keats's work is one possible allusion to *The Corsair* (1814) in a letter and a possible echo of *The Siege of Corinth* (1816) in *The Eve of St. Agnes.* If Keats did read any of the other oriental tales, they do not appear to have made a significant impression upon him.

Joan Coldwell (89) reports that the extracts in Clarke's commonplace book suggest the schoolmaster particularly valued Byron's political poems. Besides passages in *Childe Harold* and the romances, some of the Byron poems with political implications published while Clarke and Keats were intimate are the *Ode to Napoleon Buonaparte* (1814); *Lines on a Lady Weeping,* first published anonymously in the 7 March 1812 *Morning Chronicle* and reprinted in the second edition of *The Corsair* (1814); *Napoleon's Farewell,* published anonymously in the 30 July 1815 *Examiner* and reprinted in *Poems* (1816); *On the Star of "The Legion of Honour,"* published anonymously in the 7 April 1816 *Examiner* and reprinted in *Poems* (1816); and the *Sonnet on Chillon,* published in *The Prisoner of Chillon and Other Poems* (1816). Since Clarke and his father were instrumental in shaping Keats's political views, the younger Clarke may have recommended to his pupil some of Byron's political verses, especially those published in the *Examiner,* to which newspaper we know Clarke introduced Keats. It is true that *Napoleon's Farewell* and *On the Star of "The Legion of Honour"* were published anonymously in the *Examiner,* but Clarke through his acquaintance with Hunt may have been aware of Byron's authorship. Both poems were acknowledged as Byron's when published in the 1816 *Poems.*

Keats is likely to have read several other signed Byron poems published in the *Examiner: Oh! Snatched Away in Beauty's Bloom* on 23 April 1815 (reprinted in *Hebrew Melodies* [1815]); *Bright be the place of thy soul!* on 11 June 1815 (reprinted in *Poems* [1816]); and *Monody on the Death of the Right Honourable R. B. Sheridan,* along with a review of the same, on 22 September 1816 (Blunden, *"Examiner" Examined* 64).

Another Byron poem that appeared in newspapers is *Fare Thee Well!,* the first two lines of which Keats clearly echoes in *The Jealousies* (lines 610–11). Even without this direct evidence one would assume that Keats read the poem, for it created a sensation when it was published along with *A Sketch from Private Life* in the spring of 1816, in the midst of the scandal surrounding Lord and Lady Byron's separation (see Chew 19–25). *Fare Thee Well!* and *A Sketch* were first printed for private circulation, but copies came into the hands of John Scott, who published them without Byron's consent in the *Champion* on 14 April 1816. Thereafter the poems reappeared in other newspapers and in scores of pirated editions of *Lord Byron's Poems on His Domestic Circumstances.* Hunt reprinted *Fare Thee Well!* (and lines 21–36 of *A Sketch from Private Life*) in his 21 April 1816 *Examiner* article "Distressing Circumstances in High Life," in which he defends Byron's conduct in the separation affair. *Fare Thee Well!* was finally published with Byron's authorization in *Poems* (1816) (*BPW* 3:494).

Keats almost certainly read *Fare Thee Well!* in the *Examiner* and perhaps in other sources as well. (He did not become a regular reader of the *Champion* until he met Reynolds in the fall of 1816, so he may not have seen the two poems on Byron's "domestic circumstances" in that publication in April 1816.) Benjamin Bailey preserved in a scrapbook an "Original Copy of [the] first Edition of Ld Byron's 'Fare thee well'"—presumably from the privately printed edition (Rollins, "Benjamin Bailey's Scrapbook" 17)—and Haydon in an 1824 diary entry claims John Scott showed him a copy of "the Farewell" before publishing it in the *Champion* (*Diary* 2:484). Keats therefore had two close friends who had seen or possessed the first printed version of *Fare Thee Well!*

Byron's *Address, Spoken at the Opening of Drury-Lane Theatre* was first published in the 12 October 1812 *Morning Chronicle* but was then reprinted without Byron's permission in James and Horace Smith's *Rejected Addresses* (1812). Keats probably read the Smiths' volume, for he knew the brothers as part of Hunt's set, and two passages in his letters appear to allude to *Rejected Addresses* (*Letters* 1:151 and note 5; 337 and note 6). In addition, Hunt reviewed Byron's poem in the 18 October 1812 *Examiner* (Blunden,

"Examiner" Examined 29). Keats's own writing, however, betrays no famil-
iarity with Byron's Drury Lane *Address.*

The only evidence for Keats's reading of *Childe Harold's Pilgrimage,* canto
3, which appeared in November 1816, is Gittings's claim that lines 224–26
of *Sleep and Poetry* refer to Byron and Lake Leman, which is described in
canto 3 (*John Keats* 105). Gittings on this point is opposed by Woodhouse,
who noted in his copy of Keats's 1817 *Poems* that the *Sleep and Poetry*
passage in question alludes to Wordsworth (Sperry, "Woodhouse" 155).
Gittings's argument receives some support from Hunt, who in his 1 De-
cember 1816 "Young Poets" article expresses "delight at the third canto of
Lord Byron's *Child Harolde* [*sic*], in which . . . he has fairly renounced a
certain leaven of the French style, and taken his place . . . among the poets
who have a real feeling for numbers, and who go directly to Nature for
inspiration" (Blunden, *"Examiner" Examined* 125). In lines 181–206 of *Sleep
and Poetry* Keats echoed Hunt's denunciation of Pope and his "French
style," and his praise in lines 223–25 of "sweet music . . . upstirr'd / From
out its crystal dwelling in a lake" may also reflect agreement with Hunt's
good opinion of the recently published *Childe Harold,* canto 3. On the other
hand, the passages on Lake Leman occupy only a portion of canto 3—
stanzas 68 and 85 contain the only direct references to the lake—whereas
Wordsworth was universally associated with the Lake District of England.[3]
Whether or not *Sleep and Poetry* alludes to canto 3 of *Childe Harold,* Keats
may still have read the poem, particularly if he remained fond of Byron
when it appeared and if Hunt shared with Keats his own good opinion and
his copy of the work.

We know for certain that Keats read Byron's drama *Manfred* (1817), for
he directly (though slightly inaccurately) quotes from it in his 3 May 1818
letter to Reynolds (*Letters* 1:279), and scholars have detected its influence
on several other passages in the poems and letters. Moreover, Fanny
Brawne told Keats's sister that the poet considered *Manfred* one of Byron's
best works (Edgcumbe 84). Byron's drama may have appealed to Keats
because the attitude expressed in the line quoted in the letter to Reynolds—
"Sorrow is knowledge," which Keats remembered as "Knowledge is
sorrow"—paralleled the younger poet's growing awareness of the inevita-
ble union of contrary qualities in human experience and the importance of
pain and suffering for fostering intellectual and moral development. It is
interesting to note that Keats's sonnet *To Lord Byron,* with its appreciation
of "pleasing woe" and "sweetly sad" elements in Byron's verse, appears to
acknowledge a juxtaposition of contrary qualities in Byron's poetry as early
as 1814.

In February 1818 letters, Keats twice remarks the impending publication of *Childe Harold,* canto 4, which came out on 28 April 1818. The fact that Keats anticipated the fourth canto's publication does not prove he read the work, particularly since one of his references to it is disparaging (*Letters* 1:225). In addition, Hazlitt, who was in high favor with Keats in the spring of 1818, wrote a splenetic, dismissive review of canto 4 for the *Yellow Dwarf* (2 May 1818), in which he called the poem, among other things, "an indigestion of the mind" (Hazlitt 19:35). If, as is likely, Keats read this review or if he heard Hazlitt utter similar opinions, he may have been deterred from reading the poem. On the other hand, the fact that Keats twice mentions canto 4's imminent appearance reflects an interest in or at least curiosity about the work that may have prompted him to acquire and read the conclusion of the poem he had so admired in his youth. Only one Keatsian echo of *Childe Harold,* canto 4—in *Otho the Great*—has been proposed.

Another Byron publication we know for certain Keats read is the first volume of *Don Juan* (cantos 1 and 2). As with canto 4 of *Childe Harold,* Keats was aware of *Don Juan*'s existence before the poem appeared in print; he tells his brother and sister-in-law on 14 February 1819 that "another satire is expected from Byron call'd Don Giovanni" (*Letters* 2:59). Since *Don Juan* was advertised and published anonymously, Keats must have learned of Byron's authorship from one of his literary friends. Perhaps Hunt was the source of this information, since he was in touch with Shelley, who visited Byron in Venice in September 1818, shortly after canto 1 was completed (Marchand 2:754; Pratt 293). Woodhouse reports that Keats asked Hessey to procure him a copy of *Don Juan* (*Keats Circle* 1:91), and Keats himself relates hearing extracts of the poem from Richard Abbey (*Letters* 2:192). In addition, Hunt in 1831 noted that Keats "was an admirer of *Don Juan*" (*Literary Criticism* 330). Finally, Joseph Severn in 1845 gave a detailed account of Keats's hostile reaction to the storm-at-sea passage in canto 2, which the poet was reading on board the *Maria Crowther* en route to Italy (*Keats Circle* 2:134–35). These remarks by Keats and his friends, along with a fair number of echoes of *Don Juan* discovered in *Lamia* and *The Jealousies,* attest to Keats's familiarity with the only volume of Byron's comic masterpiece published in Keats's lifetime.

It is less clear how much of cantos 1 and 2 Keats read. Hunt's remark and the proposed echoes suggest extensive reading, especially in canto 1. In Severn's narrative, however, Keats opens *Don Juan* at random to canto 2's storm scene and then throws the book down in disgust. From this account, one would assume that Keats had not read much of the poem before and would not have wished to read further. Another conclusion, however, might be that Keats previously had read and enjoyed canto 1 but did not appreciate or finish reading canto 2 on the trip to Italy. This explanation would account for the discrepancy between Hunt's and Severn's way of characterizing Keats's reaction to *Don Juan*.

In weighing the evidence for Keats's reading and response to *Don Juan*, one must also question the accuracy of both Hunt's and Severn's statements. Not only did both men write their remarks years after Keats's death, but both also may have been influenced by their own opinions of Byron's poem. Hunt was one of the few reviewers to praise cantos 1 and 2 in 1819 and 1820 (see Pratt 296–97), and in his 1821 "Sketches of the Living Poets" essay on Byron he called *Don Juan* Byron's "best work, and the one by which he will stand or fall with readers who see beyond times and toilets" (Hunt, *Literary Criticism* 158). Severn's opinion of the poem is not recorded, but given the fact that he was a pious Christian, he is likely to have been offended by Byron's depiction of marriage and human nature generally, as were many contemporary readers (see Chew 28–38, and Pratt 295–97). In addition, several scholars have challenged Severn's account of Keats's reaction to canto 2. Amy Lowell (2:482) concurs with Sidney Colvin's opinion that, although Severn may be essentially correct in his representation of Keats's attitude toward the storm-at-sea episode, he does not convey Keats's ideas in the poet's customary language. W. J. Bate believes "some expansion" of the original incident may have gone into Severn's narrative (*John Keats* 664). Nonetheless, despite some question about what particular passages Keats read and how he responded to them, the evidence taken together indicates certain interest in *Don Juan* on Keats's part and some reading, especially in canto 1.

Keats does not refer to any of Byron's other satires, but several passages in Fanny Brawne's letters to Fanny Keats suggest the poet may have read *Beppo* (1818). In a letter written sometime between 17 November and 12 December 1821, Brawne says:

> Don't you or do you admire Don Juan? perhaps you like the serious parts best but I have been credibly informed that Lord B. is not *really* a great poet, have taken a sort of dislike to him when serious and only adore him for his wit and humour. . . . Comedy of all sorts pleases me. I think Beppo nearly as good as Don Juan. (Edgcumbe 51–52)

In another, undated letter, Brawne offers Fanny Keats "the serious poems of Lord Byron" which "were given me by a schoolfellow." She says she was once "half wild about them . . . but as my dear Keats did not admire Lord Byrons poetry as many people do, it soon lost its value with me. . . . Of the rest [of Byron's works] Beppo is now known to be his. . . . Beppo and the first Don Juan are considered by *all* very clever" (Edgcumbe 84–85). Brawne goes on to discuss various other literary works and figures, and after remarks on Hazlitt and Lamb concludes, "In this I give your dear brother's opinion as far as I could get it now" (Edgcumbe 85).

The question one asks after reading these passages is, did Keats read and admire *Beppo* or is Fanny Brawne giving solely her own opinion when she speaks of that work? Clearly Keats influenced her attitude toward Byron and other writers, and especially when she emphasizes that "Beppo and Don Juan are considered by *all* very clever," she may be expressing Keats's point of view. Brawne's own tastes admittedly ran to comedy, however, and she was certainly capable of independent judgment. Also, a fair amount of material comes between the remarks on *Beppo* and the comment, "In this I give your dear brother's opinion"; "this" in the statement may refer only to the passages on Lamb and Hazlitt immediately preceding it. Brawne therefore may be speaking for herself alone when she praises *Beppo*.[4]

Two further questions raised by Fanny Brawne's letter are (1) what collection of Byron's "serious" poetry did Brawne possess and (2) did Keats ever read in her edition? Perhaps, since she does not name a specific title, she owned one of the collected editions of Byron's poetry that John Murray began publishing in 1815 and regularly updated, with additional volumes, as new Byron poems appeared. One can only guess whether or not Keats read his finacee's books. By the time the young people met, as both his and her letters make clear, Keats no longer appreciated much of Byron's poetry, and if Fanny ceased to value her edition after she came to share Keats's opinion, one would assume that Keats had no interest in reading it either. The most we can say is that, through Fanny Brawne, Keats had access to a collection of Byron's poetry should he have wished to consult it.

Keats could have borrowed copies of various Byron works from several other of his friends as well. We know Reynolds owned a copy of the third edition of *Childe Harold's Pilgrimage,* cantos 1 and 2, and wished to buy his friend Dovaston's copy of the third edition of *English Bards and Scotch Reviewers* (Clubbe 164, 166). His complaint that significant additions in the fourth edition of *The Giaour* were "scandalous . . . for those who purchase the earlier copies, get imperfect ones" (Richardson, *Letters from Lambeth* 106), implies that Reynolds was the unlucky owner of an earlier edition of that poem. He probably reviewed *The Prisoner of Chillon and Other*

Poems (*Champion,* 1 December 1816; Jones 110), and his letters, essays, and poems are filled with references to nearly all of Byron's publications.[5] Byron gave Hunt a copy of *English Bards and Scotch Reviewers* with the author's handwritten revisions (Blunden, *Leigh Hunt* 94), and, as has already been noted, Hunt reviewed *Monody on the Death of the Right Honourable R. B. Sheridan, Address, Spoken at the Opening of Drury-Lane Theatre,* and *Don Juan,* cantos 1 and 2. He also reviewed Stothard's *Plates Illustrative of Lord Byron's Works* (*Examiner,* 20 August 1815; Blunden, *"Examiner" Examined* 54). During Keats's lifetime Hazlitt reviewed canto 4 of *Childe Harold.* Like Reynolds, moreover, both Hazlitt and Hunt in their published writings reveal thorough familiarity with nearly all of Byron's major poems, and they may have owned copies of many of these works. In his surviving letters Woodhouse, an avid book collector who loaned materials to Keats, quotes *Childe Harold's Pilgrimage,* canto 1, line 612; mentions *A Dream,* published in *Poems* (1816); and discusses characteristics of Byron's poetry generally (Richardson, "Richard Woodhouse" 42; *Keats Circle* 1:84, 59–60). Finally, Keats asked James Hessey for a copy of *Don Juan* (*Letters* 2:163) and may have acquired from that source the volume he took with him to Italy.[6] Keats's publishers also would have been able to supply the poet with other Byron works he wished to read.

In a 14 October 1818 letter to his brother and sister-in-law, Keats attributed to Byron two lines slightly misquoted from Hunt's *Story of Rimini:* "I am free from Men of Pleasure's cares / By dint of feelings far more deep than theirs" (*Letters* 1:396 and note 4). One wonders which of Byron's poems Keats thought these lines came from. The fact that the first edition of *Rimini* was dedicated to Byron may have helped to associate him with Hunt's verse tale, but Keats undoubtedly considered the passage Byronic in some essential way, according to his own conception of Byron's characteristic outlook and style. Robert Gittings, the only person I am aware of who has considered this issue, believes Keats had in mind *Childe Harold's Pilgrimage,* cantos 1 and 2, which express sentiments similar to those in the quotation from *Rimini* ("Byron and Keats's Eremite" 9). The one problem with this conjecture is that *Childe Harold* is written in Spenserian stanzas, and the lines Keats quotes are rhymed couplets. It is true that lines 4 and 5 and lines 8 and 9 rhyme in a Spenserian stanza, but lines 4 and 5 virtually never work together as a complete statement, as they do in the quotation Keats attributed to Byron, and line 9 is an Alexandrine rather than an iambic pentameter line. Of course, since Keats erred in his attribution of the lines' authorship, he may also have neglected to consider the verse form of the poem from which he thought the quotation derived. A number of

Byron's Eastern tales are written in rhymed couplets, however, and the heroes of these works are similar to Childe Harold in outlook and behavior. *The Corsair* and *The Siege of Corinth* are written in heroic couplets, and *The Giaour* and *Lara* in iambic tetrameter couplets. *The Bride of Abydos* alternates between iambic tetrameter couplets and other rhyme patterns. Most of Byron's lyrics are written in quatrains, and *Manfred,* another work expressing sentiments similar to those in the quotation from *Rimini,* is blank verse. If Keats was thinking of verse form as well as content when he attributed Hunt's lines to Byron, he therefore probably had in mind one of the romances cited above.

In a 20 September 1819 letter to George and Georgiana Keats, the poet explains the difference between himself and Lord Byron thus: "He describes what he sees—I describe what I imagine" (*Letters* 2:200). Several critics (Ward 217; Gittings, *John Keats* 289; Low) have tried to identify which of his own poems Keats had in mind when he wrote this statement, but Wolf Hirst (45) is the only person to consider which of Byron's poems prompted the remark, "He describes what he sees." Hirst proposes the Preface to *Childe Harold,* cantos 1 and 2, in which Byron explains that the poem's descriptions of foreign scenes are based on direct observation. Actually, the entire poem, with its travelogue quality and extensive background notes, may lie behind Keats's remark. Perhaps too Byron's dispensing with the fiction of Childe Harold and writing in his own persona in cantos 3 and 4 shaped Keats's belief that Byron expressed only his own feelings and experiences.

A comment Haydon wrote in the margins of Thomas Medwin's 1824 *Journal of the Conversations of Lord Byron* may shed light on the sources behind Keats's statement. Byron, says Haydon, "was not a creative genius in the more enlarged sense of the word—he was obliged always obliged [*sic*] to have some identity of person or thing to be poetical on—Thus he poetises on Chillon in the Prison—on Tasso in the Dungeon, in Greece on Greece in Rome on Rome—he was obliged to have some positive place or person celebrated in History or nature before his eyes, & he versified the associations which belonged [to] them from fact" (Gray and Walker 26). Haydon's criticism of Byron's lack of imagination, which is very similar to Keats's, cites as supporting evidence *The Prisoner of Chillon* (1816), *The Lament of Tasso* (1817), and, in the references to Greece and Rome, probably *Childe Harold's Pilgrimage.* Keats and Haydon may have discussed Byron and together arrived at an agreement of his shortcomings as a creative genius. If this was the case, Haydon's list of Byron poems composed in response to direct impressions may reflect those, or at least some of those, Keats had in mind when he said Byron merely "describes what he sees."

One final question related to Keats's reading of Byron is prompted by Henry Stephens's remark that in 1815 and 1816, Keats "used to go with his neck nearly bare á lá Byron" (*Keats Circle* 2:211). Did Keats see one of the portraits depicting Byron with his collar open? The portraits Keats is most likely to have seen, all of which were well known through engravings, are that by Richard Westall, painted in 1813; the two by Thomas Phillips, painted and exhibited at the Royal Academy in 1814; and that drawn by G. H. Harlow and engraved by H. Meyer for the *New Monthly Magazine*'s 1 August 1815 issue (Piper 127–34 and 209n.56). Of course, the open "Byronic" collar had become part of the conventional image of the poet by 1815, and Keats need not have seen any particular portrait of Byron to have adopted this style of dress.

In summary, we have strong evidence for Keats's reading of *Fare Thee Well!, Manfred,* and *Don Juan,* cantos 1 and 2. Keats's December 1814 sonnet *To Lord Byron* attests to enthusiastic reading of some of Byron's earlier works, possibly *Hours of Idleness, Childe Harold's Pilgrimage,* cantos 1 and 2, and one or more of the verse tales published through 1814. In addition, circumstantial evidence exists for Keats's reading of *The Siege of Corinth,* cantos 3 and 4 of *Childe Harold, Beppo,* Byron poems published in the *Examiner,* and perhaps other pre-1821 publications.

When Keats Read Byron

Most of the evidence for when Keats read Byron is presented in the previous section and can be briefly summarized here. The December 1814 sonnet *To Lord Byron* and proposed echoes from *Hours of Idleness* poems in the August 1814 *Fill for me a brimming bowl* indicate that Keats read some of Byron's works—probably *Hours of Idleness* and *Childe Harold,* cantos 1 and 2—during or before this year. The fact that Charles Cowden Clarke copied extracts from *The Giaour* (1813) and some of Byron's political poems in his commonplace book suggests that Keats may have read the same works— and possibly other of the verse tales published in 1813 and 1814—when he lived in Edmonton and regularly visited Clarke.

George Felton Mathew, Keats's friend from late 1814 or early 1815 to 1816 (Bate, *John Keats* 51), admired Byron, especially his juvenile poems (Finney 1:53) and the oriental romances, and Keats is likely to have read and discussed such works with Mathew during the period of their friendship. Henry Stephens, who lodged with Keats from October 1815 through the summer of 1816 (*Letters* 1:31–32), reported that "Byron was . . . in favor" with the young poet at this time (*Keats Circle* 2:209). Perhaps Keats read *The Siege of Corinth,* which several scholars believe is echoed in *The Eve of St. Agnes,* shortly after its publication on 13 February 1816. Keats almost certainly read several of Byron's poems published in the *Examiner* in 1815 and 1816, one of which, *Fare Thee Well!* (published also in the *Champion,* unauthorized editions of *Lord Byron's Poems on His Domestic Circumstances,* and *Poems* [1816]), Keats quotes in *The Jealousies.*

Keats may have read canto 3 of *Childe Harold* soon after its publication in November 1816 (Randolph 60). This possibility is supported by the fact that Leigh Hunt, an important influence on Keats in the fall of 1816, praised the poem in his December 1816 "Young Poets" essay. Keats also could have read the 1816 collections *Poems* and *The Prisoner of Chillon and Other Poems* in 1816 or 1817, though *Fare Thee Well!* is the only work published in either of these volumes that Keats mentions in his poems or letters.

In February 1818 Keats announced to his brothers and to Reynolds the expected publication of *Childe Harold,* canto 4, which appeared on 28 April 1818. The only indication that Keats read canto 4 is a purported echo of the poem in *Otho the Great;* if Keats really did echo canto 4 in *Otho,* then he read Byron's work sometime between late April 1818 and July 1819.

Manfred came out on 16 June 1817, and Keats quotes from that work in a letter dated 3 May 1818. Keats therefore read Byron's drama sometime between those two dates. Keats in 1818 or 1819 may also have read *Beppo,* which first appeared on 28 February 1818, though only circumstantial evidence exists for Keats's reading of that work.

We know for certain that the poet read the first volume of *Don Juan,* published 15 July 1819, although the exact dates for his reading are in question. Several scholars argue that a passage in *Lamia* (1.330–32) echoes *Don Juan* 2.118.940–44. Since part 1 of *Lamia* was finished by 11 July 1819, however (*Poems* 664), it would have been impossible for Keats to echo Byron's as yet unpublished poem. Finney (2:696) solves this problem by claiming that the *Lamia* passage in question was added to part 1 early in September 1819. The draft of *Lamia* unfortunately has not survived intact (*Poems* 664–65), so we have no way of determining the validity of Finney's hypothesis.

Finney (2:696) and Bush (*Selected Poems* 354) perceive a satirical "Byronic manner" in the opening ten lines of *Lamia's* part 2, composed the last week of August 1819 (*Poems* 664), and Finney (2:691–92) believes Keats's September 1819 revisions of *The Eve of St. Agnes* reflect a Byronic worldliness and cynicism. Woodhouse, however, reporting on a 12 September 1819 meeting with Keats in which the latter showed him recent revisions of *St. Agnes,* said that Keats had not then seen *Don Juan* (*Keats Circle* 1:91–92;

Letters 2:163). It may be, as Finney argues (2:691), that Woodhouse simply was mistaken and Keats read Byron's mock epic in August 1819. One other explanation for Byronic elements in *Lamia* and the September 1819 *St. Agnes* revisions is that their source is *Beppo* (1818) rather than *Don Juan*. *Beppo* after all is written in the same stanza form and much the same style as *Don Juan,* and we know Fanny Brawne, who adopted Keats's opinion of Byron's serious works, read and enjoyed *Beppo*. Finally, however, Werner Beyer (197–202, 212–13) believes the so-called Byronic passages in *Lamia* are actually indebted to Wieland's *Oberon*.

Keats reported hearing Abbey read to him some extracts from *Don Juan* on 13 September 1819 (*Letters* 2:192), and his manner in describing the incident suggests that the poem was then unknown to him. He does not, as one would expect, say that he already was familiar with the passages Abbey read or reveal any awareness of the context of those passages. I would guess that the 13 September meeting with Abbey constituted Keats's first encounter with *Don Juan*. Since at that time he had already asked Hessey to procure him a copy of the poem (*Letters* 2:163), and since scholars have detected its influence throughout *The Jealousies,* composed in the closing months of 1819 (*Poems* 676), Keats probably read at least canto 1, from which all the proposed echoes in *The Jealousies* derive, in the fall of 1819, perhaps soon after the 13 September interview with his guardian.

Hunt in 1831 stated that Keats "was an admirer of *Don Juan*" (*Literary Criticism* 330). The most likely time for Hunt and Keats to have discussed Byron's poem was the summer of 1820, when Keats lived near Hunt and then in Hunt's home in Kentish town. Perhaps Keats also read or reread some of *Don Juan* during this time, encouraged by Hunt's opinion that the poem was Byron's masterpiece. Hunt's enthusiasm may also have influenced Keats's decision to take a copy of *Don Juan* with him to Italy. Severn reports Keats's reading of the storm-at-sea sequence from canto 2 while on board the *Maria Crowther* in October 1820 (*Keats Circle* 2:134–35). Keats may or may not have continued reading Byron's poem on this voyage and during his brief, tragic sojourn in Italy.

Keats's Attitude toward Byron

As noted above—and as the checklist shows—many of Keats's references to Byron are concerned with the man, the image, or the general character of the poetry, rather than with specific works. Although these remarks do not clarify which of Byron's poems Keats read, they do reveal a great deal about the latter's attitude toward his successful contemporary. In particular, they help to explain why Byron evolved from a favorite poet at the beginning of Keats's career, when the sonnet *To Lord Byron* was composed, to an object of derision and resentment, as Byron appears in the majority of Keats's surviving letters, poems, and remarks reported by friends.[7]

As I explained above, the chief appeal of Byron's poetry for the adolescent Keats, to judge from the latter's 1814 sonnet, was its melancholy. Later in his career, however, Keats specifically objected to the note of gloom in Byron's verse. *Sleep and Poetry* attacks "Strange thunders" in contemporary literature, or "ugly clubs, the poets Polyphemes / Disturbing the grand sea" (lines 231, 234–35). Poetry that "feeds upon the burrs, / And thorns of life," Keats continues, "forget[s] the great end / Of poesy, that it should be a friend / To sooth the cares, and lift the thoughts of man" (lines 244–47). Richard Woodhouse glossed these lines as an "Allusion to Lord Byron, & his terrific style of poetry" (Sperry, "Woodhouse" 155). A similar passage condemning poets who disturb rather than soothe, which occurs in *The Fall of Hyperion,* is also thought by many critics to refer to Byron (see checklist, General References to Byron in Keats's Writing: Poetry). Moneta has just made her important distinction between poets and dreamers: "'The one pours out a balm upon the world, / The other vexes it'" (1.201–2). In the lines thought to refer to Byron, the speaker then castigates, presumably for their "vexing" effect, "all mock lyrists, large self worshipers, / And careless hectorers in proud bad verse" (1.207–8). Although excessive melancholy is not directly included in this list of poetic sins, "mock lyrists" might well be considered to "vex" the world by dwelling on their sorrows. Certainly the conviction that poetry ought to please and soothe rather than disturb would have alienated Keats from Byron's gloomy, withdrawn protagonists.

Several of the new literary friends Keats met in the fall of 1816 are likely to have influenced his reaction against Byron's melancholy strain. Although Hunt believed Keats's objections in *Sleep and Poetry* to "Strange thunders from the potency of song" referred to the Lake Poets rather than to Byron (see Matthews 62), Hunt himself had criticized Byron along similar lines in his 1815 edition of *The Feast of the Poets.* In Hunt's verse-satire, Apollo takes Byron to task for his misanthropic characters and dark view of the world and gives him the following advice:

> you must not be always indulging this tone;
> You owe some relief to our hearts and your own;
> For poets, earth's heav'n-linking spirits, were born,
> What they can, to amend—what they can't, to adorn;

And you hide the best proof of your office and right,
If you make not as I do a contrast with night,
And help to shed round you a gladness and light.

(1815, 12)

Keats's appreciation of Hunt was at its peak when *Sleep and Poetry* was composed, and the journalist's preference for cheerful, therapeutic literature is likely to have shaped Keats's pronouncement that the "great end" of poetry is "To sooth the cares, and lift the thoughts of man," rather than to give vent to morbid, melancholy feelings as Byron did.

William Hazlitt, another major influence on Keats's thinking about poetry and poets, also condemned Byron's melancholy, though his reasons are somewhat different from Hunt's. In his last lecture "On the English Poets," which Keats almost certainly attended, Hazlitt characterizes Byron thus:

> Lord Byron (judging from the tone of his writings) might be thought to have suffered too much to be a truly great poet. . . . [He] shuts himself up too much in the impenetrable gloom of his own thoughts, and buries the natural light of things in "nook monastic." . . . He has more depth of passion, more force and impetuosity [than Thomas Moore], but the passion is always of the same unaccountable character, at once violent and sullen, fierce and gloomy. It is not the passion of a mind struggling with misfortune, or the hopelessness of its desires, but of a mind preying upon itself, and disgusted with, or indifferent to all other things. (Hazlitt 5:152–53)

According to Hazlitt, Byron's melancholy makes for bad poetry because it produces a self-centered, claustrophobic, and monotonous effect. He also dislikes what he regards as an unmanly wallowing in grief in Byron's verse.

Of course, Keats would not have been influenced by either Hunt's or Hazlitt's opinions of Byron had they not touched chords within himself. Both the notion that poetry ought to comfort and that poets ought to be "camelions" rather than "egotists" became central to Keats's own aesthetic credo. Keats also seems to have shared Hazlitt's belief that a man ought to struggle against adversity rather than cultivate his sorrows, as attested by his oft-repeated insistence that he preferred "real grievances" to "imaginary" ones because "The imaginary nail a man down for a sufferer, as on a cross; the real spur him up into an agent" (*Letters* 2:181; see also 2:113, 185–86, 210, 329–30). Although Keats himself suffered from "a horrid

Morbidity of Temperament" (*Letters* 1:142) that found expression in such poems as *Dear Reynolds, as last night I lay in bed, On Visiting the Tomb of Burns, Why did I laugh tonight?*, and *Ode to a Nightingale*, he apparently came to dislike Byron's indulgence of similar feelings.[8]

If we again accept Woodhouse's authority, *Sleep and Poetry* praises Wordsworth just before it disapproves of the harsh and gloomy strain in Byron's verse. Lines 224–26, celebrating contemporary poetry "upstirr'd / From out its crystal dwelling in a lake, / By a swan's ebon bill" was identified by Woodhouse as a reference to "Wordsworth, who resides near one of the lakes in Cumberland" (Sperry, "Woodhouse" 155). In unfavorably contrasting Byron to Wordsworth, Keats is following a pattern that can be detected in several of his friends' writing. In an 1831 essay, Hunt claims Byron resented the fact that Hunt seldom wrote about Byron's work, "the poetry he was fondest of being of another kind," for he considered "Mr. Wordsworth the first poet of the day" (*Literary Criticism* 329). In a 9 December 1815 *Champion* article, Reynolds compares Byron, whom he used to adore, to his new favorite Wordsworth. "It is true," Reynolds writes, "there are not in [Wordsworth], that haughty melancholy and troubled spirit which so peculiarly distinguish Lord Byron. . . . The truth is, Mr. Wordsworth describes natural feeling and natural beauties,—his thoughts come from him, purified through the heart.—He indulges in calm reasonings and rich reflections" (Reynolds 25). Finally, Benjamin Bailey, in a 14 June 1824 letter to John Taylor, declares, "I prefer Wordsworth to Byron, because Wordsworth is more contemplative, and indeed in his higher flights more poetical" (*Keats Circle* 2:461).

These comments suggest that, in the Keats circle and perhaps in the literary world generally, Byron and Wordsworth represented opposite styles of contemporary poetry, so that a preference for one required a rejection of the other. We know that Keats began to develop his lifelong interest in Wordsworth in the fall of 1816. The fact that Byron fell out of favor at the same time may well have resulted from the view Keats picked up from his new set of friends that one could not like both poets, and a choice of one over the other served to define one's literary tastes. Keats, like Hunt, Reynolds, and Bailey, if forced to decide between the two would opt for the contemplative naturalism of Wordsworth over the gloomy melodrama of Byron.

In a 7 April 1817 diary entry, Haydon records the first of Keats's direct comments on Byron after the 1814 sonnet. "Keats said to me today as we were walking along," writes Haydon, "'Byron, Scott, Southey, & Shelley think they are to lead the age, but [the rest of the sentence . . . erased].' This was said with all the consciousness of Genius; his face reddened" (*Diary* 2:106–7). This passage, incomplete though it is, clearly sounds a note of rivalry that recurs in many of Keats's subsequent remarks on Byron. As Keats passed from a tentative novice to an ambitious practicing poet, Byron changed from a hero worshipped from afar to a threatening rival. Although Keats could look to great poets of the past as comforting and supportive "presiders" (*Letters* 1:142), he seems to have regarded living contemporaries as competitors whom he had to "trounce"—a word he uses in another reference to Byron (*Letters* 2:84)—in order to make a space for himself in the literary world.

Other factors probably contributed to Keats's resentment of Byron and desire to surpass him. First, Byron's immense popularity marked him as a special rival. Particularly after it became apparent that *Endymion,* like Keats's first volume of poems, was not going to sell, the young poet seems to have felt keenly the other's easy success. Several critics have remarked the notes of bitterness, resentment, and jealousy in Keats's observation to his brother and sister-in-law on 14 February 1819, "I was surprised to hear from Taylor the amount of Murray the Booksellers last sale. . . . He sold 4000 coppies of Lord Byron" (*Letters* 2:62; see Finney 2:573; Ward 248; Gittings, *John Keats* 290). Wolf Hirst (48) also points out that Keats's out-raged condemnation of the shipwreck episode in canto 2 of *Don Juan* comes shortly before the young man chose for his epitaph, "Here lies one whose name was writ in water." Keats felt alternately challenged, threatened, and defeated by Byron's commercial and critical success, and he often re-sponded by denigrating the man and the work that enjoyed such immense popularity.

When Keats himself wished to become a popular writer in the summer and autumn of 1819, however, he turned to Byron as a model. The works in which critics have perceived the most Byronic elements—*Lamia,* the September 1819 revisions to *The Eve of St. Agnes,* and *The Jealousies*—were all written with a view to disarming the critics and giving the public what Keats thought it wanted: "a sensation of some sort" (*Letters* 2:189; see also 2:162–63, 174). Clearly Keats felt ambivalent about pandering to the read-ing public, however (see *Letters* 2:144), and he is likely to have felt the same way about imitating Byron. Such ambivalence is reflected in the fact that, in *The Jealousies,* Byron's poetry and domestic affairs are among the objects of Keats's satire, for the ludicrous, philandering Emperor Elfinan is gener-ally thought to have been modeled in part on Byron and his unwanted fairy fiancée Bellanaine on Anabella Milbanke (see checklist, General References to Byron in Keats's Writing: Poetry). In addition, in an 18 September 1819 letter Keats haughtily asserts that Byron "describes what he sees" whereas "I describe what I imagine—Mine is the hardest task" (*Letters* 2:200). Keats seems to have wanted to distance himself from Byron at the very time he was echoing the latter's style more closely than ever before in his career.

Another reason Keats may have felt particularly jealous and resentful of Byron was the fact that the successful poet was also a lord, whereas Keats himself, as *Blackwood's* reviewer John Lockhart took pains to remind him, was a "Cockney" with working-class origins. In a 20 September 1818 letter to Dilke that contains a humorous catalogue of different types of paper, Keats refers to "rich or noble poets—ut Byron" (*Letters* 1:368). More gloomily, to his brother and sister-in-law he complains of a neighbor's remark that he was "quite the little Poet": "You see what it is to be under six foot and not a lord" (*Letters* 2:61).

Keats's sense of class conflict with Byron no doubt received support from a number of his liberal friends. Hazlitt in his published writings frequently attacks the "noble poet's" rank, as when he asserts in "Pope, Lord Byron, and Mr. Bowles" that "Lord Byron has been twice as much talked of as he would have been, had he not been Lord Byron" (Hazlitt 19:64), or when, in his review of *Childe Harold,* canto 4, he complains of the hero's "idle wants . . . naughty airs . . . ill humours and *ennui* . . . contempt for others, and disgust at [himself], common to exalted birth and station" (Hazlitt 19.35; see also 8:209–10; 11:74–77; 19:62). Reynolds, perhaps echoing Hazlitt, wrote in his review of *Endymion* that Byron "is liked by most of his readers, because he is a Lord. If a common man were to dare to be as moody, as contemptuous, and as misanthropical, the world would laugh at him" (Matthews 119). Leigh Hunt, who was friendly with Byron throughout Keats's lifetime, nonetheless expressed reservations about "lords who write verses" (*Feast* 1815, 12). For example, he begins his "Sketches of the Living Poets" essay on Byron by saying, "There have not been many noblemen who have written poetry. . . . They have been brought up in too artificial a state, with too many ready-made notions of superiority; and their lives have passed in a condition too easy, conventional, and to say the truth, vulgar" (*Literary Criticism* 153). Finally, Charles Brown was well known for his "great dislike [of] hereditary distinctions" and his vow "never [to] put his legs under a Lord's table" (*Keats Circle* 1:lxii; see also Edgcumbe 78). Keats therefore moved in a circle that would have fed a sense of hostility toward persons and especially poets of rank.[9]

Keats's grumbling remark, "You see what it is to be under six foot and not a lord," suggests another source of resentment: Keats's insecurity about his short stature and appeal to women, as contrasted to Byron's celebrated beauty and sexual conquests. Perhaps the fact that Fanny Brawne had been "half wild" (Edgcumbe 84) over Byron's poetry before she met Keats increased the latter's jealousy of Byron's good looks and popularity with women.

Keats's disparaging references to Byron are not entirely the result of professional, social, or sexual jealousy, however. The younger poet also genuinely objected to certain aspects of Byron's poetry. (Although it is difficult to maintain a distinction between the personal and the purely aesthetic in Keats's remarks. As with all of us, psychological, social, and other background considerations inform Keats's literary principles.) One of Keats's criticisms of Byron's poetry surfaces in a 3 February 1818 letter to Reynolds, where Keats says that his friend's "letter and its sonnets gave me more pleasure than will the 4th Book of Childe Harold & the whole of any body's life & opinions" (*Letters* 1:225). The letter previously had contrasted the "egotism" of modern writers to the selflessness of Shakespeare and Milton. Although Wordsworth and Hunt are the contemporary writers specifically accused of egotism, Keats's concluding hit at Byron implicates that poet too in the modern malady of self-absorption. In fact, Byron more than any other writer of the age was known for his self-centeredness and inability to create characters unlike himself. Hazlitt, for example, who helped shape Keats's own ideas on the importance of "disinterestedness," denounced Byron's lack of this quality in his final lecture "On the English Poets":

> There is nothing less poetical than this sort of unaccommodating selfishness. There is nothing more repulsive than this sort of ideal absorption of all the interests of others . . . in the ruling passion and moody abstraction of a single mind. . . . It is like a cancer, eating into the heart of poetry. (Hazlitt 5:153; see also 11:69, 71–72, 77)

In his review of *Endymion*, Reynolds called Byron "a splendid and noble egotist" and continued: "He visits Classical shores; roams over romantic lands . . . but no spot is conveyed to our minds, that is not peopled by the gloomy and ghastly feelings of one proud and solitary man. It is as if he and the world were the only two things which the air clothed" (Matthews 118). Finally, Woodhouse, explaining to Taylor Keats's definition of the poetical character, remarked that "Ld Byron does not come up to this Character. He can certainly conceive & describe a dark accomplished vilain in love—& a female tender and kind who loves him. Or a sated & palled Sensualist Misanthrope & Deist—But here his power ends" (*Keats Circle* 1:59–60;

Letters 1:390). For Keats and for the friends with whom he shared his literary principles, Byron's poetry exhibited a tendency Keats himself wished to avoid: a subjective, personal note absent in the great writers of the past.

Related to the criticism of Byron's egotism is Keats's contempt for the noble poet's theatrical posturing, expressed most memorably in the statement, "Lord Byron cuts a figure—but he is not figurative" (*Letters* 2:67). Here Byron is regarded as a showman concerned only with superficial, external impressions, in contrast to the consummate artist Shakespeare who explored the inner meaning reflected by outward appearances and events. In addition, in Keats's representation Byron draws attention to himself instead of losing his ego in his creations as Shakespeare did.

In the 14 October 1818 letter to George and Georgiana Keats in which he describes his encounter with Jane Cox or "Charmian," Keats appears to appreciate Byron's celebrated style. "There are two distinct tempers of mind in which we judge of things," he writes, "the worldly, theatrical and pantomimical; and the unearthly, spiritual and etherial—in the former Buonaparte, Lord Byron and this Charmian hold the first place in our Minds" (*Letters* 1:395). Keats here admits that one part of himself admires the ability of a Byron or a Jane Cox to cut a striking figure. Nonetheless, as Hirst points out (45), the passage ultimately denigrates Byron, for it excludes him from the "unearthly, spiritual and etherial" category, which is surely the more important one for serious poets. Especially the term "pantomimical" describing the class into which Keats places Byron suggests that the latter's verse is shallow and more popular entertainment than enduring art.

Keats further characterizes Byron's poetry as second rate when he writes in his 18 September 1819 letter to his brother and sister-in-law, "[Lord Byron] describes what he sees—I describe what I imagine—Mine is the hardest task" (*Letters* 2:200). Keats here touches on a major difference between himself and Byron. As Jerome McGann explains, Byron did not exalt the imagination as Wordsworth, Coleridge, and Keats did. He regarded it as merely one ingredient in the creative process and analytic or critical in nature, serving to enhance understanding of the human world rather than to create an autonomous aesthetic realm (McGann 156–65; see esp. 160, 165). Keats, who was "certain of nothing but of the holiness of the Heart's affections and the truth of Imagination" (*Letters* 1:184), perhaps regarded Byron's lack of a similar commitment to the imagination as evidence of a failure of true poetic calling.

On the other hand, Keats also lost faith in autonomous realms of imagi-

nation as he grew older and increasingly confronted, accepted, and cele-
brated the contradictions of human life. One would think that, in Septem-
ber 1819 shortly after writing *To Autumn,* Keats would have been more
sympathetic to Byron's veracity and might even have perceived in Byron's
career a development similar to his own. After all, *Childe Harold,* subtitled
"A Romaunt," and the exotic Eastern tales gave way to *Beppo* and *Don
Juan,* just as *Endymion: A Poetic Romance* was followed by the poems of
1819 that question the possibility and desirability of fleeing this earth for
"faery lands forlorn."

Despite the similarities we now are able to perceive in the shapes of
Keats's and Byron's careers, however, Keats himself was probably most
sensitive to the differences between *Childe Harold* and *Endymion, Don Juan*
and the odes or *The Fall of Hyperion.* Byron found his most natural and
successful voice in a comic mode. His satires cope with the absurdities of
human nature and disappointments of life by laughing at them. Keats's
vision in his greatest works, on the other hand, is tragic, and finds consola-
tion for human suffering in the intensity of experience and the bond of
compassion for others it produces. Byron's detached amusement at human
folly and perversity could seem cruel to Keats as when, according to Sev-
ern, he complained that canto 2 of *Don Juan* "laugh[ed] and gloat[ed] over
the most solemn & heart rending [scenes] of human misery" (*Keats Circle*
2:134–35).

One final contrast between Byron and Keats that probably prevented the
latter from appreciating the former is the difference in their writing styles.
Byron's poetry, especially in his narrative works, is fast-paced and cumula-
tive in its effect, and pausing to dwell on individual lines may actually
detract from appreciation by revealing faulty diction and syntax or clichéd
phrases.[10] Keats's poetry, by contrast, is dense with vivid imagery and
suggestive language. Keats could not have "look[ed] upon fine Phrases like
a Lover" (*Letters* 2:139) in Byron's poetry, and this fact, as much as any-
thing else, probably explains the paucity of quotations and echoes of Byron
poems in Keats's writing. The younger poet did not absorb memorable
lines and images from Byron as he did from other writers more in keeping
with his own artistic bent.

After a brief adolescent enthusiasm for Byron, aesthetic and tempera-
mental differences, professional rivalry, and personal insecurities prevented
Keats throughout most of his career from admiring his popular contempo-
rary. Still, there is something satisfying about the thought of Keats reading
Don Juan on his voyage to Italy. One thinks of Shelley, who was reading
Keats's *Lamia* volume before he drowned. Despite their conflicts, the

younger generation of Romantic poets did constitute a literary group or network whose goals, techniques, and self-images were shaped at least partly in response to one another's works.

Poems Published in *Hours of Idleness* (1807)

ECHOES/ALLUSIONS

Hours of Idleness (1807)	Keats Poem	Critic
Childish Recollections 111: "With him, for years, we search'd the classic page"	*Fill for me a brimming bowl* 20: "The classic page—the muse's lore"	Finney 1:51; Allott, *Poems* 7
To a Beautiful Quaker: story, emotion, diction, meter	*Fill for me a brimming bowl*	Finney 1:51; Gittings, *John Keats* 43; Allott, *Poems* 7

Childe Harold's Pilgrimage, Cantos 1 and 2 (1812)

ECHOES/ALLUSIONS

Childe Harold's Pilgrimage	Keats Poem or Letter	Critic
cantos 1 and 2 generally	*To Lord Byron*	Gittings, "Byron and Keats's Eremite" 8–9; Gittings, *John Keats* 43
cantos 1 and 2: sentiments expressed by hero	misattribution to Byron of lines from Hunt's *The Story of Rimini* (3.121–22); 14 October 1818 letter to George and Georgiana Keats (*Letters* 1: 396)	Gittings, "Byron and Keats's Eremite" 9
Preface: "The following poem was written . . . amidst the scenes which it attempts to describe. . . ." (*BPW* 2:3)	"[Byron] describes what he sees—I describe what I imagine"; 20 September 1819 letter to George and Georgiana Keats (*Letters* 2:200)	Hirst 45
canto 2: twilight scenes	*To Lord Byron* 8–11: images of moon and evening	Gittings, "Byron and Keats's Eremite" 9
2.1–15, 39, 46: references to Greek ruins, funeral urn, ravages of time	*Ode on a Grecian Urn*	Low

Childe Harold's Pilgrimage	Keats Poem or Letter	Critic
2.26.227: "To hear, to see, to feel, and to possess"	*Bright star* 13 (draft): "To hear, to feel her tender-taken breath" (*Poems* 328)	Gittings, "Byron and Keats's Eremite" 8
2.27.235–38: "godly Eremite . . . Watching at Eve upon the giant height . . ."	*Bright star* 4: "Like nature's patient, sleepless eremite"	Gittings, "Byron and Keats's Eremite" 8; Bush, *Selected Poems* 343; Allott, *Poems* 738
2.56.502: "Slaves, eunuchs, soldiers, guests, and santons wait"	*Dear Reynolds, as last night I lay in bed* 42: "Built by a banish'd santon from Chaldee"	de Selincourt 539; Bush, *Selected Poems* 327; Allott, *Poems* 322

Childe Harold's Pilgrimage, Canto 3 (1816)

Echoes/Allusions

Childe Harold's Pilgrimage	Keats Poem	Critic
stanzas 68, 85ff.: Lake Leman	*Sleep and Poetry* 224–26: music "has been upstirr'd / From out its crystal dwelling in a lake . . ."	Gittings, *John Keats* 105[11]

Childe Harold's Pilgrimage, Canto 4 (1818)

Direct References

"Your letter and its sonnets gave me more pleasure than will the 4th Book of Childe Harold & the whole of any body's life & opinions" (Keats to Reynolds, 3 February 1818; *Letters* 1:225).

"Lord Byron's 4th Canto is expected out" (Keats to George and Tom Keats, 21 February 1818; *Letters* 1:237).

See also second entry and note for 14 February 1819 letter to George and Georgiana Keats in General References to Byron in Keats's Writing: Prose.

ECHOES/ALLUSIONS

Childe Harold's Pilgrimage	Keats Poem	Critic
4.98.875: "like the thunder-storm *against* the wind"	*Otho the Great* 2.1.57–58: "here the thunder comes / Sullen against the wind!"	de Selincourt 553; Allott, *Poems* 567

The Corsair

ECHOES/ALLUSIONS

The Corsair	Keats Letter	Critic
general	13 March 1818 letter to Bailey: "Were I a Corsair I'd make a descent on the South Coast of Devon" (*Letters* 1:241)	Lau (present work)

The Siege of Corinth (1816)

ECHOES/ALLUSIONS

The Siege of Corinth	Keats Poem	Critic
575–82: "Like the figures on arras, that gloomily glare / Stirred by the breath of the wintry air, / So seen by the dying lamp's fitful light . . ."	*The Eve of St. Agnes* 357–60: "A chain-droop'd lamp was flickering by each door; / The arras . . . Flutter'd in the besieging wind's uproar . . ."	Allott, *Poems* 477–78; Barnard, *Poems* 627

Fare Thee Well! (1816)[12]

DIRECT REFERENCE

Fare Thee Well! 1–2: "Fare thee well! and if for ever— / Still for ever, fare thee well"

"'Farewell! farewell! and if for ever! still / For ever fare thee well!'" (*The Jealousies* 610–11).

Manfred (1817)

DIRECT REFERENCES

"My dear Keats did not admire Lord Byrons poetry as many people do. . . . If I am not mistaken he thought Manfred one of the best" (Fanny Brawne to Fanny Keats, undated [1823]; Edgcumbe 84).

1.1.10: "Sorrow is knowledge"
"In fine, as Byron says, 'Knowledge is Sorrow'" (Keats to Reynolds, 3 May 1818; *Letters* 1:279).

ECHOES/ALLUSIONS

Manfred	Keats Poem or Letter	Critic
1.1.10: "Sorrow is knowl-edge"	6 August 1818 letter to Mrs. Wylie: "It is impossible to make out, that sorrow is joy or joy is sorrow" (*Letters* 1:358)	*Letters* 1:358n.4
	Hyperion 3.113–20: Apollo's deification	Allott, *Poems* 440; Barnard, *Poems* 616
1.1.50–135: spirits of earth, ocean, air, night, mountains, winds, and Manfred's star speak	*Song of Four Fairies: Fire, Air, Earth, and Water*	Gittings, *John Keats* 306

Don Juan, Cantos 1 and 2 (1819)

DIRECT REFERENCES

"Another satire is expected from Byron call'd Don Giovanni" (Keats to George and Georgiana Keats, 14 February 1819; *Letters* 2:59).

"I sho^d have thought, [Keats] affected the 'Don Juan' style of mingling up sentiment & sneering: but that he had before asked Hessey if he co^d procure him a sight of that work, as he had not met with it, and if the E. of St A. had not in all probability been altered before his Lordship had thus flown in the face of the public" (Woodhouse to Taylor, 19 September 1819; *Keats Circle* 1:91–92; *Letters* 2:163).

"On seeing a miniature of Mr. Keats put up in Mr. Hunt's study at Pisa, [Byron] could not help expressing his astonishment, how the other could admire him. Mr. Hunt said that Mr. Keats would be sorry to hear him talk so, as he (Mr. Keats) was an admirer of *Don Juan*" (Hunt, "Lord Byron, Mr. Moore, and Mr. Leigh Hunt, with Original Letters *Not* in Mr. Moore's Work," *Tatler* 14 January 1831; Hunt, *Literary Criticism* 330).

1.218: "What is the end of fame? 'tis but to fill / A certain portion of uncertain paper . . ."
"[Abbey] began blowing up Lord Byron while I was sitting with him, however Says he the fellow says true things now & then; at which he took up a Magasine and read me some extracts from Don Juan, (Lord Byron's last flash poem) and particularly one against literary ambition" (Keats to George and Georgiana Keats, 18 September 1819; *Letters* 2:192).

2.26ff.: storm at sea passage
"When we had passed the bay of Biscay, where we had been in danger & great fright from a storm of three days—Keats took up Ld Byrons Don Juan accidentally as one of the books he had brought from England & singular enough he opened on the description of the Storm, which is evidently taken from the Medusa frigate & which the taste of Byron tryes to make a jest of—Keats threw down the book & exclaimed, 'this gives me the most horrid idea of human nature, that a man like Byron should have exhausted all the pleasures of the world so compleatly that there was nothing left for him but to laugh & gloat over the most solemn & heart rending [scenes] of human misery this storm of his is one of the most diabolical attempts ever made upon our sympathies, and I have no doubt it will fascenate thousands into extreem obduracy of heart—the tendency of Byrons poetry is based on a paltry originality, that of being new by making solemn things gay & gay things solemn—On another occasion when we were in the dull Quarantine with the other passengers (who were two English Ladies) the captain requested the sailors on deck to continue singing just to amuse us. . . . on a sudden Keats rose with rather a frantic look & exclaimed that nothing could teach him the extent of mans depravity. . . . I soon found that Keats had painfully understood they were sin[g]ing abominable songs when they knew the Ladies below in the cabin were listening—this he added is only another tho more sincere spec[i]men of the unmanly depravity which By-

ron so publicly assumes to feel or tries to make others feel—'tis all the same system of a cramped & wilfull nature the one by a preverted [sic] education—the other by no education at all" (Joseph Severn, Biographical Notes on Keats, October 1845 [?]; Keats Circle 2:134–35).

ECHOES/ALLUSIONS

Don Juan	Keats Poem	Critic
cantos 1 and 2: parodic style, social satire	The Jealousies, esp. 118–26, 208–16	de Selincourt 409, 559–60; Finney 2:735
cantos 1 and 2: realism and cynicism	September 1819 revisions of The Eve of St. Agnes (in Poems, cancelled lines 55–63, 314–22, 375–78)	Finney 2:691–92
canto 1, introduction and coda: literary satire[13]	The Jealousies	Gittings, John Keats 370
1.7.54: parenthetical remark	The Jealousies 697, 705–7, 745: parenthetical remarks	Allott, Poems 733
1.53.420; 1.201.1603: Latin tags	The Jealousies 292: "The dentes sapientiae of mice"	Allott, Poems 716
1.62.494: French phrase	The Jealousies 44, 283, 369, 759: French phrases	Allott, Poems 705
1.84.671: "This should be entre nous"	The Jealousies 299: "And master is too partial, entre nous"	Allott, Poems 717
1.205–6.1633–48: attack on current literary fashions	The Jealousies 86–95: attack on popularity of candid memoirs and autobiographies	Allott, Poems 706; Barnard, Poems 689
2.118.940–48: ". . . I've seen much finer women, ripe and real, / Than all the nonsense of their stone ideal"	Lamia 1.328–32: "There is not such a treat among them all . . . As a real woman"	Finney 2:696; Allott, Poems 631[14]

Byronic Satire (Unspecified)

ECHOES/ALLUSIONS

Reference to Byron	Keats Poem	Critic
Byronic manner	*Lamia* 2.1–10: "Love in a hut, with water and a crust, / Is—Love, forgive us!—cinders, ashes, dust . . ."	Finney 2:696; Bush, *Selected Poems* 354[15]
"flavour" of Byron's "jingling invective" (Allott)	*The Jealousies* 52–53: "He's Elfinan's great state-spy militant, / His running, lying, flying foot-man too"	Allott, *Poems* 705
Byronic satire	*The Jealousies:* burlesques	Bate, *John Keats* 622

General References to Byron in Keats's Writing

POETRY

To Lord Byron: "Byron, how sweetly sad thy melody . . ."

Speculative Cases

Sleep and Poetry 230–31, 241–42: "yet in truth we've had / Strange thunders from the potency of song"; "But strength alone though of the Muses born / Is like a fallen angel."
Woodhouse, in his copy of Keats's 1817 *Poems,* notes that these lines allude to Lord Byron (Sperry, "Woodhouse" 155).[16]

Sleep and Poetry 233–35: "But in clear truth the themes / Are ugly clubs, the poets Polyphemes / Disturbing the grand sea."
Allusion to Byron (de Selincourt 409; Allott, *Poems* 79).

The Fall of Hyperion 1.207–8: "all mock lyrists, large self worshipers, / And careless hectorers in proud bad verse."
Allusion to Byron (Finney 2:719; Gittings, *John Keats* 345; Allott, *Poems* 671; Barnard, *Poems* 680).

The Jealousies: character Elfinan
Modeled on Byron (Finney 2:735–36; Bate, *John Keats* 624; Gittings, *John Keats* 372; Barnard, *Poems* 688).

The Jealousies: name Bellanaine; 609: "Poor Bell!"
Derived from name of Byron's wife, Annabel, and her pet name, Bell (Finney 2:735; Bate, *John Keats* 624; Allott, *Poems* 704; Barnard, *Poems* 689, 693).

The Jealousies 613: "By'r Lady!"
Play on "Lady Byron" (Barnard, *Poems* 693).

PROSE

"I am quite disgusted with literary Men and will never know another except Wordsworth—no not even Byron" (8 October 1817 letter to Bailey; *Letters* 1:169).

"Fools cap—I superfine! rich or noble poets—ut Byron" (20 September 1818 letter to Dilke; *Letters* 1:368).

"There are two distinct tempers of mind in which we judge of things—the worldly, theatrical and pantomimical; and the unearthly, spiritual and etherial—in the former Buonaparte, Lord Byron and this Charmian hold the first place in our Minds" (14 October 1818 letter to George and Georgiana Keats; *Letters* 1:395).

"'I am free from Men of Pleasure's cares / By dint of feelings far more deep than theirs' This is Lord Byron, and is one of the finest things he has said" (14 October 1818 letter to George and Georgiana Keats; *Letters* 1:396).[17]

"We have seen three literary kings in our Time—Scott—Byron—and then the scotch nove[ls.] All now appears to be dead—or I may mistake—literary Bodies may still keep up the Bustle which I do not hear" (29 [?] December 1818 letter to George and Georgiana Keats; *Letters* 2:16).

"You see what it is to be under six foot and not a lord" (14 February 1819 letter to George and Georgiana Keats; *Letters* 2:61).

"I was surprised to hear from Taylor the amount of Murray the Booksellers last sale—what think you of [£]25,000? He sold 4000 coppies of Lord Byron" (14 February 1819 letter to George and Georgiana Keats; *Letters* 2:62).[18]

"Lord Byron cuts a figure—but he is not figurative" (19 February 1819 letter to George and Georgiana Keats; *Letters* 2:67).

"[Hazlitt] hath a demon as he himself says of Lord Byron" (13 March 1819 letter to George and Georgiana Keats; *Letters* 2:76).

"I[t] would be just as well to trounce Lord Byron in the same manner" (15 April 1819 letter to George and Georgiana Keats; *Letters* 2:84).

"You speak of Lord Byron and me—There is this great difference between us. He describes what he sees—I describe what I imagine—Mine is the hardest task. You see the immense difference" (18 September 1819 letter to George and Georgiana Keats; *Letters* 2:200).

Keats's References to and Opinion of Byron as Reported by Others

"Byron was also in favor. . . . [Keats] used to go with his neck nearly bare á lá Byron The collar turned down & a ribbon tied round his neck without any neckerchief" (Henry Stephens to George Felton Mathew, March [?] 1847; *Keats Circle* 2:209, 211).

"Keats said to me today as we were walking along 'Byron, Scott, Southey, & Shelley think they are to lead the age, but [rest of the sentence, consisting probably of eight or ten words, has been erased].' This was said with all the consciousness of Genius; his face reddened" (Haydon, 7 April 1817 entry; *Diary* 2:106–7).

"I have been credibly informed that Lord B. is not *really* a great poet" (Fanny Brawne to Fanny Keats, between 17 November and 12 December 1821; Edgcumbe 51).

"My dear Keats did not admire Lord Byrons poetry as many people do" (Fanny Brawne to Fanny Keats, undated [1823]; Edgcumbe 84).

CHAPTER 4

Keats's Reading of Shelley[1]

Percy Bysshe Shelley was only three years older than Keats, and although he had published or printed a number of juvenile poems, romances, and political pamphlets when the two men met in December 1816, the only work he had published with his name on the title page was the *Alastor* volume of 1816. Shelley's pre-1816 compositions were not printed in large numbers nor were they widely circulated, and it is therefore unlikely that Keats read any of these works.[2]

The one exception is the 1813 *Queen Mab,* for which there is some evidence of Keats's reading. The younger poet certainly was aware of *Queen Mab*'s reputation as a scandalous work, for in a December 1817 letter to his brothers he refers to its hostile critical reception (*Letters* 1:194). Indeed, the poem gained notoriety in the first few months of Keats's acquaintance with Shelley, for it was used as evidence against the author in the 1817 Chancery battle over custody of Shelley's children, as Leigh Hunt reported in a 26 January 1817 *Examiner* article (White, *Hearth* 109). Hunt possessed a copy of *Queen Mab* (Grannis 32), which he loaned to Haydon in December 1817, hoping thereby to confound the artist's religious beliefs (Haydon, *Diary* 2:148–66; Gray and Walker 22). Finally, as the checklist shows, three possible echoes of the poem have been detected in Keats's writing.

Two of the *Queen Mab* passages that Keats may have echoed, however, are also found in *The Daemon of the World,* part I, a reworking of parts 1 and 2 of *Queen Mab* that was published in the 1816 *Alastor* volume (Ingpen and Peck 1:421). The third alleged echo of *Queen Mab*—no more than the repetition of "pathless" followed by an initial "w"—is almost certainly mere coincidence, for it occurs in the sonnet *To My Brother George,* written at Margate in August 1816 before Keats had met either Shelley or Hunt. It is therefore possible that Keats read only *The Daemon of the World* and not the longer *Queen Mab*.

One might argue that Hunt, since he urged Haydon to read *Queen Mab*, probably recommended the poem to Keats as well. Hunt's insistence that Haydon read *Queen Mab*, however, was one of many episodes in the two men's ongoing religious controversy, during which the skeptical Hunt teased and baited the pious Haydon. Hunt would not have had the same impulse to shock or convert Keats with the poem, since he knew that Keats largely shared his and Shelley's religious views. At the time of the Chancery hearings, moreover, Shelley and Hunt tended to dismiss the poem as an immature work that did not reflect the author's present views (Hunt, *Autobiography* 268; White, *Shelley* 1:493).[3] Neither Hunt nor Shelley therefore may have advocated a reading of the poem in the early months of 1817, the period in which Keats was most intimate with both men.

Still, Keats had access to both *Queen Mab* and *The Daemon of the World* through Hunt and Shelley, and *Queen Mab*'s notoriety may have piqued his curiosity about the work. If he did read either the nine-part *Queen Mab* or the shorter version in the *Alastor* volume, he probably did so in December 1816 or early 1817, shortly after meeting Shelley.

The Shelley poem most often cited as a major influence on Keats is *Alastor; or, The Spirit of Solitude,* the title poem in the collection published in February 1816 (Reiman and Powers xviii). As the checklist shows, Leonard Brown and other critics find numerous similarities in plot, character, theme, setting, and diction between *Alastor* and *Endymion*. They also find many differences between the two poems that are believed to reflect Keats's objections to *Alastor* (see note 21).

Other critics dispute some of these arguments for *Alastor*'s influence on *Endymion*. Bradley (240) and Reiman ("Keats and Shelley" 407) point out that many of the supposed verbal echoes of Shelley's poem in Keats's could actually be shared echoes of Wordsworth, or they could derive from a fund of contemporary poetic language common to both poets. Reiman ("Keats and Shelley" 406) also protests the idea that *Endymion* is an "answer" to or rebuttal of *Alastor,* arguing that this notion is based on a misreading of Shelley's poem as sympathetic to the protagonist's quest for the visionary maid. Finally, Finney's argument (1:291–97) that *Alastor*'s neo-Platonic philosophy influenced *Endymion*'s is rejected by Keats critics who find no evidence of neo-Platonism in *Endymion*.[4]

Despite disagreement regarding how or to what extent *Alastor* influenced *Endymion,* there are enough important similarities between the two works to suggest that Keats was familiar with Shelley's poem in 1817. Circumstances at that time certainly favored Keats's reading of the work. As one of the promising "Young Poets" featured along with Keats and Reynolds in Leigh Hunt's 1 December 1816 *Examiner* article, Shelley would have been an object of interest to Keats. Henry Stephens, who shared rooms with the poet in 1815–16, later remembered Keats proudly telling him of meeting Shelley and showing him the article in which Keats's and Shelley's names appeared together (*Keats Circle* 2:211). Since in 1816 *Alastor* was Shelley's only published volume in print, as well as the only work named in Hunt's "Young Poets" article, it would have been the most obvious and accessible way for Keats to become acquainted with Shelley's poetry.

We know Hunt read *Alastor* some time between 8 December 1816 and 19 January 1817, for in his "Young Poets" article he admits he has "yet seen only one or two specimens" of Shelley's poetry and promises to "procure what he has published" (Johnson 6). Then, in an 8 December 1816 letter, Shelley tells Hunt he will send him a copy of *Alastor,* apparently in response to Hunt's request (Shelley, *Letters* 1:519). Finally, in the 19 January 1817 *Examiner,* Hunt promises to "say more on this subject [Shelley's merits] in a review of" the *Alastor* volume (Johnson 9). Hunt never did review the work, but his 19 January remark suggests that he had by then read Shelley's poem and formed his opinion of it.[5]

As an enthusiastic new member of the Hunt circle, Keats almost certainly followed the editor's example in reading Shelley's volume in December 1816 or January 1817.[6] Keats himself, however, never directly mentions *Alastor.* Neither does he allude to any of the shorter poems published in the *Alastor* volume, and no echoes of these poems—except possibly *The Daemon of the World*—have been discovered in Keats's writing.[7]

The only Shelley poem Keats does directly quote is *Hymn to Intellectual Beauty,* published in the 19 January 1817 *Examiner* and reprinted in the *Rosalind and Helen* volume. Keats may have read the poem before it appeared in the *Examiner,* since Shelley sent a copy to Hunt in late September or early October 1816. As Hunt explains in his "Young Poets" article, he subsequently mislaid the poem and wrote a letter that Shelley received on 1 December 1816 asking for another copy (Reiman, "Keats and Shelley" 401–2). We do not know for certain when Shelley sent the second copy, but he probably enclosed it in his reply to Hunt, mailed some time between 1 December, when Hunt's letter arrived, and 4 December, when Shelley left Bath for Marlow. When Shelley next wrote to Hunt on 8 December 1816, he agreed to the editor's request that the *Hymn* be printed with Shelley's name (Shelley, *Letters* 1:517; Reiman, "Keats and Shelley" 402); presumably Hunt at that time possessed the text of the poem and was proceeding to other matters concerning its publication in his newspaper. Keats therefore may have seen *Hymn to Intellectual Beauty* when it was in

Hunt's possession, before it appeared in the 19 January 1817 *Examiner,* at which point the poem definitely became available to Keats.

Both Colvin and Gittings believe Shelley's *Hymn* did not appeal to Keats. Colvin says that "Keats would have felt its strain of aspiration and invocation too painful, too near despair . . . and . . . Shelley's 'Spirit of BEAUTY' . . . would have seemed to him something abstract, remote, and uncomforting" (237). Gittings (*John Keats* 107) asserts that Keats disliked the poem's characterization of this world as "a dim, vast vale of tears," no doubt thinking, as others have, of Keats's 21 April 1819 "vale of Soul-making" letter, in which the poet rejects "the common cognomen of this world . . . [as] 'a vale of tears'" (*Letters* 2:101; see also checklist, *Hymn to Intellectual Beauty,* and note 29).

Keats obviously liked the poem well enough to remember the words quoted in his 13 March 1818 letter, however. The context in which the quotation occurs also casts doubt on the notion that Shelley's poem did not appeal to Keats, for the letter sketches a view of life balanced by skepticism and faith similar to that expressed in the *Hymn.* On the one hand, Keats says that "nothing in this world is proveable" and "I am sometimes so very sceptical as to think Poetry itself a mere Jack a lanthern to amuse whoever may chance to be struck with its brilliance"; on the other hand, he asserts, with the help of Shelley's phrase, that the "ardour of the pursuer" may endow otherwise abstract and lifeless "mental pursuits" with dignity and greatness (*Letters* 1:242–43). It is true that Keats does not find common, physical reality—in his words, "Things real"—so dreary as Shelley does, and the younger poet attributes the human mind or imagination rather than a supernatural force with the ability to "consecrate . . . all [it] dost shine upon" (*Hymn to Intellectual Beauty* 13–14 [Reiman and Powers text]). Nonetheless, the belief in abstract ideals despite their lack of objective or empirical existence expressed in both Shelley's *Hymn* and Keats's letter are similar enough to suggest that Keats did appreciate the poem from which he quoted.

Shelley's pamphlet *A Proposal for Putting Reform to the Vote* was published by Charles and James Ollier in late February or early March 1817, around the same time that the Olliers published Keats's first volume of poems. The two works in fact were advertised together in the 3 March *Morning Chronicle* and the 7 March *Times* (Robinson, "Shelley, Ollier, and Blackwood" 187–88). In February Keats was still seeing Shelley or Mary Shelley fairly regularly at Hunt's, where the *Proposal* almost certainly would have been discussed.[8] It is therefore likely that Keats heard the essay's main points described, even if he did not read the piece itself. He may also have read extracts of the work in a notice Hunt wrote for the 2 March 1817 *Examiner* (Blunden, *"Examiner" Examined* 74).

Mary Shelley's *History of a Six Weeks' Tour,* which first printed Percy Shelley's *Mont Blanc,* appeared in November 1817 (Robinson, "Shelley, Ollier, and Blackwood" 218n.42). There is no indication, however, that Keats read this publication. As far as we know he saw nothing of Shelley throughout the spring and summer of 1817, and though the two men met on 6 October (*Letters* 1:168) and 18 November 1817 (Mary Shelley, *Journals* 1:185), Keats at this time wished to avoid both Hunt's and Shelley's influence. He told Bailey on 8 October 1817 that he "refused to visit Shelley, that I might have my own unfettered scope" and on 23 January 1818 admitted that Hunt and Shelley were perhaps justly hurt because Keats had not shared the draft of *Endymion* with them (*Letters* 1:170, 214). It is unlikely, given these circumstances, that Keats would have been receptive to new Shelley publications in the fall and early winter of 1817 and 1818.

An indication of the extent to which Keats had lost touch with the Shelley-Hunt circle by the end of 1817 is the fact that he did not know Shelley wrote the 28 December 1817 *Examiner* review of Godwin's *Mandeville,* which Keats mentions in a 5 January 1818 letter to his brothers.[9] The article was signed "E. K.," which led Keats to suppose that it was written by Hunt's sister-in-law Elizabeth Kent (*Letters* 1:199). He did not recall that Shelley had first submitted *Hymn to Intellectual Beauty* to the *Examiner* under the pseudonym "Elfin Knight," as Hunt explained when he printed the poem on 19 January 1817 (Johnson 9). Keats apparently enjoyed the *Mandeville* review, for he tells his brothers he will send it to them (*Letters* 1:199). As Reiman notes, Keats probably was particularly interested in the essay's contrast between Godwin's personal integrity and Wordsworth's "servility to the wealthy and powerful" (*Shelley and His Circle* 5:444). This assumption is reinforced by the fact that, in the same letter in which he mentions Shelley's review, Keats says that he declined to have dinner with Wordsworth at the home of deputy comptroller of stamps John Kingston and expresses his surprise on finding Wordsworth dressed for the dinner in "a stiff Collar" (*Letters* 1:197; see also 1:265–66).

Shelley's major project during the time he knew Keats and lived in England was *The Revolt of Islam.* Shelley's epic poem was composed between March or April and September 1817 and first published under the title *Laon and Cyntha* in December of that year. After Charles Ollier objected to certain of the work's religious and moral sentiments, *Laon and Cyntha* was withdrawn and a revised version published in January 1818 under the title *The Revolt of Islam.*[10]

Thomas Medwin—first in 1833 in *The Shelley Papers* and again in his 1847 biography of Shelley (Reiman, "Keats and Shelley" 405n.16; Medwin 1:298)—claimed that Shelley told him *The Revolt of Islam* and *Endymion* were written in a spirit of competition, the goal being for each poet to complete his long poem in six months. Although Medwin is unreliable as a biographer, his account of the long-poem competition between Keats and Shelley is generally credited (see, for example, Blunden, "Poetry Contest"; Ward 102 and 423n.30; Reiman, "Keats and Shelley" 405–6). If the story is indeed true, Keats should have been especially interested in reading *The Revolt of Islam;* and yet we have no conclusive evidence that he did so. His only direct references to it indicate his awareness of its publication problems in December 1817 and his not having read it as of 21 February 1818 (*Letters* 1:194, 237). In the February 1818 letter, after admitting that he hasn't yet read Shelley's poem, Keats remarks to his brothers, "I don't suppose you have it at the Teignmouth Libraries" (*Letters* 1:237). Gold (74), who argues for an echo of *The Revolt* in *Lamia,* regards this statement as evidence that Keats was actively seeking a copy of Shelley's poem. Keats himself seems to realize the unlikelihood of a provincial library carrying the radical work, however, and one wonders why he didn't borrow a copy from Hunt or another literary friend, instead of half-heartedly—or ironically—inquiring after the poem in an out-of-the-way location.

The answer might be that Keats was *not* eager to read *The Revolt of Islam,* or that he was at least ambivalent about doing so. Shelley after all had finished *The Revolt* before Keats finished his long poem, and as a result Keats may have felt some hostility, born of insecurity, toward the "winning" work.[11] If it is true that *Alastor* exerted a profound influence on *Endymion,* moreover, Keats may have feared becoming similarly affected by Shelley's latest major poem. As mentioned above, it was in the fall of 1817 that Keats told Bailey he had "refused to visit Shelley, that I might have my own unfettered scope" (*Letters* 1:170). Perhaps he felt he would be better able to find his own poetic style and themes if he altogether avoided contact with Shelley's infectious compositions. Another way to interpret Keats's avoidance of Shelley and his work, however, is to say that the younger poet was pursuing his own bent and simply found Shelley's manner and preoccupations irrelevant to his needs and interests at that time.

The Revolt of Islam received extensive coverage in the *Examiner,* and if Keats did not read the entire poem he still could have learned of its plot and major themes and have read numerous extracts from it in Hunt's newspaper. The passages quoted in the *Examiner* are as follows:[12] in the 30 November 1817 issue, Hunt prints without comment canto 2, lines 181–228 of

Laon and Cyntha; in the first installment of his three-part review of *Revolt of Islam,* published 25 January 1818, Hunt quotes lines 202–7, 604–12, 640–54, 658–64, 1900–1901, 1906–8, 1919–26, 2745–48, and 4466–4530; and on 22 February 1818, the first, third, and fourth paragraphs of the Preface to the poem are quoted entire. The last installment of Hunt's review, which appeared 1 March 1818, discusses Shelley's ideas and artistic strengths and weaknesses without quoting specific passages. In the fall of 1819, Hunt wrote three articles (26 September, 3 October, 10 October) defending *The Revolt of Islam* against the *Quarterly Review*'s scathing notice, which had appeared in April 1819. In the second article (3 October), Hunt quotes lines 3389 and 3395–96 of the poem and the last three sentences of the Preface. In addition, stanza 55 from canto 5 (2299–2307) is quoted (slightly misquoted) in an article that first appeared in the *Literary Pocket-Book* for 1819 (published at the end of 1818) and was later reprinted in the 5 September 1819 *Examiner* (see Keach 194–95).

Actually, Hunt's extensive, enthusiastic commentary on *The Revolt of Islam* may have helped to bias Keats against the poem. At the same time Hunt was publicly praising *The Revolt* he was finding fault with book 1 of *Endymion* (see *Letters* 1:213–14), and he never did review Keats's long poem. Blunden justly defends Hunt against charges that he neglected Keats in 1818 by saying that the editor knew his support of *Endymion* would damage further Keats's reputation with the Tory critics, and "by not defending him directly Hunt was taking the most unselfish course, and doubtless the course which Keats wished him to take" (*"Examiner" Examined* 81). In addition, in the wake of the *Quarterly Review*'s hostile criticism of *Endymion,* Hunt did reprint or quote from defenses of the poem written by Reynolds, "J. S.," and a writer for the *Chester Guardian* (Blunden, *"Examiner" Examined* 81–82). Nonetheless, even if Keats on one level appreciated Hunt's relative silence on *Endymion,* on another level he may have resented the disproportionate support given to Shelley's long poem. This reaction, combined with some jealousy of Shelley's productivity and a desire to avoid Shelley's influence, could have made Keats reluctant to read the work or to share Hunt's good opinion of it if he did.

This is not to conclude, however, either that Keats did not read *The Revolt of Islam* or that he disliked it—he may simply have left no record of his reaction to the poem. If Gold and Keach are correct in detecting *The Revolt*'s influence on *Lamia* and *To Autumn,* Keats may have been more receptive to the poem in the summer and fall of 1819 than when it first appeared.

Keats probably read *Ozymandias* in the 11 January 1818 *Examiner*

(Reiman and Powers 103). The poem appeared over the signature "Glirastes," but Keats saw Hunt on 18 and 21 January (*Letters* 1:206, 212) and could have learned of Shelley's authorship on either of those occasions. *Ozymandias* is also likely to have come up in conversation at Hunt's house on 4 February 1818, when Keats, Shelley, and Hunt each wrote a sonnet on the Nile. Indeed, discussion of Shelley's earlier Egyptian sonnet may have provided the impetus for the Nile sonnet competition at Hunt's, especially given the fact that *Ozymandias* itself was written during a sonnet contest between Shelley and Horace Smith (Reiman and Powers 103n.5).

One final Shelley poem published in 1818 that Keats is likely to have read is *Marianne's Dream,* which appeared over the signature Δ in Hunt's *Literary Pocket-Book* for 1819 (1818) (Ingpen and Peck 3:327).[13] The same edition of the *Literary Pocket-Book* included, besides the stanza from *The Revolt of Islam* mentioned above, Keats's *Four seasons fill the measure of the year* and *To Ailsa Rock* (*Poems* 599, 612). Moreover, Hunt presented Keats with a copy of the work, which Keats later gave to Fanny Brawne (Owings 31). Keats found the publication distasteful, however; he told his brother and sister-in-law on 16 December 1818 that it was "full of the most sickening stuff you can imagine.... Hunt keeps on in his old way—I am complete[ly] tired of it all" (*Letters* 2:7). Since Shelley in general and *Marianne's Dream* in particular—which alludes to a dream Hunt's wife related to Shelley—were associated in Keats's mind with Leigh Hunt, Keats may have considered Shelley's poem one of the "sickening" items in the volume. It is possible that he did not know *Marianne's Dream* was written by Shelley, since it was printed anonymously, but Hunt probably informed Keats of the book's contributors or the younger poet may have guessed Shelley's authorship from the poem's style and content.

Shelley's major publication for 1819 was the *Rosalind and Helen* volume, which appeared in May of that year and included, besides the title poem, *Lines Written among the Euganean Hills, Hymn to Intellectual Beauty,* and *Ozymandias* (Ingpen and Peck 2:413). On 20 August 1819 Shelley wrote to his publisher Charles Ollier, "Pray send a copy of my Poem [*Rosalind and Helen*] or anything which I may hereafter publish to Mr. Keats with my best regards" (Shelley, *Letters* 2:111). There is no indication, however, that Ollier complied with Shelley's request. Surely Keats would have acknowledged the gift copy had it arrived, as he later acknowledged *The Cenci* (*Letters* 2:322), and Shelley too is likely to have saved any letters Keats sent, as he saved the one thanking him for *The Cenci*. *Rosalind and Helen* is not included in Brown's "List of Keats's Books," drawn up after the poet's death. It would appear that Ollier did not send Keats a copy of the volume as Shelley asked him to do.

Keats nonetheless may have read Hunt's or someone else's copy. Or, at the least, he may have read extracts of *Rosalind and Helen* in Hunt's 9 May 1819 *Examiner* review of the volume. In his review Hunt summarizes the poem's plot and quotes lines 291–98, 338–70, 746–50, 953–76, and 1291 (Johnson 40–43; line numbers from Hutchinson text). He also praises *Lines Written among the Euganean Hills,* saying "Some of [the lines] are among the grandest . . . that Mr. Shelley has produced," though he lacks space to quote any passages directly (Johnson 44).[14] Keats at this time may have been more favorably disposed toward Hunt's review than he was toward the *Literary Pocket-Book* the previous December, for Keats, Reynolds, and Hunt recently had worked together on responses to Wordsworth's *Peter Bell.* Keats reviewed Reynolds's parody *Peter Bell* in the 25 April 1819 *Examiner* and Hunt reviewed Wordsworth's poem in the following week's (2 May) issue (*Letters* 2:93n.9; Blunden, *"Examiner" Examined* 92). In his essay on Shelley's volume, Hunt carried on the discussion of Wordsworth's poem by comparing it to *Rosalind and Helen* and by contrasting Wordsworth's egotism to Shelley's selflessness (Johnson 41). Although Keats may not have shared fully Hunt's opinions of the two poets, the fact that Keats himself had criticized Wordsworth's egotism suggests that he would have been generally sympathetic to Hunt's remarks. Keats therefore probably read Hunt's review of Shelley's 1819 volume, where he would have encountered a summary and quotations of *Rosalind and Helen.*

In 1819 Shelley mailed to Hunt copies of several poems: *Julian and Maddalo,* sent 15 August; *The Mask of Anarchy,* sent 23 September; *Peter Bell the Third,* Shelley's own response to Wordsworth's latest lyrical ballad, sent 2 November; and *England in 1819,* sent 23 December (Shelley, *Letters* 2:108, 134–35, 167; Mary Shelley, *Letters* 1:108n.2). He also may have sent other political poems, including *Song to the Men of England,* on 16 November 1819 (*Shelley and His Circle* 6:1085 and note 13). None of these poems was published until after Keats's death, so if Keats read them he did so in the manuscript versions sent to Hunt. The most likely of these poems for Keats to have read is the sonnet *England in 1819,* about which Shelley told Hunt, "you may show it to whom you please" (Shelley, *Letters* 2:167). Keats saw very little of Hunt in the fall and winter of 1819–20, however, so that the chances of his reading Shelley manuscripts in Hunt's possession are slim.

It is more likely that Keats read *Love's Philosophy,* published in Hunt's

Indicator on 22 December 1819 (Hutchinson 583). Keats himself never mentions reading the *Indicator,* but Hunt says his friends generally regarded this as his most successful publishing venture, and Keats was able to name his favorite *Indicator* article: "A Now," published 28 June 1820 (Hunt, *Autobiography* 281; Johnson 132; Forman 5:261n). In the spring and summer of 1820 the *Indicator* published several of Keats's poems—*La Belle Dame sans Merci* on 10 May, *As Hermes once took to his feathers light* on 28 June, and lines 217–56 of *The Jealousies* on 23 August (*Poems* 644, 635, 677)—as well as Hunt's review of the *Lamia* volume (2 and 9 August; Matthews 165). It is true that all of the *Indicator* issues associated with Keats came out while the latter was living near or with Hunt in Kentish Town, but the poet also may have read the earlier, 22 December 1819 issue that printed *Love's Philosophy.*

The Shelley work for which we have the most evidence of Keats's reading is *The Cenci,* published in March 1820 (Robinson, "Shelley, Ollier, and Blackwood" 198–99). As previously mentioned, Shelley on 20 August 1819 directed Ollier to send Keats a copy of any Shelley work the firm published. Shelley repeated the request on 6 September 1819 (Shelley, *Letters* 2:118), and in this instance Ollier complied, for on 16 August 1820 Keats reported receiving the play and gave his opinion of it (*Letters* 2:322–23). In addition, Fanny Brawne in 1848 announced that she possessed "the Cenci by Shelly marked with many of Keats notes" (Rollins, "Fanny Brawne Letter" 375).[15]

Unfortunately, the book's whereabouts are presently unknown (Rollins, "Fanny Brawne Letter" 375n.8). The notes might offer revealing evidence of Keats's reaction to Shelley's work, all the more valuable given the fact that so few remarks about Shelley's poetry exist in Keats's writing. The well-known advice to Shelley in Keats's 16 August 1820 letter—"you might curb your magnanimity & be more of an artist, and 'load every rift' of your subject with ore" (*Letters* 2:323)—suggests one major response to *The Cenci* and Shelley's work generally: it was concerned too much with theme or purpose and not enough with aesthetic matters. Shelley is also accused of writing too hastily when Keats says it would be better if *Prometheus Unbound* were not yet published but "still in manuscript" undergoing revision, or not yet composed beyond the second act (*Letters* 2:323). Milne (281) thinks this remark betrays jealousy of Shelley's productivity. Perhaps the younger poet was particularly piqued over the fact that Shelley's last two major works were dramas, since he himself wished to excel in that genre and so far had only co-written the mediocre melodrama *Otho the Great* and composed a fragment of *King Stephen.* Keats may be forgiven, however, if he did feel some resentment of Shelley's output at this time. After all, he knew he was fatally ill and could not look forward to composing any more plays or poems himself.

Shelley assumed Ollier would send Keats a copy of *Prometheus Unbound . . . With Other Poems* (Shelley, *Letters* 2:221), published in August 1820 (Robinson, "Shelley, Ollier, and Blackwood" 198), and Keats reported in his 16 August letter to Shelley that he was "in expectation of Prometheus every day" (*Letters* 2:323). As was the case with *Rosalind and Helen,* however, there is no evidence that Keats received the volume: no letter to Shelley acknowledging its arrival survives, and it does not appear in Brown's "List of Keats's Books." Keats may have heard the work discussed when the Gisbornes were in London in the summer of 1820. Maria Gisborne's journal records visits to Hunt when Keats was present on 22 June and 12 July, although Shelley is not mentioned as a topic of conversation (Gisborne and Williams 36, 40). A 22 August entry reports a discussion of *Prometheus* with Godwin the previous day (45), and in a 23 August 1820 letter to Shelley, Hunt announces that he has "just seen" the work (Hunt, *Correspondence* 1:158). These remarks suggest that Shelley's volume did not appear in print and become a topic of conversation until the latter part of August 1820. By this time, however, Keats had left Hunt's house and moved in with the Brawnes, and on 17 September he boarded the *Maria Crowther* for Italy.

It is nonetheless possible, as Little argues (41, 42n.3), that Keats acquired some familiarity with *Prometheus Unbound* through Hunt. On August 13, the day after he abruptly left Hunt's house, Keats wrote inviting Hunt to visit at the Brawnes' "whenever you can get time," and Hunt replied immediately that he would come that afternoon "& most probably every day" (*Letters* 2:316–17). If Hunt did visit Keats frequently at the Brawnes'—he visited at least once after August 13, for when he wrote Shelley on the 23rd he knew about Keats's 16 August letter to Shelley and was able to report on Keats's health (Hunt, *Correspondence* 1:158)—he may on one of these occasions have brought *Prometheus Unbound* for Keats to read. Or, he may at least have discussed the volume and read extracts from *Prometheus* and some of the shorter poems published with it.[16] Hunt especially liked *To a Skylark;* in a 23 June 1822 defense of the volume against the *Quarterly Review*'s hostile notice, he quotes the poem entire and remarks, "I know nothing more beautiful than this,—more choice of tones, more natural in words, more abundant in exquisite, cordial, and most poetical associations. One gets the stanzas by heart unawares, and repeats them like 'snatches of old tunes'" (Johnson 75). One would like to think that Keats at least once heard or read this Romantic songbird poem so often linked with his own *Ode to a Nightingale*. The evidence for Keats's familiarity with the *Prometheus* volume, however, remains scanty and conjectural.

Ultimately, too, a sense of futility haunts the question of whether or not Keats read *Prometheus Unbound . . . With Other Poems*. Even if he did, it was too late for these works to figure in his poetic development. In fact, one of the most unfortunate aspects of Keats's association with Shelley is that the younger poet did not live to read and respond to Shelley's best works. During the period of his own activity, Keats's impression of Shelley as a poet was based on a knowledge of *Alastor . . . and Other Poems, Hymn to Intellectual Beauty*, a handful of sonnets, and possibly *The Revolt of Islam*, the *Rosalind and Helen* volume, and *Queen Mab*, or more likely the shorter *Daemon of the World* and extracts of the former volumes in reviews.

On a more positive note, however, with Shelley more so than with any of the other Romantic poets Keats must have felt a sense of contemporaneity. Indeed, the two poets' careers run remarkably parallel courses: breakthrough meetings with Leigh Hunt and his London literary circle in late 1816; apprenticeship long poems in 1817; Shakespearean tragedies in the summer of 1819; most important single volumes (*Lamia* and *Prometheus Unbound*, respectively) published a month apart in 1820; early deaths in Italy and burial in the same Roman cemetery.[17] Moreover, Shelley was the most talented "young poet" of Keats's generation and acquaintance, a fact that Keats seems to have acknowledged when he told Haydon in 1817, "Byron, Scott, Southey, & Shelley think they are to lead the age, but [the rest of the sentence . . . erased]" (Haydon, *Diary* 2:106–7; see checklist, Keats's References to and Opinion of Shelley as Reported by Others). The fact that Keats classifies Shelley with the other, immensely popular writers, all of whom he regards as significant rivals for dominance of the period's literary scene, reflects a high opinion of Shelley's abilities.[18]

Moreover, even if Keats did not read all or the best of Shelley's publications, Shelley may have had an important influence on Keats's career in other respects. The very differences in their temperaments and poetic styles may have helped Keats to define by contrast his own goals and techniques, as is suggested by his criticism of Shelley's poetry in his 16 August 1820 letter and, perhaps, by the ways in which *Endymion* differs from *Alastor*. In addition, Stuart Sperry refers to Shelley as "a fellow protégé of Hunt's whose progress Keats followed and measured himself against throughout his career" (*Keats the Poet* 94). In fact, Keats may on some level have felt engaged in a race with Shelley, not just during the composition of *Endymion*, but to the end of his life. It was Keats's astonishingly rapid progress during the three years that constitute his poetic career that enabled him to achieve his place "among the English Poets" (*Letters* 1:394). If a spirit of rivalry with Shelley helped lend a sense of urgency to Keats's development, we must count Shelley's influence as very healthy indeed.

Queen Mab; A Philosophical Poem (1813)

DIRECT REFERENCES

"Shelley's poem is out & there are words about its being objected too, as much as Queen Mab was" (Keats to George and Tom Keats, 27 [?] December 1817; *Letters* 1:194).

ECHOES/ALLUSIONS

Queen Mab and *The Daemon of the World*[19]	Keats Poem or Letter	Critic
Mab 1.59ff.: "the chariot of the Fairy Queen"; *Daemon* 1.57 ff.: "The chariot of the Daemon of the World"	*Sleep and Poetry* 125–54: chariot of the imagination	Finney 1:164n; Bush, *Selected Poems* 312[20]
Mab 2.16: "far clouds of feathery gold"; *Daemon* 204: "those far clouds of feathery purple gleam"	*To My Brother George* (sonnet) 4: "from the feathery gold of evening lean"	Allott, *Poems* 48
Mab 9.144: "pathless wilderness"	*Addressed to Haydon* 4: "In noisome alley, and in pathless wood"	Allott, *Poems* 66

Alastor; or, The Spirit of Solitude: and Other Poems (1816)

ECHOES/ALLUSIONS[21]

Alastor[22]	Keats Poem or Letter	Critic
#1: *General similarities between* Alastor *and* Endymion		
neo-Platonic philosophy	neo-Platonic philosophy	Finney 1:295–96[23]
themes (conflict between self / solitude and love / humanitarian actions; choice between mortal and immortal realms; authenticity of visionary imagination)	themes	Stillinger, *Hoodwinking* 23–26; Stillinger, *Complete Poems* 431

Alastor	Keats Poem or Letter	Critic
myth of androgyn; quest for unity and wholeness through imagination	myth of androgyn; quest for unity and wholeness through imagination	Baer
plot: union with visionary woman and subsequent pursuit of her	plot	Bradley 227, 241; Allott, "*Endymion* and 'Alastor'" 159–60
romantic, wondrous scenery (see also in section #2 *Endymion* 1.214–16 and passim, and in section #3 *Alastor* 235; 363–65, 369–70; 377–81; 590ff.)	scenery	Allott, "*Endymion* and 'Alastor'" 160
landscape systematically symbolic	landscape not systematically symbolic	Allott, "*Endymion* and 'Alastor'" 160, 162–65
visionary maid dark and philosophical	moon goddess fair and sensuous	Allott, "*Endymion* and 'Alastor'" 164

#2: *Passage not specified for* Alastor *but specified for Keats poem or letter*

Poet dies before his time; Shelley in writing *Alastor* fails as poet	10 May 1817 letter to Hunt: "Tell [Shelley] there are stran[ge] Stories of the death of Poets—some have died before they were conceived" (*Letters* 1:140)	Brown 622–23
Poet solitary and philosophic by nature	*Endymion* 1: Endymion naturally robust and sociable	Bradley 241; Allott, "*Endymion* and 'Alastor'" 163–64
Poet detached from community	*Endymion* 1: Endymion detached from community	Baer 35
Poet wanders through "country of sharp chiaroscuro" (Brown)	*Endymion* 1.214–16 and passim: landscape rich, abundant with life	Brown 629

Alastor	**Keats Poem or Letter**	**Critic**
Poet's vision not challenged	*Endymion* 1.721–60: Peona admonishes Endymion for pursuing dream	Brown 633
Poet achieves kinship with past; Poet's pursuit of visionary maid is quest for friendship and love	*Endymion* 1.769ff.: "fellowship with essence" passage	Brown 633
Poet forgoes human love	*Endymion* 2.1–43: invocation to love	Brown 636
quest for visionary maid is journey into increasing self-consciousness	*Endymion* 2: descent into underworld is journey into recesses of self	Baer 32, 39
no acceptance of human life at corresponding point in plot	*Endymion* 2.153–60: temporary acceptance of human life	Brown 637
poem generally	*Endymion* 2.284: "The deadly feel of solitude"	Brown 638
Poet cherishes solitude	*Endymion:* 2.681–82: Endymion learning to suspect solitude	Brown 638–39
Poet succumbs to sorrow	*Endymion* 4.146–290: way to banish sorrow is to forget self and enter life	Brown 647–49
endorses visionary idealism	*Endymion* 4.646–55: rejection of visionary idealism	Allott, *Poems* 272; Barnard *Poems* 585[24]

#3: *Specific passages in* Alastor *and in Keats poem or letter*

Preface: before vision, Poet studies nature and is content; after vision, loses interest in nature and is restless	*Endymion* 3.172–77: visionary maid supplants Endymion's love of the moon and destroys his tranquillity	Bradley 242

Alastor	Keats Poem or Letter	Critic
Preface: distinction between "self-centered seclusion" of Poet and moral torpor of "meaner spirits"	*Fall of Hyperion* 1.147–59: distinction between those who suffer from human misery and those who do not	Bradley 242–43; de Selincourt 583; Bush, *Selected Poems* 357; Allott, *Poems* 667; Allott, *"Endymion* and 'Alastor'"* 168; Barnard, *Poems* 679
	Endymion 1.777ff.: "pleasure thermometer" passage and dramatization of gradations of happiness in subsequent books	Allott, *"Endymion* and 'Alastor'"* 168
Preface: "The Poet's self-centred seclusion was avenged"	16 August 1820 letter to Shelley: "[an artist] must have 'self concentration'" (*Letters* 2:322–23)[25]	Bradley 244
line 1: "Earth, ocean, air, beloved brotherhood"	*Endymion:* settings (books 1 and 2, earth; book 3, water; book 4, air)	Brown 628
1–149: invocation, summary of youth's life and surroundings, preparation for vision	*Endymion* 1.1–572: invocation, etc.	Brown 628
opening passage: Poet engaged in solitary pursuit of knowledge	*Endymion:* opening passage (Endymion introduced in midst of merrymaking)	Brown 628–29
lines 75–128: Poet seeks universal knowledge	*Endymion* 1.288–89: Pan is "Dread opener of the mysterious doors / Leading to universal knowledge"	Brown 629
lines 110–12: "the fallen towers / Of Babylon, the eternal pyramids, / Memphis and Thebes"	*Endymion* 3.849: "Memphis, and Babylon, and Ninevah"	Allott, *Poems* 238
lines 129–39: Arab Maid— Poet ignores	*Endymion* 4: Indian Maid— Endymion pities and loves	Brown 645–49; Bush, *Selected Poems* 323

Alastor	**Keats Poem or Letter**	**Critic**
lines 149–91: Poet falls asleep, has dream-vision of union with beautiful woman, returns to sleep	*Endymion* 1.578–678: Endymion falls asleep, etc.	Brown 630–32[26]
lines 149–91: "nympholeptic dream" (Finney)	*Endymion* 2.709–873: "nympholeptic dream"	Finney 1: 296, 304, 309, 322
lines 178–82, 489–92: contrast between dark visionary maid and blue-eyed spirit at well	*Endymion* 4.57–66: contrast between fair moon goddess and dark Indian maid	Allott, *Poems* 247; Allott, *"Endymion* and 'Alastor'"* 165
lines 192–207: Poet wakes from dream to find earth dreary	*Endymion* 1.681–705: Endymion finds earth dreary when awakens from dream	Bradley 241; Brown 632; Bush, *Selected Poems* 319; Allott, *"Endymion* and 'Alastor'"* 167; Baer 36
lines 205–6: "He eagerly pursues / Beyond the realms of dream that fleeting shade"	*Endymion* 1.857: "A hope beyond the shadow of a dream"	Allott, *"Endymion* and 'Alastor'"* 166
lines 205–22: determines to pursue vision	*Endymion* 1.970ff.: determines to renounce thoughts of vision	Brown 634
line 210: "pathless desart of dim sleep"	*Addressed to Haydon* 4: "pathless wood"	Allott, *Poems* 66
lines 224–27: vision returns to Poet	*Endymion* 1.918ff.: vision returns three times to Endymion	Brown 634
lines 227–307: Poet moves from earth to sea, rejecting earth in pursuit of vision	*Endymion* 2: Endymion moves from earth to sea and in process learns compassion for others	Brown 635–40
line 235: "Through tangled swamps and deep precipitous dells"	*Endymion* 2.49: "Through wilderness, and woods of mossed oaks"	Brown 636
line 257: "mountaineer"	*Endymion* 2.51: "the lone woodcutter"	Brown 636

Alastor	Keats Poem or Letter	Critic
line 299: "A little shallop floating near the shore"	*Endymion* 1.423: "A little shallop, floating there hard by"	Brown 629
line 308ff.: Poet trusts self to sea, journey ends in death	*Endymion* 3: Endymion trusts self to sea, restores drowned lovers to life	Brown 643–45
line 308ff.: Poet suffers and dies as a result of abandoning this world for pursuit of visionary woman	*Endymion* 3.314ff.: Glaucus suffers as a result of leaping into the sea in pursuit of water nymph	Brown 642–43
lines 363–65, 369–70: cavern	*Endymion* 2: underworld landscape	Finney 1:252, 306
	Endymion 4.651–53: "Caverns lone, farewel! . . ."	Finney 1:252
lines 377–81: chasm and whirlpool	*Endymion* 2.601–4: chasm, subterranean streams, fountains	Allott, *Poems* 187–88; Barnard, *Poems* 574
lines 479–92: vision in well	*Endymion* 1.895–905: vision in well	Allott, *Poems* 159; Allott, "*Endymion* and 'Alastor'" 164–66
lines 494–505: defeated Poet sees stream that seems to be emblem of his own life	*Endymion* 4.782–96: discouraged Endymion encounters landscape reminiscent of his life	Brown 651–52
line 590ff.: landscape	*Endymion* 2: landscape	Brown 638
lines 627–30; 634, 645	*Endymion* 4.957–58; 917–61	Brown 653[27]
conclusion: Poet apathetic, resigned to death	*Endymion* 4.933–36: Endymion apathetic, resigned to death	Brown 653
lines 672–720: survey of forces that drove Poet to solitude	*Endymion* 3.1–40: condemnation of political leaders	Brown 641n.24

Alastor	Keats Poem or Letter	Critic
conclusion: Poet dies without being reunited with visionary maid	*Endymion* 4: conclusion (Endymion is reunited with moon goddess and gains eternal happiness)	Bradley 241; Brown 628, 653; Stillinger, *Hoodwinking* 25; Allott, *"Endymion* and 'Alastor'"* 165–66, 169; Baer 32, 41

Hymn to Intellectual Beauty
Examiner 19 January 1817; rpt. *Rosalind and Helen* 1819

DIRECT REFERENCES

Lines 13–14: "Spirit of BEAUTY, that dost consecrate / With thine own hues all thou dost shine upon" (Reiman and Powers text).
"Which by the by stamps the burgundy mark on the bottles of our Minds, insomuch as they are able to '*consec[r]ate whate'er they look upon*'" (Keats to Bailey, 13 March 1818; *Letters* 1:243).

ECHOES/ALLUSIONS

Hymn to Intellectual Beauty	Keats Poem or Letter	Critic
neo-Platonic philosophy	*Endymion*	Finney 1:295[28]
line 17: "This dim vast vale of tears"	21 April 1819 letter to George and Georgiana Keats: "The common cognomen of this world among the misguided and superstitious is 'a vale of tears'" (*Letters* 2:101).	*Letters* 2:101n; Reiman, "Keats and Shelley" 411n.35[29]
lines 25–28: "No voice from some sublimer world hath ever / To sage or poet these responses given . . ."	*Why did I laugh tonight? No voice will tell*	Ryan 195n.21

Review of William Godwin's *Mandeville* (signed "E. K.") *Examiner* 28 December 1817

DIRECT REFERENCES

"There is an article in the sennight Examiner—on Godwin's Mandeville signed E. K. I think it Miss Kents—I will send it" (Keats to George and Tom Keats, 5 January 1818; *Letters* 1:199).

Laon and Cyntha (1817) / *The Revolt of Islam* (1818)

DIRECT REFERENCES

"Shelley's poem is out & there are words about its being objected too, as much as Queen Mab was" (Keats to George and Tom Keats, 27 [?] December 1817; *Letters* 1:194).

"I have not yet read Shelly's Poem—I don't suppose you have it at the Teignmouth Libraries" (Keats to George and Tom Keats, 21 February 1818; *Letters* 1:237).

ECHOES/ALLUSIONS

The Revolt of Islam (Hutchinson text)	Keats Poem or Letter	Critic
1.37.452–53: "A woman's heart beat in my virgin breast, / It had been nurtured in divinest lore"	*Lamia* 1.189–90: "A virgin purest lipp'd, yet in the lore / Of love deep learned to the red heart's core"	Gold 75
5.55.2209–2307: bounty of Autumn provides victory feast for rebels that allows them momentary sense of well-being, before they are attacked once again by tyrant's allies (stanza quoted in "September" article in *The Literary Pocket-Book* [1818], reprinted in 5 September 1819 *Examiner*)	*To Autumn* 8–9: bees lulled into assumption that "warm days will never cease"	Keach 194–95

Month after month the gather'd rains descend
(composed 4 February 1818; first published 1876)

DIRECT REFERENCES

"The Wednesday before last Shelley, Hunt & I wrote each a Sonnet on the River Nile, some day you shall read them all" (Keats to George and Tom Keats, 14 [?] February 1818; *Letters* 1:227–28).

Rosalind and Helen, A Modern Eclogue; With Other Poems (1819)

DIRECT REFERENCES

"Pray send a copy of my Poem or anything which I may hereafter publish to Mr. Keats with my best regards" (Shelley to Charles Ollier, 20 August 1819; Shelley, *Letters* 2:111).[30]

Song to the Men of England (1819; published 1839)

ECHOES/ALLUSIONS

Song to the Men of England	Keats Poem	Critic
lines 9–12: "Wherefore, Bees of England, forge / Many a weapon, chain, and scourge, / That these stingless drones may spoil / The forced produce of your toil?" (Hutchinson text)	*To Autumn:* 9–11: bee image	Keach 195–96[31]

The Cenci (1820)

DIRECT REFERENCES

"I always tell Ollier to send you Copies of my books. . . . The Cenci I hope you have already received" (Shelley to Keats, 27 July 1820; Shelley, *Letters* 2:221).

"I received a copy of the Cenci, as from yourself from Hunt. There is only one part of it I am judge of; the Poetry, and dramatic effect, which by many spirits now a days is considered the mammon. A modern work it is said must have a purpose, which may be the God—*an artist* must serve Mammon—he must have 'self concentration' selfishness perhaps. You I am sure will forgive me for sincerely remarking that you might curb your magnanimity and be more of an artist, and 'load ever rift' of your subject with ore" (Keats to Shelley, 16 August 1820; *Letters* 2:322–23).

"Shelley's Cenci" (Charles Brown's "List of Keats's Books," July [?] 1821; *Keats Circle* 1:254).

"If Medwin had known that I possessed the Cenci by Shelly marked with many of Keats notes he would have been miserable till he got it, but I kept that and others out of his way" (Fanny Brawne Lindon to Maria Dilke, November 1848; Rollins, "Fanny Brawne Letter" 375).

Prometheus Unbound. A Lyrical Drama in Four Acts. With Other Poems
(1820)

Direct References

"I always tell Ollier to send you Copies of my books.—'Prometheus Unbound' I imagine you will receive nearly at the same time with this letter" (Shelley to Keats, 27 July 1820; Shelley, *Letters* 2:221).

"I am in expectation of Prometheus every day.[32] Could I have my own wish for its interest effected you would have it still in manuscript—or be but now putting an end to the second act. I remember you advising me not to publish my first-blights on Hampstead heath—I am returning advice upon your hands" (Keats to Shelley, 16 August 1820; *Letters* 2:323).

Influence of Shelley (Conversation or Unspecified Works) on Keats's Poetry: Speculative Cases

Written in Disgust of Vulgar Superstition (22 December 1816)
Influenced by Shelley's religious views (Finney 1:158; Bate, *John Keats* 133–36; Gittings, *John Keats* 110).[33]

Sleep and Poetry 125–54: vision of charioteer
Derived via Shelley's conversation from Plato's *Phaedrus* (Finney 1:164).

Prefatory note in Keats's *Poems* (1817): "The Short Pieces in the middle of the Book, as well as some of the Sonnets, were written at an earlier period than the rest of the Poems" (*Poems* 736).
Influenced by Shelley's advice that Keats should not publish his earliest work (Gittings, *John Keats* 114. For Shelley's advice see *Letters* 2:323 and checklist, *Prometheus Unbound*).

Endymion 1.347–54: Argonauts see Apollo
Derived via Shelley's conversation from Apollonius Rhodius' *Argonautica* 2.676 (de Selincourt 423; Barnard, *Poems* 564).

Endymion (passage unspecified but perhaps 1.816–42)[34]
"The second fault I allude to I think we have noticed—The approaching inclination [*Endymion*] has to that abominable principle of *Shelley's*—that *Sensual Love* is the principle of *things*. Of this I believe him to be unconscious, & can see how by a process of imagination he might arrive at so false, delusive, & dangerous conclusion" (Bailey to Taylor, 29 August 1818; *Keats Circle* 1:34–35).

General References to Shelley in Keats's Prose

"Does Shelley go on telling strange Stories of the Death of kings? Tell him there are stran[ge] Stories of the death of Poets—some have died before they were conceived 'how do you make that out Master Vellum' Does M^rs S— cut Bread and Butter as neatly as ever? Tell her to procure some fatal Scissars and cut the th[r]ead of Life of all to be disappointed Poets. . . . Remember me to them all" (Keats to Hunt, 10 May 1817; *Letters* 1:139–40).

"From No 19 I went to Hunt's and Haydon's who live now neighbours. Shelley was there. . . . You see Bailey how independant my writing has been—Hunt's dissuasion was of no avail—I refused to visit Shelley, that I might have my own unfettered scope" (Keats to Bailey, 8 October 1817; *Letters* 1:168, 170).[35]

"Shelley's poem is out & there are words about its being objected too, as much as Queen Mab was. Poor Shelley I think he has his Quota of good qualities, in sooth la!!" (Keats to George and Tom Keats, 27 [?] December 1817; *Letters* 1:194).

"the fact is he [Hunt] & Shelley are hurt & perhaps justly, at my not having showed them the affair officiously & from several hints I have had they appear much disposed to dissect and anatomize, any trip or slip I may have made" (Keats to George and Tom Keats, 23 January 1818; *Letters* 1:214).

"Remember me to Shelley and Kingston" (Keats to Horace Smith, 19 February 1818; *Letters* 1:234).

"Yesterday I received an invitation from Mr Shelley, a Gentleman residing at Pisa, to spend the Winter with him: if I go I must be away in a Month or even less" (Keats to Fanny Keats, 13 August 1820; *Letters* 2:314).

"I do not think I mentioned any thing of a Passage to Leghorn by Sea. Will you join that to your enquiries, and, if you can, give a peep at the Birth, if the Vessel is in our river?" (Keats to John Taylor, 14 August 1820; *Letters* 2:318).

"Last week I received a letter from Shelley, at Pisa, of a very kind nature, asking me to pass the winter with him" (Keats to Brown, 14 August 1820; *Letters* 2:321).[36]

Keats's References to and Opinion of Shelley as Reported by Others

"I remember [Keats's] also telling me of an introduction he had to two or three Young Poets of Promise & among them I remember well the name of Shelley—I also remember his showing me some time afterwards 'the Examiner' in which was an Article under the Title of 'the Rising Poets' or 'the Young Poets' or some such Title in which the names of several were inserted with a brief sketch of them & a Specimen of their Poetry, and the name of John Keats appeared among them, with that of Shelley" (Henry Stephens to George Felton Mathew, March [?] 1847; *Keats Circle* 2:211).

"Keats did not take to Shelley as kindly as Shelley did to him. . . . Keats, being a little too sensitive on the score of his origin, felt inclined to see in every man of birth a sort of natural enemy. Their styles in writing also were very different; and Keats, notwithstanding his unbounded sympathies with ordinary flesh and blood, and even the transcendental cosmopolitics of *Hyperion,* was so far inferior in universality to his great acquaintance, that he could not accompany him in his daedal rounds with nature, and his Archimedean endeavors to move the globe with his own hands" (Hunt, *Autobiography* 273–74).

"Keats said to me today as we were walking along 'Byron, Scott, Southey, & Shelley think they are to lead the age, but [the rest of the sentence, consisting probably of eight or ten words, has been erased].' This was said with all the consciousness of Genius; his face reddened" (Haydon, 7 April 1817 entry; *Diary* 2:106–7).

"Dear Keats got entangled with them [Shelley, Mary Shelley, and their set] inextricably he said to me it was too late—with an agony of expression I shall never forget—When Wilkie was sitting to me once in 1815 . . . Keats called, walked about the room as I drew—a Picture of misery & disappointment—Wilkie said he never saw such an instance—he dined with us and staid all day" (Haydon's annotation to Thomas Medwin's *Conversations of Lord Byron* [1824]; Gray and Walker 23).[37]

"[Shelley] offered Keats an asylum after his ill usage—Hunt lived just below in Lisson Grove North—Keats called on me just after Shelley had done this & told me so—" (Haydon's annotation to Thomas Medwin's *Conversations of Lord Byron* [1824]; Gray and Walker 22).

"When Shelley left England for Italy, Keats told me that he had received from him an invitation to become his guest, and, in short, to make one of his household. It was upon the purest principle that Keats declined his noble proffer, for he entertained an exalted opinion of Shelley's genius—in itself an inducement; he also knew of his deeds of bounty, and, from their frequent social intercourse, he had full faith in the sincerity of his proposal; for a more crystalline heart than Shelley's has rarely throbbed in human bosom. . . . Keats said that in declining the invitation his sole motive was the consciousness, which would be ever prevalent with him, of his being, in its utter extent, not a free agent, even within such a circle as Shelley's—he himself, nevertheless, being the most unrestricted of beings" (Clarke and Clarke 150–51).[38]

Notes

Introduction

1. *Addressed to the Same*. Keats's poetry is quoted from Stillinger's 1978 edition, hereafter referred to as *Poems*.

2. I am indebted to Kim Blank's *Wordsworth's Influence on Shelley* (11–13) for bringing Shelley's remarks on contemporary influence to my attention.

3. Donald Reiman argues that Keats came of age at the end of the historical movement in which Wordsworth, Coleridge, Byron, and Shelley participated and regards Keats as one of "the last generation of Romantic poets" whose other members include "Reynolds, Jeremiah Holmes Wiffen, Charles Jeremiah Wells, George Darley, William Sidney Walker, and John Chalk Claris ('Arthur Brooke')" ("Keats and the Abyss" 264). George Cheatham (24) also refers to Keats as a third generation Romantic. Such classifications are in keeping with my perception that Keats occupied a unique position with respect to the other major Romantic poets—a position not shared even by Shelley, only three years his senior.

4. Harold Bloom, on the contrary, asserts that "The strength of [past writers' influence] . . . increases as the struggling poet's distance from them lengthens in time" (*Map of Misreading* 17). Although Bloom's formulation may apply in some cases, it does not appear to in Keats's. Blank finds that for Shelley too "The voices of the past do not . . . speak as loudly as those of the present" (12).

5. The Shelley essay, because of its brevity and the nature of the material, considers both issues together in one section. The Byron chapter, for reasons explained therein, includes a third section on Keats's attitude toward Byron.

6. John Hollander's *The Figure of Echo: A Mode of Allusion in Milton and After* outlines "a kind of rhetorical hierarchy . . . of allusive modes" (64). At the top is quotation, in which the writer directly acknowledges his borrowing from another. Next comes allusion, which is defined as a conscious and intentional reference to another work that the writer expected his audience to recognize. Finally there are echoes, which are less overt and faithful borrowings and may be either conscious or unconscious on the writer's part. (For other definitions and classifications of various types of influence, see Lonsdale xvi–xvii; Chandler 463; Newlyn viii–ix; Stein 3, 222–23n.3.)

In the "Direct References" sections of my checklists I generally have included only statements that are surrounded by quotation marks, that are introduced by tags like "as Byron says," or that name a particular poem. However, I also include a few cases that appear to be undoubted allusions, as when Keats tells Bailey, "I am troubling you with Moods of my own Mind," or when he tells Reynolds that the attendant at Burns's cottage "drinks glasses five for the Quarter and twelve for the hour" (*Letters* 1:287, 324). In these examples, a passage from one of the other poets' works (a section title in Wordsworth's *Poems in Two Volumes* and line 10 of Coleridge's *Christabel,* respectively) is repeated closely, and the recipients of Keats's letters knew the works in question and would have recognized them as the sources of Keats's remarks. All other, less certain allusions, echoes, and other forms of influence (such as similarities in genre or structure) are entered into the "Echoes/ Allusions" sections of the checklists.

7. For discussions of these and other problems inherent in source studies see Muir and Bateson, "Editorial Commentary"; Lonsdale xvi–xvii; Stillinger, "John Keats" 699; Stein 2; Blank ix. Lonsdale, Stein, and Blank go on to counter some of the attacks on source study and explain the validity and usefulness of such work.

Chapter 1

1. For descriptions of Wordsworth's volumes I have consulted the British Library Catalogue; Wise, *Wordsworth* 37, 50–51, 52, 59–60, 87–88; and Curtis 718. These sources, plus de Selincourt's and Darbishire's edition of Wordsworth's *Poetical Works* (hereafter referred to as *WPW*), Healey, and Moorman have been used throughout for bibliographical information about Wordsworth's writings.

2. See Reynolds 27, 70, 72, 74–75, 80–81. Reynolds also includes a "Supplementary Essay" in his 1819 parody *Peter Bell* (260–61).

3. Volume and page numbers in parenthesis refer to *The Friend,* ed. Rooke. Line numbers are taken from *WPW; The Prelude* (1850 text), ed. Maxwell; and, for *The Female Vagrant,* Brett and Jones, eds., *Lyrical Ballads.* Unless otherwise noted, Wordsworth was identified as the author of works and passages printed in *The Friend.*

4. My conclusions differ from Balslev's (see esp. 11, 27, 64, 68, 82) in that I find more evidence of Keats's familiarity with *Lyrical Ballads* poems and *The Excursion* than Balslev does.

5. Altick (30) recounts Clarke's first meeting with Hunt, at a party shortly before Hunt's imprisonment on 3 February 1813. The two men's friendship thereafter grew as Clarke regularly sent fresh eggs and vegetables to Horsemonger Lane Gaol and periodically visited Hunt there (Altick 30–31). Hunt's opinion of Wordsworth clearly underwent a change some time between the first, 1811 version of *The Feast of the Poets,* in which Wordsworth is ridiculed, and the 1814 version, in which Hunt explains that since the last edition he has read and come to admire much of Wordsworth's poetry. Since the 1811 *Feast* was published at the end of that year and the second edition early in 1814 (Blunden, *Leigh Hunt* 61, 79–80), Hunt's conversion must have taken place in 1812 or 1813. Blunden (*Leigh Hunt* 67) believes Hunt began to reassess his opinion of Wordsworth soon after the 1811 *Feast* was published.

6. A good summary of the evolution of Hunt's attitude toward Wordsworth

as reflected in revisions to *The Feast of the Poets* can be found in Thorpe's "Leigh Hunt as a Man of Letters" (32–36).

7. In addition to the Thorpe essay cited in the previous note, see Finney (1:73–77) for an account of Hunt's assessment of Wordsworth in 1816–18.

8. Woodhouse thought the lines in *Sleep and Poetry* referred to "Lord Byron, & his terrific Style of poetry—to Christabel by Coleridge &c" (Sperry, "Woodhouse" 155). Although Woodhouse might seem to contradict Hunt, the two men's statements are not necessarily in conflict. Coleridge, of course, was considered one of the "Lake Poets," and therefore may have been intended along with Wordsworth in Hunt's remark. Moreover, in *The Feast of the Poets* (1815, 12), Hunt upbraids Byron for his melancholy and misanthropy. Even though Hunt doesn't mention Byron in his gloss on *Sleep and Poetry,* he nonetheless may have taught Keats to criticize both Byron and the Lake Poets for their "morbid" qualities. Finally, Woodhouse's list of poets intended by Keats ends with "&c" and therefore is meant to be illustrative rather than exhaustive or exclusive.

9. See also the *Diary* entry for 25 October 1816—soon after Haydon had met Keats—where the artist writes: "If I ever adored another [man], it was Wordsworth" (2:63n). At some later date Haydon substituted "is not" for "was," thereby revealing the shifts in attitude toward Wordsworth to which he was liable.

10. Both Bate (*John Keats* 96) and Finney (1:148) believe Keats, Clarke, and Haydon discussed Wordsworth the evening of 19 November 1816 and that this conversation inspired Keats's remarks on Wordsworth the following day in *Addressed to the Same.*

11. In addition to *Character of the Happy Warrior,* Haydon's 1842 *Diary* entry (5:234) lists as Wordsworth's best works *Laodamia* (1815), *The Old Cumberland Beggar* (1800), and *Tintern Abbey* (1798). Keats frequently quotes or echoes the latter two poems, but he never directly or indirectly alludes to *Laodamia.* If he read this work, he seems not to have shared Haydon's enthusiasm for it.

12. See "Mr. Wordsworth's Poetry," "The Pilgrimage of the Living Poets to the Stream of Castaly," "On Egotism in Literature," "Popular Poetry—Periodical Criticism, &c.," and "Wordsworth's Thanksgiving Ode" (all reprinted in Reynolds). See also note 2.

13. Bate (*John Keats* 194) says that, between late June and September 1817, "What social life [Keats] had was subdued; he was obviously preoccupied." For the dating of *Endymion*'s composition, see *Poems* (571). All references to the dates of Keats's poetry derive from *Poems.*

14. One might suppose that Bailey could have possessed the 1815 edition of Wordsworth's *Poems,* rather than the two earlier collections. Bailey had been a reader and supporter of Wordsworth for several years before the 1815 edition appeared, however, as we know from his own statement to Milnes and from quotations of Wordsworth poems in Bailey's handwriting, dating from 1814, in the Leigh sisters' commonplace books (*Keats Circle* 2:286; Hudnall, esp. 12–13, 17, 24–25). Bailey clearly knew poems from the *Lyrical Ballads* and 1807 volumes before March 1815, when the new edition was published (Moorman 269), and since he seems to have made a practice of purchasing Wordsworth's books there is little reason to suppose he did not buy the earlier collections.

15. Finney believes that Keats is following Bailey whenever he regards Words-

worth "as a sympathetic poet of the human heart" (1:324; see also 1:394–401, 2:459–60). Finney's dates for Keats's acceptance and rejection of Wordsworth's humanitarianism, however, are unconvincing.

16. For Keats's comments on Wordsworth's visit see checklist, General References to Wordsworth in Keats's Writing: Prose. Other anecdotes from Wordsworth's stay in the capital are conveniently gathered by Thorpe, "Wordsworth and Keats" 1010, 1015–19, and Bate, *John Keats* 265–73.

17. Evidence suggests that Haydon and Reynolds may also have been disappointed with Wordsworth during the latter's visit to London. In his diary for 22 December 1817, Haydon compares Wordsworth's introspection to Shakespeare's empathy in terms very similar to Keats's own in the spring of 1818 (*Diary* 2:171–72; Bate [*John Keats* 268] makes this point). Reynolds's parody *Peter Bell* includes a reference to one of the haughty remarks—concerning Walter Scott's *Rob Roy*—that Wordsworth uttered during his 1817–18 visit (Reynolds 260). Keats's most critical remarks about Wordsworth in the spring of 1818 were written to Haydon and Reynolds (see checklist, General References to Wordsworth in Keats's Writing: Prose). All three friends may have helped shape one another's opinions of Wordsworth during this period.

18. Owings (27) says that "it is the general consensus of Keats biographers that he did buy, read, and annotate this copy by January of 1818."

19. Hazlitt's influence on Keats's remarks in this letter has frequently been noted. See, for example, *Letters* 1:223n.6; Muir, "Keats and Hazlitt" 147; Ward 160; Allott, "Keats and Wordsworth" 29.

20. Stillinger believes Wordsworth's tales of abandoned women and betrayal generally in *Lyrical Ballads* and *The Excursion* influenced *Isabella,* written in the spring of 1818. Stillinger also argues that *Isabella*'s realism and concern with psychology owe a debt to *Lyrical Ballads* ("Wordsworth and Keats" 183–84).

21. For the sake of convenience and consistency, titles, quotations, and line numbers from Wordsworth poems are cited from *WPW*. In composing the present work, however, I found Curtis's edition of *Poems in Two Volumes* and Brett and Jones's edition of *Lyrical Ballads* most helpful.

22. J. Burke Severs, however, argues against parallels between *Tintern Abbey* and the passages in Keats's poem and letter.

23. This poem was composed by both Keats and Charles Brown. It is fairly safe to assume, however, that if Keats was not responsible for the epigraph, he either was familiar with or would have made himself familiar with the passage his co-author proposed as an epigraph. For discussion of *Beauley Abbey*'s composition and textual history see *Poems* (617–18).

24. A direct reference to another piece published in *Poems in Two Volumes*—the sonnet *Composed in the Valley near Dover, on the Day of Landing*—occurs in *"The House of Mourning" written by Mr. Scott*. This poem was once attributed to Keats, but Stillinger classifies it as a "questionable attribution" and believes the sonnet may have been written by Woodhouse (*Poems* 754).

25. Allott (*Poems* 273) calls Keats's "mountain tarn" merely "A Wordsworthian detail," and Gittings (*John Keats* 158) believes the phrase derives from Coleridge's *Dejection: An Ode*.

26. Manning (190–91) points out that line 13 of *O Nightingale! thou surely art* was

quoted by Wordsworth in the Preface to his *Poems* (1815); Keats could have encountered the line in that context instead of or in addition to reading it in the poem. Manning further suggests that some of the language of the Preface's commentary on line 13 may have influenced *Ode to a Nightingale*.

27. Balslev says Keats may have been struck by lines 59–60 of *Resolution and Independence* while reading Wordsworth's Preface to *Poems* (1815), where the passage that includes these lines is quoted.

28. As Muir points out ("Keats and Hazlitt" 145–46), Hazlitt quotes from line 4 of *To the Cuckoo*—"that wandering voice"—in the fifth of his *Lectures on the English Poets* ("On Thomson and Cowper"). Keats may have been struck by the phrase during Hazlitt's lecture rather than while reading Wordsworth's poem.

29. Balslev (30–31) says that both Wordsworth and Keats may have derived the association between sleep and flies from Shakespeare's *Henry IV, Part 2* 3.1.5ff.

30. As all of the above critics point out, Wordsworth himself seems in this line to be echoing Spenser's *Colin Clout's Come Home Again* 244–45.

31. See also Coleridge checklist, Poems from Other Publications/Problematic Cases.

32. Finney, and Rollins citing Finney, give 5.1207ff. as the *Excursion* passage in question. Book 5 ends with line 1016, however, and 4.1207ff. corresponds to the passage Finney describes.

33. See also notes 26 and 27 above.

34. This poem also was published in *Annals of the Fine Arts, for 1817* (1818). See Healey 99.

35. Allott also comments on "din" in *Endymion* 1.40, saying the word is "used by Wordsworth and Coleridge" (*Poems* 122).

36. Healey (17) gives 31 March—not 4 February "as is usually stated"—as the date *To B. R. Haydon* was published in the *Champion*. Also, unlike Wise and *WPW*, Healey (106) records the sonnet's appearance in *Annals of the Fine Arts, for 1817* (1818).

37. My examination of *Two Addresses to the Freeholders of Westmorland* in Owen and Smyser's edition of Wordsworth's *Prose Works* revealed no mention of Robert Saunders Dundas. Neither is Dundas listed in Owen and Smyser's detailed index.

38. This echo is surely invalid, for *When they were come unto the Faery's court* was written on 15 April 1819, before *Peter Bell* was published.

39. Gittings, however, believes the lines refer to Lake Leman and Lord Byron (*John Keats* 105). For a discussion of these conflicting views, see chap. 3, "Which of Byron's Works Keats Read."

40. Woodhouse glossed these lines as an "Allusion to Lord Byron, & . . . Christabel by Coleridge" (Sperry, "Woodhouse" 155). See note 8 above for a discussion of Hunt's and Woodhouse's statements.

Chapter 2

1. A few Coleridge poems proposed as influences on Keats that are not included in any of the principal editions cited above are discussed in the checklist section Poems from Other Publications/Problematic Cases. My bibliographical sources have been Wise, *Coleridge,* and E. H. Coleridge's two-volume edition of *The Com-*

plete Poetical Works of Samuel Taylor Coleridge, hereafter referred to as *CPW.* The chronology at the beginning of *Biographia Literaria* (Engell and Bate ed.) occasionally corrects errors or fills gaps in these two major bibliographies. All of Coleridge's poems are cited from *CPW.*

2. Hyder Rollins conjectures that, when Keats in his 3 May 1818 letter to Reynolds refers to "resting places in reasoning," he "Possibly . . . was thinking of the 'Landing Places' in Coleridge's *The Friend*" (*Letters* 1:281n.7). The "Landing-Places," or groups of "Essays Interposed for Amusement, Retrospect, and Preparation," however, were introduced for the first time in the 1818 edition of *The Friend,* which was not published until November of that year (*The Friend* 1:xxxiii), six months after Keats wrote his letter to Reynolds.

3. See Hazlitt's anticipatory review of *The Statesman's Manual* in the 8 September 1816 *Examiner* (Hazlitt 7:114–18); his review of the same on 29 December 1816 (7:119–28); his 15 December 1816 essay "On Modern Apostates" (7:131–37); and "Mr. Coleridge's Lay Sermon" and "On the Connection between Toad-Eaters and Tyrants," both in the 12 January 1817 *Examiner* (7:128–29, 145–52).

4. Besides Coleridge's aesthetic merits of "delicacy . . . simplicity of . . . sentiments, and . . . morality" (Jackson 236), Mathew no doubt approved the older man's conservative political views. When Mathew wrote his review of *Christabel* nearly all criticism of Coleridge's work was favorable or unfavorable depending on whether the reviewer agreed or disagreed with the author's politics, and we know from a letter he wrote to Milnes that Mathew in 1815 "loved the institutions of [his] country" (*Keats Circle* 2:186).

5. Hunt's 1821 essay on Coleridge is printed in Hunt, *Literary Criticism* 166–76. In their note to this essay (643–45), Houtchens and Houtchens survey the history of Hunt's attitude toward Coleridge. See also Thorpe's introductory essay in the same volume (32, 36, 58–70).

6. Even *Christabel,* according to Leonidas Jones (68), fascinated Reynolds and influenced the latter's 1816 poem, *The Naiad.*

7. It is also possible that both Keats and Reynolds were echoing Hazlitt in their misquotation of *Christabel.* Jones says Reynolds frequently "repeated [Hazlitt's] quotations" (Jones 83), and Muir regards Keats's 1817 *Champion* essay on Kean as an "obvious" imitation of Hazlitt ("Keats and Hazlitt" 141).

8. Haydon's statement is somewhat puzzling, since Coleridge had attended an exhibit of Haydon's students' drawings only six years earlier—on 30 January 1819 (see *Diary* 2:218n.1). Either Haydon in 1825 forgot about the 1819 encounter or he did not see Coleridge at the exhibit. It seems clear at any rate that the two men did not meet frequently.

9. Ryan (145–46) believes Keats picked up "penetralium" from Bailey, who uses "penetralia" in a 22 February 1818 letter to Taylor (*Keats Circle* 1:9). Stillinger ("Keats and Coleridge" 24n.25) remarks that Keats actually may have written "penetralia" and John Jeffrey, whose transcription is the only surviving manuscript of the December 1817 letter, have miscopied the word as "penetralium."

10. See, for example, Thayer 271; Daniel 137; Gittings, *John Keats* 302; Randel 51. In addition, a number of critics have argued that Coleridge's conversation itself influenced some of Keats's poems and letters. See Garrod 128–29; Finney 2:585; Ryan 202; Beer, *Poetic Intelligence* 281.

11. A few critics have argued for echoes of *Frost at Midnight* in *On the Grasshopper and Cricket* and *Endymion*, book 1, written before *Frost at Midnight* was published in *Sibylline Leaves*. See checklist, Poems from Other Publications/Problematic Cases, for a discussion of the plausibility of these echoes.

12. Coleridge's poem, and perhaps Keats's as well, echoes *Paradise Lost* 9.445.

13. Randel actually argues that Keats's nightingale is both happy and unhappy—that Keats agrees with both Milton and Coleridge in the debate over the bird's disposition. Sato, on the other hand, argues that Keats's poem rejects both Milton's and especially Coleridge's characterization of the nightingale ("'Nightingales'"; see especially 22). Sato reads *Ode to a Nightingale* as a parodic response to Coleridge's *The Nightingale: A Conversation Poem*.

14. For a discussion of this echo's validity, see "Which of Coleridge's Works Keats Read."

15. Stillinger ("Keats and Coleridge" 12n.8) says line 231 of *Sleep and Poetry* "probably has nothing to do with *Christabel*, but Woodhouse's annotation shows that he knew of, or else assumed, Keats's familiarity with the poem."

16. For this echo Sato cites Takeshi Saito, ed., *Christabel* (Tokyo: Kenkyusha, 1930), 42.

17. As Stillinger observes ("Keats and Coleridge" 15), the phrase "high disdain" occurs in *Paradise Lost* 1.98.

18. Both Kohli (21–24) and Stillinger ("Keats and Coleridge" 24–25) point out that Hazlitt is usually credited with shaping Keats's ideas about the egoless poet, but Coleridge's discussion in *Biographia Literaria* of Shakespeare's lack of individuality predates Hazlitt's similar remarks in his 27 January 1818 lecture "On Shakespeare and Milton."

19. *"The House of Mourning" written by Mr. Scott*, which Stillinger regards as a questionable attribution (*Poems* 754), refers in line 10 to "The voice of Mr. Coleridge" (*Poems* 756).

Chapter 3

1. E. H. Coleridge (180–84) lists the short poems published with the various editions of *Childe Harold's Pilgrimage;* see also Randolph 102–3. The "Thyrza" poems are *To Thyrza* ("Without a stone to mark the spot"), *Stanzas* ("Away, away, ye notes of woe!"), *To Thyrza* ("One struggle more, and I am free"), *Stanzas* ("And thou art dead, as young and fair"), and *Stanzas* ("If sometimes in the haunts of men"). The notes to these poems in Byron's *Complete Poetical Works*, edited by Jerome J. McGann (hereafter refered to as *BPW*), identify them as part of the Thyrza cycle. All publication information about Byron's poems is taken from *BPW* unless otherwise noted.

2. Walker (2, 3n.8, 11) cites other references in contemporary magazines and one private letter to the lyrics published with *Childe Harold*.

3. See also "Keats's Attitude toward Byron," where I cite evidence that *Sleep and Poetry* criticizes Byron's work.

4. De Selincourt (460), in discussing Keats's use of the ottava rima stanza form in *Isabella*, notes that "This measure . . . had been recently reintroduced into English poetry by Hookham Frere . . . and by Byron" in *Beppo*, published in February 1818.

Finney (1:379) and Allott (*Poems* 327), however, claim Keats was not influenced by *Beppo* but by Fairfax's translation of *Jerusalem Delivered*. Most recently, Susan Wolfson (285–86, 285n.20) finds similarities between Keats's use of the ottava rima stanza in *Isabella* and Byron's in *Beppo,* although she does not directly argue that Byron's poem influenced Keats's. She does, however, suggest that cantos 3 and 4 of *Don Juan* may owe something to Byron's reading of *Isabella*.

5. The indexes in Jones, Reynolds, and Richardson, *Letters from Lambeth* list Reynolds's many references to Byron. For a discussion of Reynolds's youthful enthusiasm for Byron see Jones 39 and Clubbe 154–55.

6. Keats's copy of *Don Juan* has not survived, although Severn preserved the copy of Shakespeare's *Poetical Works* that Keats took to Italy and bequeathed to the painter (see Owings 53). Bate (*John Keats* 664) thinks it was Severn rather than Keats who brought *Don Juan* on board the *Maria Crowther,* though Severn's 1845 account clearly states that the book belonged to Keats.

7. For a fuller discussion of Keats's attitude toward Byron, including ways in which Keats throughout his life continued to appreciate Byron's work, see Lau, "Keats and Byron."

8. Or, perhaps Keats wished to distance himself from Byron's melancholy because it was a quality he disliked in himself. Hirst says about another of Keats's criticisms of Byron that Keats "merely objectifies a tendency within himself, and, in the guise of attacking Byron, attacks himself" (47). This type of defense mechanism may be at work in a number of Keats's hostile remarks about Byron—as well as in Byron's hostile remarks about Keats. On the latter point see Cheatham 24–25.

9. Critics who discuss class implications in Keats's literary career and in the Byron-Keats relationship include Cheatham (22–24), Barnard (*John Keats* 3–5, 8, 48), and Levinson (*Keats's Life of Allegory,* esp. 1–44). In their consideration of class conflicts between Keats and Byron, however, these critics cite only Byron's remarks on Keats; they do not also consider Keats's and Keats's friends' comments on Byron.

10. Grant (179–80) remarks these characteristics of Byron's poetry and suggests that, in our century, "we may have lost the art of reading Byron" (180).

11. Woodhouse, however, believes the lines refer to Wordsworth (Sperry, "Woodhouse" 155).

12. For *Fare Thee Well!*'s publication history see "Which of Byron's Works Keats Read."

13. It is not entirely clear what Gittings means by the "introduction" to *Don Juan*. If he means the Dedication, his argument for the work's influence on Keats is unfounded, for the Dedication was not published until 1832.

14. Barnard (*Poems* 666) says that *Lamia* 1.328–39 is indebted to Byron generally. Elsewhere (670) he cites *Don Juan,* without specifying a particular passage, as an influence on *Lamia* 1.328–33. Beyer, however, says the *Lamia* passage is indebted to Wieland's *Oberon* rather than to Byron (212).

15. Beyer (197–202) says the *Lamia* passage is indebted not to Byron but to Wieland's *Oberon*.

16. Leigh Hunt, however, believed the lines allude to "the Lake Poets" (Matthews 62).

17. As explained in "Which of Byron's Works Keats Read," the quotation is not

in fact from Byron but, apparently, from Leigh Hunt's *Story of Rimini* 3.121–22: "And had been kept from men of pleasure's cares / By dint of feelings still more warm than theirs" (Milford ed.); see *Letters* 1:396n.4.

18. The Byron work to which Keats is alluding is probably canto 4 of *Childe Harold's Pilgrimage*, 4,000 copies of which had been advance ordered by February 1818 (*Letters* 2:62n.4). The poem was not published until 28 April 1818.

Chapter 4

1. In this chapter, the issues of which Shelley works Keats read and when he read them are discussed in one section.

2. The information about Shelley's early publications is taken from Grannis 3–38, and Reiman, *Shelley* 17–35. Reiman ("Keats and Shelley") most accurately and comprehensively presents the known facts about the two poets' first meeting, subsequent encounters, and attitudes toward one another.

3. Hunt also excused the poem in this way, according to Haydon, when the artist returned Hunt's copy of *Queen Mab* with critical notes (Gray and Walker 22).

4. See Bate (*John Keats* 172–73) for a summary of objections to neo-Platonic interpretations of *Endymion*.

5. Hunt's copy of *Alastor . . . and Other Poems*, with Hunt's marginal markings, is in the Department of Special Collections, University of California at Santa Barbara (see Quinn 18 and note 5).

6. Reiman draws the same conclusion ("Keats and Shelley" 407).

7. The shorter poems published with *Alastor* are *To*——("O! there are spirits of the air"); *Stanzas: April, 1814; Mutability; The pale, the cold, and the moony smile; A summer-evening church-yard; To Wordsworth; Feelings of a Republican on the Fall of Bonaparte; Superstition; Sonnet from the Italian of Dante; Translated from the Greek of Moschus; The Daemon of the World*, parts 1 and 2 (Ingpen and Peck 1:xx).

8. Reiman ("Keats and Shelley" 404–5) lists the February 1817 meetings between Keats and Shelley or Mary Shelley. See also Bate (*John Keats* 142n) and "Events in the Life of Keats" (*Letters* 1:33).

9. Just before Keats comments on the *Mandeville* review he remarks, "I have not seen Hunt, he was out when I called" (*Letters* 1:199). Had Hunt been at home Keats might have learned about Shelley's most recent literary activities.

10. See Reiman and Powers xviii, 96n.1, and Reiman, *Shelley* 51. The fullest discussion of the poem's composition and publication history can be found in *Shelley and His Circle* 5:141–67.

11. Both Ward (132, 135) and Gittings (*John Keats* 155) point out that when Keats returned to London from Oxford in October 1817, Shelley had finished *Laon and Cyntha* whereas Keats still had a thousand lines of *Endymion* to compose.

12. Line numbers from *Laon and Cyntha* are taken from the Ingpen and Peck text; line numbers from *The Revolt of Islam* derive from the Hutchinson text. Hutchinson numbers the lines consecutively throughout the poem. Hunt's reviews are printed in Johnson (12–35).

13. Shelley composed *Marianne's Dream* at Marlow in May 1817 and sent it to Hunt to insert in the *Examiner*. Hunt advertised the poem early in 1818 but then decided to publish it in the *Literary Pocket-Book* instead of in the *Examiner* (Ingpen

and Peck 3:327; Blunden, *"Examiner" Examined* 82). It is possible that Keats saw the poem in manuscript before it was published but more likely that he did not, since he saw little of Hunt and Shelley after February 1817.

14. Both White (*Hearth* 153n) and Barcus (146n) mistakenly claim that Hunt printed the entire *Lines Written among the Euganean Hills* in a footnote to his review. This misconception may have resulted from the fact that Johnson (44–47) prints lines 70–205 of the poem in a footnote to his edition of Hunt's review. The note in this case is Johnson's, not Hunt's, as a consultation of the actual *Examiner* text makes clear.

15. Richardson (*Fanny Brawne* 72) thinks Keats gave Fanny *The Cenci* before leaving for Italy. Since it was in Keats's "chest of books" when the poet died, however, it is more likely that Fanny received *The Cenci* from Brown (*Keats Circle* 1:254, 259, 259–60n.67).

16. The poems published with *Prometheus Unbound* are *The Sensitive Plant; A Vision of the Sea; Ode to Heaven; An Exhortation; Ode to the West Wind; An Ode, Written October, 1819, before the Spaniards Had Recovered Their Liberty; The Cloud; To a Skylark; Ode to Liberty.* Hunt's copy of the volume, which contains many marginal markings by Hunt, is presently held by the Henry Huntington Library (Quinn 19–20, 20n.9).

17. Ward (367) and Reiman ("Keats and Shelley" 399) provide similar—though not identical—lists of parallel events in Keats's and Shelley's careers.

18. Reiman ("Keats and Shelley" 405) makes a similar point. Allott (*"Endymion* and 'Alastor'"* 159) regards Keats's lack of intimacy with Shelley as the result simply of a lack of rapport between the two men, noting that Keats got along perfectly well with John Hamilton Reynolds, the other "young poet" featured with Keats and Shelley in Hunt's 1 December 1816 *Examiner* article. Reynolds, however, never posed the same threat as a rival to Keats that Shelley did. He was less ambitious and confident than Shelley, to say nothing of his talents. A favorite genre of Reynolds was poems bidding farewell to the muses, one of which he wrote on 14 February 1818 in the copy of Shakespeare he later gave to Keats (Jones 140–41). Moreover, on 14 October 1818 he wrote to Keats, "I can never write anything now—my mind is taken the other way:—But I shall set my heart on having you, high, as you ought to be. Do *you* get Fame,—and I shall have it in being your affectionate and steady friend" (*Keats Circle* 1:44). Perhaps one of the reasons why Keats and Reynolds were compatible was Reynolds's deference to Keats as the superior poet. The prolific, single-minded Shelley was clearly a more serious contender for high literary honors than was Reynolds, and this fact may well have contributed to Keats's coolness toward Shelley—although other factors, including temperamental differences, no doubt also played a part.

19. As explained elsewhere, revised versions of parts 1 and 2 of *Queen Mab* were published in the *Alastor* volume of 1816 as *The Daemon of the World.* The text of *Queen Mab* is taken from Reiman and Powers; *The Daemon of the World* from Hutchinson.

20. Neither Finney nor Bush explicitly argues that Keats was influenced by the chariot image in Shelley's poetry. Finney believes Keats's chariot of the imagination derived from Shelley's conversations concerning Plato's *Phaedrus,* though he adds that Shelley used the image in *Queen Mab* and *The Daemon of the World* (1:164 and

note). Bush (*Selected Poems* 312) says merely that "The chariot of the imagination is an image more characteristic of Shelley than of Keats (cf. *The Daemon of the World . . .* lines 56 f.)."

21. Several of the critics cited below believe that significant differences, as well as similarities, between *Alastor* and *Endymion* reflect the influence of Shelley's poem on Keats's. According to these critics, where *Endymion* departs from *Alastor* Keats is directly commenting on, responding to, or rebutting Shelley's poem.

22. The only other poem from the 1816 volume for which there is evidence of Keats's reading is *The Daemon of the World,* which is included in the checklist section on *Queen Mab.* The text of *Alastor* is quoted from Reiman and Powers.

23. See note 4.

24. As mentioned earlier, Reiman ("Keats and Shelley" 406–7) rejects the notion that *Alastor* endorses the pursuit of visionary ideals.

25. Little (42) argues that the passage in Keats's letter alludes not to Shelley but to Satan's single-mindedness in book 1 of *Paradise Lost.*

26. Besides outlining general plot similarities, Brown notes a number of verbal parallels between the two passages.

27. Brown cites these lines as examples of similar settings in *Alastor* and *Endymion,* but few of the lines in either poem describe physical surroundings. It is not clear what similarity relating to setting Brown perceives in these passages.

28. See note 4.

29. Ryan (198 and note) questions whether Keats in his letter was alluding to Shelley's poem. The phrase "vale of tears," Ryan notes, "has a very long history in Christian writing" and "does not seem to have been closely identified with Shelley." The rest of the passage that includes Keats's reference to the "vale of tears," moreover, does not suggest that Keats had Shelley in mind when he wrote it. The entire sentence reads: "The common cognomen of this world among the misguided and superstitious is 'a vale of tears' from which we are to be redeemed by a certain arbitrary interposition of God and taken to Heaven" (*Letters* 2:101–2). Keats would not have characterized Shelley, of all people, as a "superstitious" believer in God and heaven.

30. Frederick Jones (Shelley, *Letters* 2:111n.7) identifies the poem alluded to as *Rosalind and Helen.* In August 1819 this was the most recently published of Shelley's poems and is mentioned earlier in Shelley's letter. On 6 September 1819 Shelley repeated his request that Ollier send Keats copies of all Shelley works the firm published (Shelley, *Letters* 2:118). As explained in the essay section of this chapter, Keats does not appear to have ever received *Rosalind and Helen* from Ollier.

31. Keach does not directly argue that *To Autumn* was influenced by *Song to the Men of England* but merely suggests that the bees in Keats's poem may have the same political implications as those in Shelley's. For the possibility that Keats could have read a manuscript version of *Song to the Men of England,* see the essay section of this chapter.

32. As I explain elsewhere, Keats does not appear to have ever received the volume.

33. Ryan (94–99) concedes that Shelley's presence at Hampstead in December 1816 may have encouraged the sentiments expressed in Keats's sonnet, but he does not regard Shelley as the major influence on Keats's religious views at this time.

Ryan argues that Hunt and various aspects of the contemporary intellectual and religious milieu were chiefly responsible for shaping Keats's beliefs.

34. Bush (*Selected Poems* 319), Allott (*Poems* 157), and Barnard (*Poems* 568) apply Bailey's remarks to this passage. Bush also cites *Endymion* 2.1ff., and Finney (1:322) believes Bailey was referring to book 4 of *Endymion*.

35. Bate (*John Keats* 219) believes the statement "There's Hunt infatuated" in the same letter (*Letters* 1:169) refers to Hunt's infatuation with Shelley.

36. Two other passages in Keats's letters are believed by certain critics to refer to Shelley. Ward (109) says the comment in Keats's 11 May 1817 letter to Haydon— "[Hunt's] self delusions . . . have inticed him into a Situation which I should be less eager after than that of a galley Slave" (*Letters* 1:143)—refers to Hunt's financial indebtedness to Shelley. Gittings (*John Keats* 357) asserts that Keats is alluding to Shelley when the former tells Haydon on 3 October 1819, "Could I have dated from my Palace in Milan you would have heard from me" (*Letters* 2:219). Shelley went first to Milan when he traveled to Italy in the spring of 1818.

37. Gray and Walker (32) say that this passage "should almost certainly be accepted as characteristic exaggeration." The incident, if it ever occurred, could not have taken place in 1815, as Keats had met neither Shelley nor Haydon at this time.

38. Rollins (*Letters* 2:323n.3) thinks this remark refers to Shelley's 27 July 1820 letter inviting Keats to Pisa. Clarke had lost touch with Keats in 1820, however; he told Milnes in 1846 that he last saw Keats "in fine health and spirits" shortly after the latter had written *The Eve of St. Agnes* (*Keats Circle* 2:151–52; see also *Letters* 2:37, 60). Gittings (*John Keats* 207) concludes that Clarke's statement must refer to an earlier invitation Keats received to live with the Shelleys in Italy. Gittings believes Shelley asked Keats to accompany him and his family to Italy in March 1818. Since no such invitation is mentioned by the people involved, however, it is more likely that Clarke confused the invitation Keats received to join Shelley in Italy with that the younger poet received to visit the Shelleys at Marlow in the spring of 1817. Keats was still in touch with Clarke at this time, and the reason Clarke gives for Keats's not wishing to visit Shelley is similar to the one the poet himself reported to Bailey in an 8 October 1817 letter (see checklist, General References to Shelley in Keats's Prose).

Abbreviations

BPW	Byron, George Gordon, Lord. *The Complete Poetical Works*. Ed. Jerome J. McGann. 5 vols. to date. Oxford: Clarendon, 1980–.
CPW	*The Complete Poetical Works of Samuel Taylor Coleridge*. Ed. Ernest Hartley Coleridge. 2 vols. Oxford: Clarendon, 1912.
Keats Circle	*The Keats Circle*. Ed. Hyder E. Rollins. 2d ed. 2 vols. Cambridge: Harvard University Press, 1965.
Letters	*The Letters of John Keats*. Ed. Hyder E. Rollins. 2 vols. Cambridge: Harvard University Press, 1958.
Poems	*The Poems of John Keats*. Ed. Jack Stillinger. Cambridge: Harvard University Press, 1978.
Shelley and His Circle	*Shelley and His Circle: 1773–1822*. Ed. Kenneth Neill Cameron and Donald H. Reiman. 8 vols. to date. Cambridge: Harvard University Press, 1961–.
WPW	*The Poetical Works of William Wordsworth*. Ed. Ernest de Selincourt and Helen Darbishire. 5 vols. Oxford: Clarendon, 1940–49.

Works Cited

Allott, Miriam. "Keats and Wordsworth." *Keats-Shelley Memorial Bulletin* 22 (1971): 28–43.

———. "Keats's *Endymion* and Shelley's 'Alastor.'" In *Literature of the Romantic Period,* ed. R. T. Davies and B. G. Beatty, 151–70. New York: Barnes and Noble, 1976.

———, ed. *The Poems of John Keats.* 3d impression with corrections. London: Longman, 1975.

Altick, Richard D. *The Cowden Clarkes.* London: Oxford University Press, 1948.

Baer, Cynthia. "'Lofty Hopes of Divine Liberty': The Myth of the Androgyn in *Alastor, Endymion,* and *Manfred.*" *Romanticism Past and Present* 9, no. 2 (1985): 24–49.

Balslev, Thora. *Keats and Wordsworth: A Comparative Study.* Copenhagen: Munksgaard, 1962.

Barcus, James E., ed. *Shelley: The Critical Heritage.* London: Routledge and Kegan Paul, 1975.

Barnard, John, ed. *The Complete Poems.* By John Keats. 2d ed. Harmondsworth: Penguin, 1977.

———. "An Echo of Keats in 'The Eolian Harp.'" *Review of English Studies* 28 (1977): 311–13.

———. *John Keats.* Cambridge: Cambridge University Press, 1987.

Bate, Walter Jackson. *The Burden of the Past and the English Poet.* Cambridge: Harvard University Press, 1970.

———. *John Keats.* 1963. Reprinted. New York: Oxford University Press, 1966.

Beer, John. *Coleridge's Poetic Intelligence.* New York: Barnes and Noble, 1977.

———. *Coleridge the Visionary.* 1959. Reprinted. New York: Collier Books, 1962.

Beyer, Werner. *Keats and the Daemon King.* New York: Oxford University Press, 1947.

Blank, G. Kim. *Wordsworth's Influence on Shelley: A Study of Poetic Authority.* London: Macmillan, 1988.

Bloom, Harold. *The Anxiety of Influence: A Theory of Modern Poetry.* New York: Oxford University Press, 1973.

———. *A Map of Misreading.* New York: Oxford University Press, 1975.

———. *The Visionary Company: A Reading of English Romantic Poetry.* 1961. Rev. ed. Ithaca: Cornell University Press, 1971.

Blunden, Edmund. "Keats's Odes: Further Notes." *Keats-Shelley Journal* 3 (1954): 39–46.

———. "The Keats-Shelley Poetry Contest." *Notes and Queries* 199 (1954): 546.

———. *Leigh Hunt: A Biography*. London: Cobden-Sanderson, 1930.

———. *Leigh Hunt's "Examiner" Examined*. London: Cobden-Sanderson, 1928.

Bonnerot, Louis. "Keats and Wordsworth." *Times Literary Supplement* 9 February 1946, 67.

Bradley, A. C. "The Letters of John Keats." In *Oxford Lectures on Poetry*, 209–39. London: Macmillan, 1909.

Brett, R. L., and A. R. Jones, eds. *Lyrical Ballads*. By William Wordsworth and Samuel Taylor Coleridge. London: Methuen, 1963.

Brooks, Elmer L. "Byron and the *London Magazine*." *Keats-Shelley Journal* 5 (1956): 49–67.

Brown, Leonard. "The Genesis, Growth, and Meaning of *Endymion*." *Studies in Philology* 30 (1933): 618–53.

Bush, Douglas. "Notes on Keats's Reading." *PMLA* 50 (1935): 785–806.

———, ed. *Selected Poems and Letters*. By John Keats. Boston: Houghton Mifflin, 1959.

———. "Some Notes on Keats." *Philological Quarterly* 8 (1929): 313–15.

Byron, George Gordon, Lord. *The Complete Poetical Works*. Ed. Jerome J. McGann. 5 vols. to date. Oxford: Clarendon, 1980–.

Cameron, Kenneth Neill, and Donald H. Reiman, eds. *Shelley and His Circle: 1773–1822*. 8 vols. to date. Cambridge: Harvard University Press, 1961–.

Chandler, James R. "Romantic Allusiveness." *Critical Inquiry* 8 (1982): 461–87.

Cheatham, George. "Byron's Dislike of Keats's Poetry." *Keats-Shelley Journal* 32 (1983): 20–25.

Chew, Samuel C. *Byron in England: His Fame and After-Fame*. 1924. Reprinted. New York: Russell and Russell, 1965.

Chilcott, Tim. *A Publisher and His Circle: The Life and Work of John Taylor, Keats's Publisher*. London: Routledge and Kegan Paul, 1972.

Clarke, Charles Cowden, and Mary Cowden Clarke. *Recollections of Writers*. New York: Charles Scribner's Sons, 1878.

Clubbe, John. "The Reynolds–Dovaston Correspondence." *Keats-Shelley Journal* 30 (1981): 152–81.

Coldwell, Joan. "Charles Cowden Clarke's Commonplace Book and Its Relationship to Keats." *Keats-Shelley Journal* 29 (1980): 83–95.

Coleridge, Ernest Hartley. "A Bibliography of the Successive Editions and Translations of Lord Byron's *Poetical Works*." In *The Works of Lord Byron*, ed. E. H. Coleridge, 7:89–348. London: John Murray, 1904.

Coleridge, Samuel Taylor. *Biographia Literaria*. Ed. James Engell and Walter Jackson Bate. 2 vols. Vol. 7 of *The Collected Works of Samuel Taylor Coleridge*. Princeton: Princeton University Press, 1983.

———. *Collected Letters of Samuel Taylor Coleridge*. Ed. Earl Leslie Griggs. 6 vols. Oxford: Clarendon, 1956–71.

———. *The Complete Poetical Works of Samuel Taylor Coleridge*. Ed. Ernest Hartley Coleridge. 2 vols. Oxford: Clarendon, 1912.

————. *The Friend*. Ed. Barbara E. Rooke. 2 vols. Vol. 4 of *The Collected Works of Samuel Taylor Coleridge*. Princeton: Princeton University Press, 1969.

————. *Lay Sermons*. Ed. R. J. White. Vol. 6 of *The Collected Works of Samuel Taylor Coleridge*. Princeton: Princeton University Press, 1972.

————. *The Notebooks of Samuel Taylor Coleridge*. Ed. Kathleen Coburn. 4 vols. New York: Bollingen, 1957–89.

————. *Shakespearean Criticism*. Ed. Thomas Middleton Raysor. 2 vols. Cambridge: Harvard University Press, 1930.

Colvin, Sidney. *John Keats: His Life and Poetry, His Friends, Critics, and After-Fame*. 3d ed. New York: Charles Scribner's Sons, 1925.

Curtis, Jared, ed. *Poems, in Two Volumes, and Other Poems, 1800–1807*. By William Wordsworth. Ithaca: Cornell University Press, 1983.

Daniel, Robert. "Odes to Dejection." *Kenyon Review* 15 (1953): 129–40.

Davenport, Arnold. "A Note on *To Autumn*." In *John Keats: A Reassessment*, ed. Kenneth Muir, 95–101. Liverpool: Liverpool University Press, 1958.

de Selincourt, Ernest, ed. *The Poems of John Keats*. 5th ed. London: Methuen, 1926.

Dudley, O. H. T. "Pure Serene." *Times Literary Supplement* 23 September 1944, 463.

Edgcumbe, Fred, ed. *Letters of Fanny Brawne to Fanny Keats, 1820–1824*. New York: Oxford University Press, 1937.

Finney, Claude Lee. *The Evolution of Keats's Poetry*. 2 vols. in one. 1936. Reprinted. New York: Russell and Russell, 1964.

Ford, N. F. "Some Keats Echoes and Borrowings." *Modern Language Quarterly* 8 (1947): 455–58.

Forman, Harry Buxton, ed. *The Poetical Works and Other Writings of John Keats*. Rev. Maurice Buxton Forman. 8 vols. New York: Charles Scribner's Sons, 1938–39.

Garrod, H. W. *Keats*. 2d ed. Oxford: Clarendon, 1939.

Gerber, Richard. "Cybele, Kubla Khan, and Keats: An Essay on Imaginative Transmutation." *English Studies* 46 (1965): 369–89.

Gisborne, Maria, and Edward E. Williams. *Maria Gisborne and Edward E. Williams, Shelley's Friends: Their Letters and Journals*. Ed. Frederick L. Jones. Norman: University of Oklahoma Press, 1951.

Gittings, Robert. "Byron and Keats's Eremite." *Keats-Shelley Memorial Bulletin* 7 (1956): 7–10.

————. *John Keats*. Boston: Little, Brown, 1968.

Gold, Elise M. "Keats Reads Shelley: An Allusion to *The Revolt of Islam* in *Lamia*." *American Notes and Queries* 23 (1985): 74–77.

Grannis, Ruth S. *A Descriptive Catalogue of the First Editions in Book Form of the Writings of Percy Bysshe Shelley*. New York: Grolier Club, 1923.

Grant, Douglas. "Byron: The Pilgrim and Don Juan." In *The Morality of Art*, ed. D. W. Jefferson, 175–84. New York: Barnes and Noble, 1969.

Gray, Duncan, and Violet W. Walker. "Benjamin Robert Haydon on Byron and Others." *Keats-Shelley Memorial Bulletin* 7 (1956): 14–26.

Hardy, Barbara. "Keats, Coleridge, and Negative Capability." *Notes and Queries* 197 (1952): 299–301.

Haydon, Benjamin Robert. *The Autobiography and Memoirs of Benjamin Robert Haydon*. Ed. Tom Taylor. 2 vols. New York: Harcourt, Brace, 1926.

———. *The Diary of Benjamin Robert Haydon*. Ed. Willard Bissell Pope. 5 vols. Cambridge: Harvard University Press, 1960–63.

Hazlitt, William. *The Complete Works of William Hazlitt*. Ed. P. P. Howe. 21 vols. London: J. M. Dent, 1930–34.

Healey, George Harris. *The Cornell Wordsworth Collection*. Ithaca: Cornell University Press, 1957.

Hirst, Wolf. "Lord Byron Cuts a Figure: The Keatsian View." *Byron Journal* 13 (1985): 36–51.

Hollander, John. *The Figure of Echo: A Mode of Allusiveness in Milton and After*. Berkeley and Los Angeles: University of California Press, 1981.

Hudnall, Clayton E. "John Hamilton Reynolds, James Rice, and Benjamin Bailey in the Leigh Browne-Lockyer Collection." *Keats-Shelley Journal* 19 (1970): 11–32.

Hunt, Leigh. *The Autobiography of Leigh Hunt*. Ed. J. E. Morpurgo. London: Cresset, 1949.

———. *The Correspondence of Leigh Hunt*. Ed. Thornton Hunt. 2 vols. London: Smith, Elder, 1862.

———. *The Feast of the Poets, With Other Pieces in Verse*. London, 1814. 2d ed. 1815.

———. *Foliage; or Poems Original and Translated*. London, 1818.

———. *Imagination and Fancy*. 1844. Reprinted. New York: AMS, 1972.

———. *Leigh Hunt's Literary Criticism*. Ed. Lawrence Huston Houtchens and Carolyn Washburn Houtchens. New York: Columbia University Press, 1956.

———. *The Poetical Works of Leigh Hunt*. Ed. H. S. Milford. London: Oxford, 1923.

Hutchinson, Thomas, ed. *Poetical Works*. By Percy Bysshe Shelley. Corr. G. M. Matthews. London: Oxford University Press, 1970.

Ingpen, Roger, and Walter E. Peck, eds. *The Complete Works of Percy Bysshe Shelley*. 10 vols. London: Ernest Benn, 1926–30.

Jackson, J. R. de J, ed. *Coleridge: The Critical Heritage*. New York: Barnes and Noble, 1970.

Johnson, R. Brimley. *Shelley-Leigh Hunt: How Friendship Made History*. London: Ingpen and Grant, 1928.

Jones, Leonidas M. *The Life of John Hamilton Reynolds*. Hanover: University Press of New England, 1984.

Keach, William. "Cockney Couplets: Keats and the Politics of Style." *Studies in Romanticism* 25 (1986): 182–96.

Keats, John. *The Letters of John Keats*. Ed. Hyder E. Rollins. 2 vols. Cambridge: Harvard University Press, 1958.

———. *The Poems of John Keats*. Ed. Jack Stillinger. Cambridge: Harvard University Press, 1978.

Kohli, Devindra. "Coleridge, Hazlitt and Keats's Negative Capability." *Literary Criterion* 8 (1968): 21–26.

Lange, Donald. "A New Reynolds-Milnes Letter: Were There Two Meetings between Keats and Coleridge?" *Modern Language Review* 72 (1977): 769–72.

Lau, Beth. "Keats and Byron." In *Critical Essays on John Keats,* ed. Hermione de Almeida, 206–22. Boston: G. K. Hall, 1990.

Levinson, Marjorie. *Keats's Life of Allegory: The Origins of a Style*. Oxford: Blackwell, 1988.

————. *The Romantic Fragment Poem: A Critique of a Form*. Chapel Hill: University of North Carolina Press, 1986.

Little, Jeffrey. "Serving Mammon: Keats's Reply to Shelley." *Romanticism Past and Present* 5, no. 2 (1981): 41–43.

Lonsdale, Roger, ed. *The Poems of Thomas Gray, William Collins, and Oliver Goldsmith*. London: Longmans, 1969.

Low, Donald A. "Byron and the 'Grecian Urn.'" *Times Literary Supplement* 26 October 1973, 1314.

Lowell, Amy. *John Keats*. 2 vols. Boston: Houghton Mifflin, 1925.

Maier, Rosemarie. "The Bitch and the Bloodhound: Generic Similarity in 'Christabel' and 'The Eve of St. Agnes.'" *Journal of English and Germanic Philology* 70 (1971): 62–75.

McFarland, Thomas. *Originality and Imagination*. Baltimore: Johns Hopkins University Press, 1985.

McGann, Jerome J. *Don Juan in Context*. Chicago: University of Chicago Press, 1976.

Manning, Peter J. "Keats's and Wordsworth's Nightingale." *ELH* 17 (1980): 189–92.

Marchand, Leslie. *Byron: A Biography*. 3 vols. New York: Knopf, 1957.

Matthews, G. M., ed. *John Keats: The Critical Heritage*. New York: Barnes and Noble, 1971.

Medwin, Thomas. *The Life of Percy Bysshe Shelley*. 2 vols. London: Thomas Cantley Newby, 1847.

Milne, Fred L. "Shelley on Keats: A Notebook Dialogue." *English Language Notes* 13 (1976): 278–84.

Moorman, Mary. *William Wordsworth: The Later Years, 1803–50*. Oxford: Clarendon, 1965.

Muir, Kenneth. "Keats and Hazlitt." In *John Keats: A Reassessment*, ed. Kenneth Muir, 139–58. Liverpool: Liverpool University Press, 1958.

————. "Three Notes on Keats." *Notes and Queries* 195 (1950): 364.

Muir, Kenneth, and F. W. Bateson. "Editorial Commentary." *Essays in Criticism* 4 (1954): 432–40.

Murry, John Middleton. "Keats and Coleridge: A Note." *Keats-Shelley Memorial Bulletin* 3 (1950): 5–7.

————. "Keats and Wordsworth." In Murry, *Keats*, 269–91. New York: Noonday Press, 1955.

————. *Studies in Keats*. London: Oxford, 1930.

Newlyn, Lucy. *Coleridge, Wordsworth, and the Language of Allusion*. Oxford: Clarendon, 1986.

O'Loughlin, J. L. N. "Coleridge and 'The Fall of Hyperion.'" *Times Literary Supplement* 6 December 1934, 875.

Owings, Frank N., Jr. *The Keats Library*. London: Keats-Shelley Memorial Association, 1978.

Pearce, Frank W. "Keats and the Ancient Mariner: Book III of *Endymion*." *Keats-Shelley Journal* 24 (1975): 13–15.

Piper, David. *The Image of the Poet: British Poets and Their Portraits*. Oxford: Clarendon, 1982.

Pratt, Willis W. *Notes on the Variorum Edition*. Vol. 4 of *Byron's Don Juan: A Variorum Edition*, ed. Truman Guy Steffan and Willis W. Pratt. 2d ed. Austin: University of Texas Press, 1971.

Quinn, Mary A. "Leigh Hunt's Presentation Copy of Shelley's *Alastor* Volume." *Keats-Shelley Journal* 35 (1986): 17–20.

Randel, Fred V. "Coleridge and the Contentiousness of Romantic Nightingales." *Studies in Romanticism* 21 (1982): 33–55.

Randolph, Francis Lewis. *Studies for a Byron Bibliography*. Lititz, Pa.: Sutter House, 1979.

Reiman, Donald H. "Christobell; or, The Case of the Sequel Preemptive." *The Wordsworth Circle* 6 (1975): 283–89.

———. "Keats and the Abyss." In Reiman, *Intervals of Inspiration: The Skeptical Tradition and the Psychology of Romanticism*, 263–305. Greenwood: Penkevill, 1988.

———. "Keats and Shelley: Personal and Literary Relations." In *Shelley and His Circle*, ed. Donald H. Reiman, 5:399–427. Cambridge: Harvard University Press, 1973.

———. *Percy Bysshe Shelley*. New York: Twayne, 1969.

Reiman, Donald H., and Sharon B. Powers, eds. *Shelley's Poetry and Prose*. New York: Norton, 1977.

Reynolds, John Hamilton. *Selected Prose of John Hamilton Reynolds*. Ed. Leonidas M. Jones. Cambridge: Harvard University Press, 1966.

Richardson, Joanna. *Fanny Brawne: A Biography*. New York: Vanguard, 1952.

———, ed. *Letters from Lambeth: The Correspondence of the Reynolds Family with John Freeman Milward Dovaston*. Woodbridge, Eng.: Boydell, 1981.

———. "Richard Woodhouse and His Family." *Keats-Shelley Memorial Bulletin* 5 (1953): 39–44.

Rivers, Charles L. "Influence of Wordsworth's 'Lines Composed a Few Miles above Tintern Abbey' upon Keats's 'Ode to a Nightingale.'" *Notes and Queries* 196 (1951): 142–43.

Robinson, Charles E. "Percy Bysshe Shelley, Charles Ollier, and William Blackwood: The Contexts of Early Nineteenth-Century Publishing." In *Shelley Revalued: Essays from the Gregynog Conference*, ed. Kelvin Everest, 183–226. Totowa, NJ: Barnes and Noble, 1983.

———. "The Shelley Circle and Coleridge's *The Friend*." *English Language Notes* 8 (1971): 269–74.

Rollins, Hyder E. "Benjamin Bailey's Scrapbook." *Keats-Shelley Journal* 6 (1957): 15–30.

———. "A Fanny Brawne Letter of 1848." *Harvard Library Bulletin* 5 (1951): 372–75.

———, ed. *The Keats Circle*. 2d ed. 2 vols. Cambridge: Harvard University Press, 1965.

Routh, James. "Parallels in Coleridge, Keats, and Rossetti." *Modern Language Notes* 25 (1910): 33–37.

Rutherford, Andrew, ed. *Byron: The Critical Heritage*. New York: Barnes and Noble, 1970.

Ryan, Robert M. *Keats: The Religious Sense*. Princeton: Princeton University Press, 1976.

Sato, Toshihiko. "Extemporization and Elaboration: Keats's 'Faery Court' and 'La Belle Dame.'" *Hiroshima Studies in English Language and Literature* 29 (Feb. 1985): 1–20.

———. "'Nightingales': Coleridge's Challenge to a Future Poet and Keats's Probable Reply." *The University of Saga Studies in English* 13 (March 1985): 11–24.

Severs, J. Burke. "Keats's 'Mansion of many Apartments,' *Sleep and Poetry*, and *Tintern Abbey*." *Modern Language Quarterly* 20 (1959): 128–32.

Shelley, Mary Wollstonecraft. *The Journals of Mary Shelley*. Ed. Paula R. Feldman and Diana Scott-Kilvert. 2 vols. Oxford: Clarendon, 1987.

———. *The Letters of Mary Wollstonecraft Shelley*. Ed. Betty T. Bennett. 3 vols. Baltimore: Johns Hopkins University Press, 1980–88.

Shelley, Percy Bysshe. *The Letters of Percy Bysshe Shelley*. Ed. Frederick L. Jones. 2 vols. Oxford: Clarendon, 1964.

Slote, Bernice. *Keats and the Dramatic Principle*. Lincoln: University of Nebraska Press, 1958.

Spens, Janet. "A Study of Keats's 'Ode to a Nightingale.'" *Review of English Studies*, n.s., 3 (1952): 234–43.

Sperry, Stuart M., Jr. *Keats the Poet*. Princeton: Princeton University Press, 1973.

———. "Richard Woodhouse's Interleaved and Annotated Copy of Keats's *Poems* (1817)." *Literary Monographs* (Univ. of Wisconsin–Madison) 1 (1967): 101–64, 308–11.

Stein, Edwin. *Wordsworth's Art of Allusion*. University Park: Pennsylvania State University Press, 1988.

Stillinger, Jack, ed. *Complete Poems*. By John Keats. Cambridge: Harvard University Press, 1982.

———. *The Hoodwinking of Madeline and Other Essays on Keats's Poems*. Urbana: University of Illinois Press, 1971.

———. "John Keats." In *The English Romantic Poets: A Review of Research and Criticism*, ed. Frank Jordan, 665–718. 4th ed. New York: MLA, 1985.

———. "Keats and Coleridge." In *Coleridge, Keats, and the Imagination: Romanticism and Adam's Dream*, ed. J. Robert Barth, S.J., and John L. Mahoney, 7–28. Columbia: University of Missouri Press, 1990.

———. "Wordsworth and Keats." In *William Wordsworth and the Age of English Romanticism*, ed. Kenneth R. Johnston and Gene W. Ruoff, 173–95. New Brunswick: Rutgers University Press, 1987.

Thayer, Mary R. "Keats and Coleridge: 'La Belle Dame sans Merci.'" *Modern Language Notes* 60 (1945): 270–72.

Thorpe, Clarence DeWitt. "Keats and Hazlitt: A Record of Personal Relationship and Critical Estimate." *PMLA* 62 (1947): 487–502.

———. "Leigh Hunt as a Man of Letters." In *Leigh Hunt's Literary Criticism*, ed. Lawrence Huston Houtchens and Carolyn Washburn Houtchens, 3–73. New York: Columbia University Press, 1956.

———. "Wordsworth and Keats—A Study in Personal and Critical Impression." *PMLA* 42 (1927): 1010–26.

Twitchell, James B. "Porphyro as 'Famish'd Pilgrim': The Hoodwinking of Madeline Continued." *Ball State University Forum* 19 (1978): 56–65.

Vendler, Helen. *The Odes of John Keats*. Cambridge: Harvard University Press, 1983.

Waldoff, Leon. *Keats and the Silent Work of Imagination*. Urbana: University of Illinois Press, 1985.

Walker, Keith. *Byron's Readers: A Study in Attitudes Towards Byron 1812–1832*. Salzburg: Institut fur Anglistik und Amerikanistik, 1979.

Ward, Aileen. *John Keats: The Making of a Poet*. New York: Viking, 1963.

Watson, George, ed. *Biographia Literaria*. By Samuel Taylor Coleridge. New York: Dutton, 1956.

White, Newman Ivey. *Shelley*. 2 vols. New York: Knopf, 1940.

———. *The Unextinguished Hearth: Shelley and His Contemporary Critics*. Durham: Duke University Press, 1938.

Wigod, J. D. "Negative Capability and Wise Passiveness." *PMLA* 67 (1952): 383–90.

Wise, Thomas J. *A Bibliography of the Writings in Verse and Prose of George Gordon Noel, Baron Byron*. 2 vols. London, 1932–33.

———. *A Bibliography of the Writings in Prose and Verse of Samuel Taylor Coleridge*. London: Richard Clay and Sons, 1913.

———. *A Bibliography of the Writings in Prose and Verse of William Wordsworth*. London: Richard Clay and Sons, 1916.

Wolfson, Susan J. *The Questioning Presence: Wordsworth, Keats, and the Interrogative Mode in Romantic Poetry*. Ithaca: Cornell University Press, 1986.

Wordsworth, William. *The Poetical Works of William Wordsworth*. Ed. Ernest de Selincourt and Helen Darbishire. 5 vols. Oxford: Clarendon, 1940–49.

———. *The Prelude: A Parallel Text*. Ed. J. C. Maxwell. Harmondsworth: Penguin, 1971.

———. *The Prose Works of William Wordsworth*. Ed. W. J. B. Owen and Jane Worthington Smyser. 3 vols. Oxford: Clarendon, 1974.

Wordsworth, William, and Dorothy Wordsworth. *The Letters of William and Dorothy Wordsworth: The Middle Years, Part II, 1812–1820*, 2d ed. Ed. Ernest de Selincourt; rev. Mary Moorman and Alan G. Hill. Oxford: Clarendon, 1970.

Index of Keats's Writing